THE TRUTHTELLERS

THE
TRUTHTELLERS

Jane Austen   George Eliot
D. H. Lawrence

LAURENCE LERNER

SCHOCKEN BOOKS

NEW YORK

Published in U.S.A. in 1967
by Schocken Books Inc.
67 Park Avenue, New York, N.Y. 10016
Copyright © Laurence Lerner 1967
Library of Congress Catalog Card No. 67-12148

Printed in Great Britain

To
WAYNE BOOTH

CONTENTS

PREFACE

Parts of this book (not always in their present form) have already appeared in print. Some of the ideas were tried out in two Third Programme talks: 'The Cool Gaze and the Warm Heart' (on *Middlemarch*), published in *The Listener*, 29 September 1960; and 'This Old Maid' (Lawrence's view of Jane Austen), published in *The Listener*, 21 February 1963. The Introduction is based on an article called 'Love and Gossip; or How Moral is Literature?', published in *Essays in Criticism*, April 1964. The discussion of 'How Beastly the Bourgeois is' was published in the *Critical Survey*, Spring 1963; that of *Daniel Deronda* in the *Critical Quarterly*, Winter 1965.

Many people (not all of them known to me personally) have helped in the writing of this book. I cannot thank all the critics who have lent me ideas: probably I do not know who they all are. Because I have tried to write direct from the novels, saying as little as possible about the critical debates, I ought to mention in this preface those to whom I know that I owe a debt: Marvin Mudrick, C. S. Lewis, D. W. Harding and Lionel Trilling on Jane Austen; Eliseo Vivas and Eugene Goodheart on D. H. Lawrence; and (with a different kind of debt) Gordon Haight for his magnificent editing of the George Eliot letters. To all of these I give the impersonal thanks of a fellow-worker; and to some of my friends I owe a warmer, more personal gratitude. Geoffrey Carnall had many valuable arguments with me when the book was still a few germinating ideas; the members of my graduate seminar on George Eliot at the University of Illinois listened patiently to some of it, and helped me to express what was still inchoate; and, most valuable of all, a few friends read parts of it in typescript and gave me their comments—Leigh Gibby, Cecil Jenkins, Gāmini Salgādo and Tony Nuttall. My strongest thanks are to Wayne Booth, who read it all, then fed his comments into the running literary argument that has lasted the five years of our friendship, and whose grandfather makes a brief appearance on p. 43.

L. D. L.

January 1966

A*

Lawrence on Jane Austen:

This old maid typifies 'personality' instead of character, the sharp knowing in apartness instead of knowing in togetherness, and she is, to my feeling, thoroughly unpleasant, English in the bad, mean, snobbish sense of the word.

Apropos of Lady Chatterley's Lover

and the central sentence of George Eliot's novels:

Her trust had been delusive, but she would have chosen over again to have acted on it rather than be a creature led by phantoms and disjointed whispers in a world where there was the large music of reasonable speech, and the warm grasp of living hands.

Romola, Ch. 36

INTRODUCTION

THIS book is about the view of man and the moral attitudes that inform the work of Jane Austen, George Eliot and D. H. Lawrence. The first part deals mainly with what they have in common; the second part draws a contrast and fits them into it. If these three authors had been chosen merely because they fit a scheme, readers would rightly complain that I was using literature as the tool of criticism. I must therefore say at the outset that I have chosen them for their greatness—George Eliot because she is the finest of all English novelists; Jane Austen because her social comedy is unparalleled in its ability to entertain immediately, and stand up to almost endless re-readings; and Lawrence, the crude uneven, dangerous giant, because he looms over all modern fiction, threatening, inspiring, delighting; and because for all the long quarrel I have had with him, and shall re-enact in these pages, he is part of my life, as he is of the life of most modern readers.

That is my justification for writing about each. The justification for writing about them together must be that thinking about one helps us to understand the others, and with the understanding that they call for, not one that we have imposed on them. The scheme of this book may be wrong-headed, but it has not been imposed: it grew. I have tried never for a moment to treat these writers as if their importance was merely to illuminate a thesis. Their importance is their own: if they do illuminate my thesis, that matters because it helps to illuminate them.

All of them are writers who compel us to reconsider our view of man; and the pattern which this book traces is really a pattern of ways to think about the nature of man. Is this the sort of response appropriate to a novel? Does the novelist intend to make us examine our moral position? Some will say yes; some no; some that it depends on the novelist; some that it depends on us. The first need, then, is to set against each other the view of literature that says yes to this question, and that which says no. I shall call these the committed and the dramatic. To expound them will involve going over some familiar ground, and I must begin with Keats and Wordsworth without, perhaps, saying anything very new about those authors,

'A poet', wrote Keats

> is the most unpoetical of anything in existence, because he
> has no identity—he is continually informing and filling some
> other body. . . . When I am in a room with people, if ever I am
> free from speculating on creations of my own brain, then not
> myself goes home to myself, but the identity of every one in
> the room begins to press upon me, so that I am in a very little
> time annihilated.[1]

The quality Keats is describing in this famous letter is what he
elsewhere refers to as Negative Capability, and attributes to
Shakespeare:

> It struck me what quality went to form a Man of Achievement,
> especially in Literature, and which Shakespeare possessed so
> enormously—I mean *Negative Capability*, that is, when a man
> is capable of being in uncertainties, mysteries, doubts, without
> any irritable reaching after fact and reason.[2]

This poetical character Keats contrasts with another, that of
Shelley ('you might curb your magnanimity and be more of an
artist') and Wordsworth ('the Wordsworthian or egotistical sublime'). Now it is quite true that Wordsworth could never have
said, 'not myself goes home to myself', could not have had 'as
much delight in conceiving an Iago as an Imogen.' 'What shocks
the virtuous philosopher delights the chameleon poet'—but it
shocks the virtuous Wordsworth too.

> *Economists will tell you that the State*
> *Thrives by the forfeiture—unfeeling thought,*
> *And false as monstrous! Can the mother thrive*
> *By the destruction of her innocent sons?*[3]

Not, of course, a specimen of Wordsworth at his best: but an
example of his willingness to preach. When Wordsworth writes
badly, it is as the virtuous philosopher; when Keats writes badly,

> *—When it is moving on luxurious wings*
> *The soul is lost in pleasant smotherings:*
> *Fair dewy roses brush against our faces,*
> *And flowering laurels spring from diamond vases—*[4]

---

[1] Letter to Richard Woodhouse, 27 October, 1818
[2] Letter to George and Thomas Keats, 22 December, 1817
[3] *The Excursion*, VIII, 283ff
[4] 'I stood tiptoes upon a little hill', ll. 130ff

it is because he is the chameleon poet recklessly indulging himself
in experience. But though a distinction is often most neatly illus-
trated from poets' bad verses, this distinction runs through all
they wrote.

> *Milton! thou shouldst be living at this hour:*
> *England hath need of thee: she is a fen*
> *Of stagnant waters: altar, sword, and pen,*
> *Fireside, the heroic wealth of hall and bower,*
> *Have forfeited their ancient English dower*
> *Of inward happiness. We are selfish men;*
> *Oh! raise us up, return to us again;*
> *And give us manners, virtue, freedom, power.*
> *Thy soul was like a star, and dwelt apart;*
> *Thou hadst a voice whose sound was like the sea;*
> *Pure as the naked heavens, majestic, free,*
> *So didst thou travel on life's common way*
> *In cheerful godliness; and yet thy heart*
> *The lowliest duties on herself did lay.*[1]

The intention of this poem is obviously ethical: Milton is needed,
not to provide aesthetic pleasure for the lovers of poetry, but to
cleanse the fen of stagnant waters—and since the professed aim
of *Paradise Lost* was ethical and theological, we can assume that
he would have been pleased at this invocation. More important
than professed intentions are actual achievements; and the power
of this sonnet does, in fact, lie very close to its ethical purpose.
There are two great and obviously Wordsworthian lines, that
reverberate back and forth through the whole poem:

> *Thy soul was like a star, and dwelt apart;*
> *Thou hadst a voice whose sound was like the sea.*

What gives Wordsworth's imagery this holy quality—what charges
his simple natural objects (rocks and stones and trees; stars, seas
and mountains) with an awe as if no one had ever mentioned them
in a poem before? Not the chameleon delight of Keats; but (as we
see in this poem) their power to symbolise the simplest human
virtues. The star and the sea contrast both with the selfishness of
'this hour' and the lowliness of 'life's common way'—they show us
Milton's vast superiority to modern man, and also the vast contrast
within him, a contrast that has about it some of the awe we feel for

---

[1] 'London 1802'

13

Incarnation. It is this moral concern with experience that infuses Wordsworth's finest use of natural imagery, and gives it its power.

In the *Ode to Autumn*, on the other hand, the immersion in experience is a forgetfulness of self and its identity:

> *To bend with apples the mossed cottage trees*
> *And fill all fruit with ripeness to the core ;*
> *To swell the gourd, and plump the hazel shells*
> *With a sweet kernel; to set budding more,*
> *And still more, later flowers for the bees,*
> *Until they think warm days will never cease,*
> *For Summer has o'erbrimmed their clammy cells.*[1]

This verse is about not being Keats, not myself going home to myself: it is a rendering of natural process, its exultation is in becoming the rising sap, the growing tissue, the drowsy heat. 'If a sparrow come before my window I take part in its existence and pick about the gravel.' This is why the work of these two Romantic poets of Nature can never be confused: the self that judges, the moral self, that 'puts its hand in its breeches pocket', is ever-present in Wordsworth, constantly banished from Keats.

All this is well known, and often said. I have begun by showing this contrast in two poets, but I wish to apply it to the novel, and I wish to ask just what it is that we are contrasting. We need a novel that deals with urgent issues, depicts our fen of stagnant waters and engages the sympathies and judgements of the moral self; and I choose *The Quiet American*, by Graham Greene. I want to set down a dispute about this book between two critics. I dare not call them Wordsworth and Keats (what do I know of the opinions either would have held on Communism, on American intervention, even on some of the critical points that will be raised— and how could I ever write in the style of either?); but since one believes in the palpable design and the other in negative capability, I will call them W and K. W begins by summarising the book.

W: This is a political novel, set in Indo-China, where the French are fighting the Communists, while the Americans stand by, offering aid and advice. The story is told by a degenerate, cynical, worldly-wise Englishman called Fowler, who doesn't believe in getting involved—and who understands the local situation far better than the starry-eyed college boy from Boston who blunders

---

[1] 'Ode to Autumn', ll. 5-11

in, eating Vit-health sandwich spread and talking about a Third Force. He has got his ideas from reading too many books before he came, and when he finds his third force it is in the form of a ruthless general with a private army: so that the main result of his interference is a lot of unnecessary civilian deaths. The moral of this is clear and explicit: beware of the innocent. 'Innocence is like a dumb leper who has lost his bell, wandering the world, meaning no harm.'

K: But why are you so sure that the book comes down in favour of Fowler? Not just because he's the narrator—none of us is so naïve nowadays. Fowler is jealous of Pyle, who stole his girl; a part of him is longing for death, and he is not at all grateful when Pyle saves his life with a schoolboyish bravery that Fowler despises: to him it is just another sign that Pyle has no imagination. Surely Greene has gone out of his way to throw doubt on Fowler's motives for having Pyle killed. It's up to us to choose whether we prefer Fowler or Pyle—as men, and as politicians.

W: But it isn't—Greene has chosen. The book is obviously anti-American. Americans thought it was, and it aroused some resentment there. And look at all the touches that have nothing to do with Pyle or Fowler—Joe, for example, the Economic Attaché, complaining that his driver always pretends not to understand French. 'I was three years in Paris. My accent's good enough for one of these damned Vietnamese.' Isn't that the arrogant voice of naïvety? Isn't that a voice that reminds us that Pyle, and all he stands for, is dangerous?

K: Yes but Greene plays very fair. If he gives us the case against Pyle explicitly, he provides all the evidence for the case against the French. Fowler is horrified (and so is Greene!) by the deaths during General Thè's 'demonstration'—using Pyle's bombs; but the French planes are murdering civilians just as savagely up in the north, dropping napalm: 'the poor devils are burnt alive,' says the pilot, 'the flames go over them like water. They are wet through with fire.' These people are just as innocent as General Thè's victims; and though Fowler doesn't react in quite the same way, Greene puts the facts in front of us, for us to do so, if we wish.

W: Are you sure we are never told in the book that Fowler is right in his judgement of Pyle?

K: But of course not. This is a book in which the author never intrudes his own opinions.

W: It needn't be done as a comment. The plot itself might expose Fowler as right and Pyle as wrong—as it does, surely. When Pyle makes his way to Phat Diem, risking his life, Fowler despises him for his courage: 'he was as incapable of imagining pain or danger to himself as he was incapable of conceiving the pain he might cause to others'. You might shrug that aside as being only Fowler's view, but it's made perfectly clear to us, as we go on, that he's right. After the bomb outrage, Pyle looks down at the blood on his shoes, and says, 'I must get a shine before I see the minister'. That isn't something passed on to us, perhaps exaggerated, by Fowler, that's what Pyle said. He can't conceive what has happened to the victims.

K: Well of course the book isn't perfect: I do find some of Pyle's remarks out of character. And the reason for this, I presume, is Greene's own politics. Perhaps, as a man, he is anti-American, or at any rate opposed to American interference in Asia; perhaps he couldn't resist a few digs at Pyle, but we must ignore these. They are touches that the author of *The Quiet American* ought to have prevented Mr Graham Greene from putting in.

W: And in making out your case for Greene's fairness to Pyle you'd ignore these touches?

K: Yes.

W: But that's dreadful—that's the sort of irresponsibility a critic should never allow himself. By picking and choosing what you like in the character of Pyle, you could easily make him admirable—you could make anyone admirable.

K: But we have to pick and choose, as soon as we pass from interpretation to criticism. As soon as we start judging the success of a book, weighing what the author has done against our own experience of life (or, as in this case, our own political judgement) we must, unless the book is perfect, find some dead wood. And how little we find in *The Quiet American*. Greene is a true novelist: which means that whatever his own opinions, they have hardly interfered with his portrayal of both sides. He writes as if he was a chameleon delighting in Iago as much as Imogen. He gives us both sides and allows us to choose.

'His opinions haven't interfered.' The essence of K's position is that a work which depicts a conflict must depict each side with total sympathy, that creative power consists precisely in this, the ability to enter into the identity of everybody. But for W every work of literature has positives, leads us to prefer some attitudes to others; and if we come down on the other side, we are disagreeing with the author. It is clear, I hope, that these terms are not formal ones: a play can be committed, a poem can be dramatic, a novel (as we see) can be taken as either. Jane Austen, George Eliot and Lawrence are all committed writers: their novels have positives.

That was a contrast between two kinds of (or two ways of regarding) literature. I turn now to a contrast between two kinds of criticism.

The literary critic can be pulled in the direction of remembering that art is a unique human activity, which can only be understood and described in its own terms; or that of seeing it as a *human* activity, fed with the same food, hurt with the same weapons, subject to the same diseases as the rest of our lives. I shall describe these two critics as the Aristotelian and the Platonist. The Aristotelian critic is concerned with form: that is, with the organising principles of works of art, the principles that organise them *artistically*. He may, like the Romantics, despise the *genres*, or he may, like the neo-classics, take them seriously; if he does classify, he will do so by formal resemblance, not by similarities in world view, or in the poet's emotion, or in intellectual content. The Platonic critic is concerned with content: and his method of classifying authors, if you take it to an extreme, yields the simple division into those who shall be admitted to the community, for their doctrines are wholesome, and those who should be banished or condemned to silence. His evaluation of a work will involve his own position on whatever issues it treats of.

Now if we state the contrast like this, it seems all in favour of the Aristotelian. For he at least knows what art is: whereas the history of criticism is littered with Platonists (Zhdanov, Tolstoi, Stephen Gosson, and so back to Plato himself) whose hatred of a work's extra-literary intention rendered them unable to listen to it. The Platonist must be able to tell true poetry from false, must possess himself of a poem on its own terms, must enter the world of art, before he can begin to be any sort of critic: otherwise he is merely a censor. We do not care to hear that Lawrence is a fascist or Greene a misanthrope except from those who can tell Lawrence from Céline, Greene from Ian Fleming. A critic can be a mere Aristotelian, but to be a Platonist at all he must be something of an Aristotelian first.

But the Platonist has an advantage too. He will not forget (as the Aristotelian might) that sooner or later formal beauty bores us, unless the material of it is urgent. The Platonist will not mind admitting that movements which revivify art are usually impure, that writers have often been drawn towards their subject for reasons more personal and more savage than its artistic possibilities. He will not forget that literature matters.

The Platonist, being less concerned with form will be tempted to assimilate *The Mill on the Floss* to George Eliot's *Journal*, *Women in Love* to *Psychoanalysis and the Unconscious, Jude the Obscure* to *The Dynasts*. The Aristotelian will be suspicious of such resemblances: a novel is not a discursive treatise, a novel is not a journal, a novel is not an epic drama, he tells us, and these distinctions must be remembered if we are to understand the form of each. One kind of Aristotelian (happily rare today) is uneasy about the very existence of such a mixed form as epic drama; another kind (much commoner today) subdivides forms—the realistic and the symbolic novel, the picaresque and the plotted novel, the comedy of manners and the satire of morals.

It is easy now to bring together these two kinds of critic and these two kinds of literature. The Platonist is likely to write about the committed writer; and quite likely to believe that all writers are, if you look closely, committed. The Aristotelian may believe that all writers are dramatic, but there is no need for him to: he may equally well believe that both kinds are possible, he might even believe that all writers are committed—though if he does he will not consider that this has anything to do with what makes them great. He is as likely to study one kind as another.

And now for the point of this theoretical introduction. This is a highly Platonic book—dogmatically so, some will think, polemically, even fanatically so. Its aim is to discover and compare the values of these three writers—their human, not their artistic values. This may be enough to make some readers decide to read no further. There is, of course, no reason why they should: but though any reader is at liberty to ignore this book, it is not at liberty to ignore them, and I have felt it necessary to ask myself constantly if what I have written is proof against the central objection to the Platonist: the objection that he unwrites literature.

We care about George Eliot's view of life because she was a great novelist: we read her letters and journals because she wrote

Middlemarch. But to study her view of man—to hunt out her ideas, to relate her to Utilitarianism, to Positivism, to Herbert Spencer, to the decline of religious belief—is not this to pounce on those moments in the novels when she leaves fiction to offer an aside, is it not to lean more and more heavily on the journals and letters, on the essays and on *Theophrastus Such*, as if *they* were what mattered most?

And if we go further: if we not only chase after the opinions that she built into her novels, but also try and find, in her emotional life, the compost that made one opinion grow and not another; if we remind ourselves that the intellect takes no interest in an idea or situation unless that has been invested with libido, and so (having gone behind the novels to the opinions) we go behind the opinions to the life and inner stresses of the writer—then we have really unwritten everything. We are back then 'where all the ladders start, In the foul rag-and-bone shop of the heart,' and George Eliot herself will rebuke us:

> Something should be done by dispassionate criticism towards the reform of our national habits in the matter of literary biography. Is it not odious that as soon as a man is dead his desk is raked, and every insignificant memorandum, which he never meant for the public, is printed for the gossiping amusement of people too idle to reread his books? 'He gave the people of his best. His worst he kept, his best he gave'; but there is a certain set, not a small one, who are titillated by the worst and indifferent to the best. I think this fashion is a disgrace to us all. It is something like the uncovering of the dead Byron's club-foot.[1]

An example from Lawrence will be topical here. During the trial of *Lady Chatterley's Lover* the defence witnesses (Platonists to a man) defended the high ethical seriousness implied in the book. Stressing the responsibility which Mellors feels towards Connie, recalling his wish to marry and live with her at the end, they insisted that so far from being a defence of promiscuity, it was a novel deeply concerned with the bond established by sex: that its implications led us to fidelity, not promiscuity. To which Mr Colin Welch:

> One difficulty about Mellors assuming much responsibility for Connie is his apparent failure to assume any responsibility for

[1] Letter to John Blackwood, 20 February, 1874

19

any of the women he has previously bedded, including his wife and the long list of conquests of which he boasts to Connie. Admittedly his sexual experiences with these women, though varied, are uniformly unsatisfactory. . . . Thus is established another point that Lawrence wished to make: that no responsibility whatever is inherent in the sexual act as such. It is inherent only in the *perfect* sexual act. If this is an argument against promiscuity, it seems a very dubious one.[1]

This is unanswerable, but wrong—so wrong, we want to say, that he has not seen the difference between a novel and a treatise. These other women do not exist in the book, the way Connie does: Mellors' desertion of them is not an artistic fact, the way his desertion of Connie would be. Such systematic applications of hypothetical cases is the way we talk of ethical treatises, not of novels. But can we blame Mr Welch? He is only answering (he claims) the assertion of the defence that the book *is* a treatise, or at any rate that it can be read like a treatise: that is, that the moral positives we can extract from it are as systematic as a code. But would this not be an absurd claim—the claim of Platonism run mad (as mad as Plato)? Without, for the moment, pausing to discuss who is at fault here—Mr Welch, or the defence, or Lawrence himself—let us simply note that this is no way to talk about novels.

The remedy is to remember constantly that a belief or a value only matters artistically if it is artistically present in the book. In deducing the beliefs and opinions of these three authors, it is not enough to recall that one 'when a child had strong political opinions, especially about the affairs of the sixteenth and seventeenth centuries', that another had read Comte and translated Strauss, that the third was a pacifist and a wanderer of Nonconformist mining stock. The beliefs that matter are the beliefs of their books; and that means the beliefs that have been really tested, really applied, really brought to life in the imagined world of fiction. The theme and content of a novel matter, and can be discussed: but they matter when—and because—they are embodied in creative achievement.

[1] 'Black Magic, White Lies', *Encounter*, February, 1961

PART ONE

THE TRUTHTELLERS

1 The Absence of God in Jane Austen

JANE AUSTEN, George Eliot and D. H. Lawrence had one important thing in common: they none of them believed in God. Since Henry Austen refers to his sister as 'thoroughly religious and devout', and James Edward Leigh-Austen speaks, in his *Memoir* of his aunt, about 'the piety which ruled her in life, and supported her in death'; since Lawrence called himself, in a letter to Edward Garnett, 'a passionately religious man', and in another letter urged Lady Cynthia Asquith to learn to believe in God ('Believe me, in the end, we will unite in our knowledge of God'); since even George Eliot conveyed her dislike of Buckle by calling him 'irreligious'—this assertion may seem surprising. When we say that Jane Austen did not believe in God, we are giving a special meaning either to 'Jane Austen' or to 'believe'. There is nothing odd or arbitrary about this: it is a meaning well known and well used in literary criticism. In fact, without such a distinction, literary criticism is impossible. We need to say that whatever Miss Austen the sister of Henry may have believed, Jane Austen the novelist did not believe in God; or else we need to say that though her piety 'ruled her life', though, as Henry Austen tells us, in his solemn and splendid Pecksniffian style,

> On Serious religious subjects she was well-instructed, both by reading and meditation, and her opinions accorded strictly with those of our Established Church,[1]

yet she did not arrange, control or interpret her deepest experience in the light of these opinions or this piety—did not, in such a sense, believe. It does not matter which of these we say, for they mean the same: Jane Austen the writer is an instrument for disentangling in the mind and character of Miss Austen what beliefs were, on the deepest level, really accepted.

I say that Jane Austen the novelist did not believe in God because God is totally absent from her work. A person may remain silent about a deeply held and genuine belief, but not a writer:

[1] 'Biographical Notice of the Author', by Henry Austen; prefixed to the posthumous edition of *Northanger Abbey* and *Persuasion*, 1818

all that exists in a writer's work is what he creates. I cannot of course prove that God is absent from Jane Austen's work, because no one can prove an absence: but there is quite a lot of circumstantial evidence. There is, for instance, the question of the duties of the clergy. In one splendid passage, Jane Austen describes what the duties of a clergyman are not:

> . . . it shall be my earnest endeavour to demean myself with grateful respect towards her ladyship, and be ever ready to perform those rites and ceremonies which are instituted by the Church of England.[1]

Her contempt for Mr Collins was complete, and she enjoyed satirising him:

> The rector of a parish has much to do. In the first place, he must make such an agreement for tithes as may be beneficial to himself and not offensive to his patron. He must write his own sermons; and the time that remains will not be too much for his parish duties, and the care and improvement of his dwelling, which he cannot be excused from making as comfortable as possible. And I do not think it of light importance that he should have attentive and conciliatory manners towards everybody, especially towards those to whom he owes his preferment.[2]

What is wrong with Mr Collins as a clergyman? His selfishness, his lack of imagination, would be faults in anyone: what is more specific is that he regards religion as a social institution, not as a personal experience. But so does Henry Tilney, in *Northanger Abbey*—so, even, does Edmund Bertram:

> I cannot call that situation nothing which has the charge of all that is of the first importance to mankind, individually or collectively considered, temporally and eternally—which has the guardianship of religion and morals, and consequently of the manners which result from their influence.[3]

How much should we read into 'consequently'? Is Edmund saying that religion and morals matter in so far as they influence manners? Certainly 'religion' is an automatic word here—it is not by awakening faith that Jane Austen's clergyman will wield influence. As we read on, the stress on manners becomes even clearer:

[1] *Pride and Prejudice*, ch. 13   [2] Ibid., ch. 18   [3] *Mansfield Park*, ch. 9

It is not in fine preaching only that a good clergyman will be useful in his parish and his neighbourhood, where the parish and neighbourhood is of a size capable of knowing his private character and observing his general conduct, which in London can rarely be the case. The clergy are lost there in the crowds of their parishioners. They are known to the largest part only as preachers.[1]

It is only as a man, we here realise, that the clergyman will be watched, not as a priest. His manners will be better observed by country neighbours, it is true; but the depth of religious experience does not rub off in neighbourly contact—indeed, it is probably better seen in preaching. Even to Edmund, there will be nothing *religious* about the duties of the admirable clergyman he will (of course) make. And when we turn to their wives, we see that even as a social function the office of the clergyman is slight. Mrs Elton does little for the parish—but then, after all, she is Mrs Elton. Mrs Grant, however, whom Jane Austen likes, hardly does more:

Mrs Grant, having by this time run through the usual resources of ladies residing in the country without a family of children— having more than filled her favourite sitting room with pretty furniture and made a choice collection of plants and poultry— was very much in want of some variety at home.[2]

That is all very well for a lady residing in the country: but Mrs Grant is not simply that, she is a parson's wife. Is there no more for her to do?

The characters of Henry Tilney and Edmund Bertram are very different from that of Mr Collins. As clergymen, they will be less gross in their deference to rank, and more delicate in their patronage of inferiors. But it is not at all clear just how their duties will differ from those which Mr Collins set himself. They will defer, and they will patronise; they will not be any more religious than he is, and they certainly will not show enthusiasm. If they are better clergymen, that will simply be because they are better men.

And it need not surprise us to find that what Jane Austen has satirised with such verve and bite is not far from what she believes herself. The same is true of her views on marriage:

[1] Ibid., ch. 9   [2] Ibid., ch. 4

About thirty years ago, Miss Maria Ward, of Huntingdon, with only seven thousand pounds, had the good luck to captivate Sir Thomas Bertram, of Mansfield Park, in the county of Northampton, and to be thereby raised to the rank of a baronet's lady, with all the comforts and consequences of a handsome house and a large income. All Huntingdon exclaimed on the greatness of the match; and her uncle, the lawyer, himself allowed her to be at least three thousand pounds short of any equitable claim to it.[1]

Here is Jane Austen's satire at its calmest and most deadly. Without raising her voice, she sets to and outlines the view that marriage is a transaction. It could, as we read casually, sound like a neutral, factual account of what happens, though one or two words might make us raise an eyebrow: 'luck', 'captivate', 'comforts and consequences' as the fruits of marriage. ('Captivate' is not only deadly, but neat: it could so easily mean, in such a context, 'infatuate', and yet it firmly doesn't.) The one touch that is violently and obviously satiric is 'equitable': only as the sentence ends are we given the metaphor of a transaction so grossly that we are *forced* to see what is being said, and to realise openly what this view of marriage is.

We applaud: we see in this a standard to condemn the fortune-hunting of Willoughby and General Tilney. And yet Jane Austen's heroines have the same good luck as Miss Ward: even those who love men without prospects have good fortune thrust upon them, in the end, by the kindly authoress. A remark by Lord David Cecil that has become celebrated sums up her view of marriage: 'It was wrong to marry for money, but it was silly to marry without it'.[2] Several critics have objected to this, saying it is refuted by, or at any rate denied in, *Persuasion*. '*Persuasion*,' writes D. W. Harding,[3] 'deliberately states the obligation to treat love as the *only* allowable basis of marriage.' (My italics.) The alternative basis is, of course, money: and the *only* way to demonstrate that love is the only allowable basis would be to show a match where there was love and not money. I doubt if there is such a match in Jane Austen, but the nearest thing is probably Mrs Price, who

[1] *Mansfield Park*, ch. 1

[2] *Jane Austen*, by Lord David Cecil (Leslie Stephen Lecture, 1936), p. 33

[3] 'The Character of Literature: Jane Austen and Moral Judgement', in *From Blake to Byron* (Pelican Guide to English Literature, vol. 5), p. 54

married 'in the common phrase, to disoblige her family', and we (and Fanny) see the dreadful consequences. Anne Elliott married for love, but she did not marry a poor man: Cecil is therefore right. Further, Anne is made to draw the moral of *Persuasion* for us, quite explicitly: and the moral is not that she should have defied Lady Russell and held to her engagement with the then penniless Captain Wentworth. She was right to take the advice (family approval is another—and essential—basis for marriage) and Anne even hesitates to assert that Lady Russell was wrong to give it:

> I am not saying that she did not err in her advice. It was, perhaps, one of those cases in which advice is good or bad only as the event decides; and for myself, I certainly never should, in any circumstance of tolerable similarity, give such advice. But I mean, that I was right in submitting to her . . . .[1]

'As the event decides': I cannot believe that this merely means 'as the marriage is happy or not', for such a qualification is true of all advice, and Jane Austen does not usually utter such tautologies. She means 'as the man makes his fortune or not', as we soon realise if we read on and see where the blame principally lies—in Captain Wentworth. He should have come back to Anne as soon as he had made his fortune, and then she would have renewed the engagement: then she would have had the other 'allowable basis' besides love. Jane Austen believed that love was a necessary but not a sufficient condition of marriage.

And so she is able to put into the mouth of Mary Crawford a piece of irony so delicate that it is hard to be quite sure if it really is ironic:

> I would have everybody marry if they can do it properly. I do not like to have people throw themselves away; but everybody should marry as soon as they can do it to advantage.[2]

'Properly'; 'to advantage'—yes, there is a grain of coarseness in this that labels it as Mary Crawford. Yet what is 'coarseness' but frankness?—for the content of this is a pure summary of what Jane Austen herself thought.

From these two instances we can now generalise about Jane Austen's satire. Her neatest and most deadly attacks are always upon something which she is not too far away from herself: the

---

[1] *Persuasion*, ch. 23   [2] *Mansfield Park*, ch. 4

selfishness of Emma, the catty brilliance of Mary Crawford, like the view of marriage as a transaction, like the triviality of Mr Collins' pastoral duties, are only tactless and too explicit versions of some of the bases of Jane Austen's world. Her finest satire is directed at a distorted image of herself.

More of this later: my concern here has been to find in Jane Austen's conception of the clerical life as complete an absence of the religious dimension as she found in Mr Collins' conception. It would be absurd to underrate the force of her satire against Mr Collins: but what she is satirising is his folly and selfishness as a man. Clerical virtue is not, for her, essentially different from secular virtue. And she is no devout anti-clerical either: if there is a special religious quality, the place to look for it will be in the clergy. We can only conclude that for Jane Austen the novelist there is no such quality.

2 *The Absence of God in George Eliot*

The absence of God in George Eliot is more difficult to establish. For in her novels religious experience is not, as it is in Jane Austen, simply omitted: it is, on the contrary, very prominent. Her first book was about clergymen; and almost all the novels have a clergyman in them. Religious experience is—or seems to be—a main theme of at least two: *Janet's Repentance* and *Adam Bede*.

Janet's Repentance is the story of a conversion. Janet Dempster is the wife of a lawyer who has led the movement to persecute the local evangelical clergyman, Mr Tryan. She is a tall, dark, proud woman, hungry for love, intense with sympathy, bitter at the neglect and cruelty her husband shows her—a Dorothea Brooke, even a Marian Evans. She supports her husband in his attacks on Tryan, partly because she is glad to do anything that will renew sympathy between them, but also because she is sure that Tryan must be self-righteous and insensitive. One day she happens to visit a sick girl, and overhears Mr Tryan comforting her: his humility, his fellowship in the girl's suffering, and his glance as he comes out (his 'one, direct, pathetic look') impress her deeply; and when, later, her trouble with her husband comes to a head she sends for Mr Tryan. They become close friends for the short remainder of his life—a friendship tinged, at the end, with sexual attraction, but never dangerously.

It is difficult, now, to understand the delighted reception which *Scenes from Clerical Life* met with when it came out in 1858: enthusiastic letters came from Froude, from Mrs Carlyle, from Dickens, who wrote

> to express my admiration of their extraordinary merit. The exquisite truth and delicacy, both of the humour and the pathos of these stories, I have never seen the like of.[1]

Were they all delighting in what we now prefer to overlook—the sentimentality, the occasional facetiousness, the lurid melodrama— or were they remarkably perceptive, disengaging from all these the seeds of her greatness? For to us, who know and admire the later novels, the *Scenes* are full of fascinating anticipations; and one of the obvious faults of *Janet's Repentance* (the fact that it is clogged with too many characters, with a sprinkling of every age and trade in the village) seems, to the eyes of hindsight, rich with the promise of *Middlemarch*. In discussing George Eliot's treatment of conversion I have chosen to begin with *Janet's Repentance*, because she began with it, and because it is all set out so neatly there; but before discussing its likeness to the works that followed I will begin with a remark on its difference—that is, on its inferiority. For this in turn ought to throw light on the greatness to come.

George Eliot has not yet learned, in his book, to state her ethical position with the flexibility that will adjust it to real human cases; nor to body it forth dramatically. It must strike any reader of *Janet's Repentance* how much stating there is, how much telling instead of showing:

> Assuredly Milby had that salt of goodness which keeps the world together, in greater abundance than was visible on the surface: innocent babes were born there, sweetening their parents' hearts with simple joys. . . .[2]

> He is stumbling, perhaps; his heart now beats fast with dread, now heavily with anguish; his eyes are sometimes dim with tears, which he makes haste to dash away; . . .[3]

Such passages breathe the mingling of melodrama and uplift that the Victorian public loved, and it doesn't matter whether we

---

[1] Letter from Dickens to George Eliot, 18 January, 1858; published in *George Eliot's Life as Related in her Letters and Journals*, ed. Cross, vol. 2
[2] *Janet's Repentance*, ch. 2   [3] Ibid., ch. 10

censure George Eliot for truckling to her readers or for sharing their tastes: the result is what matters. But it would be wrong to think that their badness is connected with their explicitness. It would be wrong, first, because parts of the 'showing' are at least as bad (Mr Tryan's dialogue is slush; his flashback into his past as a seducer is lurid and ludicrous); second, because what maturity this book has comes not only in the conversations in the Red Lion, but also in the explicitness:

> We have all of us considerable regard for our past self, and are not fond of casting reflections on that respected individual by a total negation of his opinions. . . .[1]

> It is because sympathy is but a living again through our own past in a new form, that confession often prompts a response of confession. . . .[2]

In these sentences the great George Eliot is already emerging: that wiry intellect, bent to the springy shape of sympathy by the intense heat of her intuitive understanding. Such sentences are as much the product of a creative act as any dialogue: and this is the final and important reason why the badness of *Janet's Repentance* must not be attributed to its explicitness. The greatness of the mature George Eliot consists so often in her ability to move from a dramatic scene to its generalised implications without her language withdrawing to the level of fact and logic only, that if we read her with the prejudice that showing is the mode of literature, and telling merely that of the commentator, we cripple our appreciation from the start. I do not illustrate this further now: it will, I hope, demonstrate itself in the course of the book; and I shall be discussing it, from a different direction, in a later part.

To take *Janet's Repentance*, now, as a study in conversion. It is conversion by a clergyman, in the name of Christianity: but what Janet gets from Mr Tryan is wholly human. What first touches her heart is the look he gives her when they meet accidentally at Sally Martin's. Expecting to hear only 'self-satisfied unction', she is surprised when she overhears Mr Tryan comforting Sally by talking about his own weaknesses, and saying 'Pray for me, Sally, that I may have strength too when the hour of great suffering comes'. The surprise grows, and deepens to respect, when he comes out of Sally's room, and they look at each other gravely for a few

---

[1] *Janet's Repentance*, ch. 12   [2] Ibid., ch. 18

moments. What arrested Janet in Mr Tryan's voice was a 'fellow-ship in suffering'; what moves her in his look is 'the direct glance of a sincere and loving human soul'. The divine is not merely absent here, it is explicitly replaced by the human.

Mr Tryan's influence on Janet is due entirely to this human contact; and George Eliot says so:

> The tale of the Divine Pity was never yet believed from lips that were not felt to be moved by human pity.[1]

The same point is made when she comes again to Mr Tryan, and eases her wild need for comfort by confessing to him her despair and her temptation to drink.

> Then poor Janet poured forth her sad tale of temptation and despondency; and even while she was confessing she felt half her burden removed. The act of confiding in human sympathy, the consciousness that a fellow-being was listening to her with patient pity, prepared her soul for the stronger leap by which faith grasps the idea of the divine sympathy.[2]

Since Mr Tryan is, after all, a clergyman, and will therefore himself offer a religious view of what he has succeeded in doing ('I am very thankful that He has chosen to work through me'), George Eliot cannot omit the Divine pity from her analysis; but she is as careful as Hawthorne ever was not to give it an independent status. The 'stronger leap by which faith grasps the idea of the Divine sympathy' could take us the further step into religious belief; and indeed some Christians might insist as strongly as she does that the path to Divine sympathy must lie through human sympathy, and might claim that this is the significance of the Incarnation—that only as it is made flesh can the divine be apprehended. Though George Eliot is careful not to deny this step, she is equally careful not to take it: and perhaps there are hints that she is not encouraging her readers to take it. 'That stronger leap by which *faith grasps* the idea of the Divine sympathy': is there not something in the syntax that puts the responsibility on faith, that suggests that God is the product of faith, rather than the reverse? The *idea* of the Divine sympathy may underline this. It is the gentlest of emphases but is it not a shadow of denial that the Divine is 'out there', waiting for us? If the Incarnation is a way of telling us that the human can be a metaphor for the divine, George Eliot seems to be closer, here, to saying that the divine is a metaphor for the human. There is little doubt that this is what Marian Evans believed: writing to Mrs Henry Ponsonby nearly twenty years later, she described the 'conclusion without which I could not have cared to write any representation of human life', and it is exactly the conclusion we have been drawing out of *Janet's Repentance*:

> that the fellowship between man and man which has been the principle of development, social and moral, is not dependent on conceptions of what is not man: and that the idea of God, as far as it has been a high spiritual influence, is the ideal of a goodness entirely human (i.e. an exaltation of the human).[1]

Turning back to *Janet's Repentance*, we can find this conclusion repeatedly confirmed:

> In this artificial life of ours, it is not often we see a human face with all a heart's agony in it, uncontrolled by self-consciousness; when we do see it, it startles us as if we had suddenly walked into the real world of which this everyday one is but a puppet-show copy. For some moments Mr Tryan was too deeply moved to speak.[2]

Here surely the core of the experience is its purely human quality. The phrase 'the real world of which this everyday one is but a puppet-show copy' seems the natural vocabulary of anyone wishing to contrast our glimpses of the divine with the merely human; but it is used here with a different purpose, to contrast a glimpse of the human with the merely conventional.

George Eliot felt it necessary to give Mr Tryan at any rate one heresy: it keeps his human quality from being too completely absorbed in his calling. And it is worth noting what the heresy is:

> My friend used to urge me that my sin against God was greater than my sin against her; but—it may be from want of deeper spiritual feeling—that has remained to this hour the sin which causes me the bitterest spiritual pang.[3]

[1] Letter to Mrs Henry Frederick Ponsonby, 10 December, 1874
[2] *Janet's Repentance*, ch. 18   [3] Ibid., ch. 18

By causing him—uneasily of course, for he is a clergyman—to suggest that God can look after himself, George Eliot has extricated him, if ever so gently, from the religion he professes.

The conversion of Janet Dempster is the pattern of all George Eliot conversions. The interpretation I have outlined is one that she never changed, though she learned to weave it more and more intricately into a situation more and more deeply understood. In her next book, *Adam Bede*, she placed a conversion at the climax: the opening of Hetty's heart in prison by Dinah Morris. *Adam Bede* is much longer than *Janet's Repentance*, and the treatment of Hetty is more sustained and ambitious than that of Janet. It is in one important respect more religious: and less successful.

There are three phases in the treatment of Hetty: her initial egoism, the suffering that makes her accessible to influence, and her yielding and confession. Though, strictly, it is only the third which concerns my present argument, I shall say something about the others first.

Hetty as we first see her is locked completely in herself: her 'narrow bit of an imagination' is not large enough for her to enter into what anyone else is feeling or even saying. When she reads Arthur Donnithorne's letter explaining at length why their affair is over, she takes in nothing of his eloquence, merely the one fact that impinges on her wishes: 'Reasons why he could not marry her had no existence for her mind.' (Here, with unusual economy, George Eliot in showing us Hetty's selfishness has also shown us Arthur's—Hetty's unimaginative pouncing on the one central fact amid his easy phrases reminds us that it *is* the central fact, that they *are* easy phrases.) This egoism of Hetty's, this limited imagination, issues in an inability to listen. So when Adam, about to hand over this same letter to her, tries to tell her how useless it is to love Arthur, she hears all he says but takes in only those points that answer or don't answer to what she wants—to deceive her family, to prevent Adam telling anybody what he knows, and above all to keep Arthur:

> Hetty said nothing: she felt a revival of hope at the mention of a letter which Adam had not read. There would be something quite different in it from what he thought.[1]

[1] *Adam Bede,* ch. 30

Letters, to Hetty, don't contain what they are likely to contain, but what she wishes them to: it is the narrowness of her imagination that makes self-deception so easy to her.

In Hetty lie the seeds of Proust's Odette. During a long, subtle and eloquent speech of self-deceiving analysis by Swann, explaining why it would be wrong, even degrading, even against her own interests, for her to go to the *Opera-Comique* that evening ('tu es une eau informe qui coule selon la pente qu'on lui offre'), Odette's reaction is this:

> Odette depuis un moment donnait des signes d'émotion et d'incertitude. A défaut du sens de ce discours, elle comprenait qu'il pouvait rentrer dans le genre commun des 'laius' et scènes de reproches ou de supplications, dont l'habitude qu'elle avait des hommes lui permettait, sans s'attacher aux détails des mots, de conclure qu'ils ne les prononceraient pas s'ils nétaient pas amoureux, que du moment qu'ils étaient amoureux il était inutile de leur obéir, qu'ils ne le seraient que plus après. Aussi aurait-elle écouté Swann avec le plus grand calme si elle n'avait vu que l'heure passait et que pour peu qu'il parlât encore quelque temps, elle allait, comme elle le lui dit avec un sourire tendre, obstiné et confus, 'finir par manquer l'Ouverture'![1]

To measure early George Eliot against Proust at his most deadly and most subtle may be unfair, so I will merely remark in passing how perfectly we are shown Odette's inability to listen because she has brought to such intuitive perfection her ability to take from such a speech exactly what she needs to know: egoism narrows the imagination by sharpening one part of it. Nor has Proust any need to moralise and shake his head: his novel does not offer morals, merely the material for us to draw them if we wish. Only occasionally in *Adam Bede* do we catch the clear note of George Eliot's maturity, the note of reporting a truth that is too disquieting and too clearly seen to be messed up with comment:

> Hetty did not understand how anybody could be very fond of middle-aged people.[2]

This is the most frightening sentence in the whole book. Its wording is so mild it could be uttered, in all innocence, by Hetty herself; its content so horrible that it suggests, as none of the moralising

[1] *Du Coté de chez Swann*, Gallimard edition, vol. II, p. 97
[2] *Adam Bede*, ch. 15

can, the constricted vision of the totally selfish. This sentence is buried in a paragraph of sad analysis of Hetty's selfishness—good enough paragraph in its way, but it weakens the sharp effect of this one sentence. It was not till she came to write *Middlemarch* that George Eliot was able to keep up this terrible cool gaze, reporting the narrowness of Rosamund's imagination in a voice that never softens, wails or falters—the nearest thing in English to the voice of Proust. It is this selfishness that causes Hetty to present so tough a front to Dinah Morris: Dinah's offers of help and sympathy are seen merely as a threat to the boundaries of her imagination. To become capable of yielding, Hetty has first to suffer.

Hetty's suffering is the finest thing in *Adam Bede*. The two chapters (36 and 37) that describe her journey to Windsor and back, and Hetty's own confession in chapter 45, display a widening of George Eliot's powers: a vision of ultimate pain and distress that recalls Dostoyevsky. They show, incidentally, how foolish is that school of novel criticism for which characterisation is the only fit aim of the novelist: as Hetty is impersonalised, her story moves to a deeper level. Of course this is still not the George Eliot of *Middlemarch* or even of *The Mill on the Floss*: the touches of power are often softened. When the coachman, with laborious archness, teases Hetty about her sweetheart, 'Hetty felt her face flushing and then turning pale. She thought this coachman must know something about her.' The directness of this corresponds perfectly to the naïve alarm that Hetty felt; but this was not the moment to soften the effect with an explanatory generalisation beginning 'It is difficult for country people to believe . . .'

The narrowness of Hetty's imagination is both a help and a hindrance to George Eliot in these two chapters. So simple a sensibility is exactly the right medium to show us the numbing effect of the wretched journey, and when we are stood back to see Hetty's sufferings (as she can't see them herself) in a larger context, the simple contrast is very impressive. But George Eliot's leisurely style, the unsubtle, even laborious methods that she has not yet learnt to concentrate and explore with, is too greatly encouraged by the need to fit the slow-moving mind of Hetty. The result, until the birth of the baby, is good writing but not great. The only touch before that which shows the full range of the author's power, is Hetty's irrational decision, when she finds that Arthur is not at

Windsor, to go back the way she came, acting on the trivial reason that there was a good place to drown herself at Stratford on Avon.

But after the baby is born, Hetty's simplicity is completely universalised, and can no longer be felt as a limitation on the writing. And the shift in viewpoint that the plot imposed on George Eliot (or that she was enlightened enough to impose on the plot) has had excellent results. Because Hetty will not talk at the trial, the birth and abandoning of the baby are described by others, and shown wholly from the outside: only later do we get Hetty's version, in her confession to Dinah. This means that George Eliot is unable to comment: and the factual account that Sarah Stone and John Olding give at the trial forces her towards a style so unlike her accustomed style that we could mistake it for the work of another novelist, a novelist as different as can be from George Eliot—Hemingway, say:

> My name is Sarah Stone. I am a widow, and keep a small shop licensed to sell tobacco, snuff, and tea, in Church Lane, Stoniton. The prisoner at the bar is the same young woman who came, looking ill and tired, with a basket on her arm, and asked for a lodging at my house on Saturday, evening the 27th of February. . . .

> My name is John Olding. I am a labourer, and live at Tedd's Hole, two miles out of Stoniton. A week last Monday, towards one o'clock in the afternoon, I was going towards Hetton Coppice, and about a quarter of a mile from the coppice I saw the prisoner, in a red cloak, sitting under a bit of a haystack not far off the stile. She got up when she saw me, and seemed as if she'd be walking on the other way. . . . I should have thought she was a beggar-woman, only for her good clothes. I thought she looked a bit crazy, but it was no business of mine. I stood and looked back after her, but she went right on while she was in sight. . . .[1]

The power of this comes not simply from the omission of comment (though certainly it would be weakened by the use of words like 'pity', 'compassion' or—later—'conscience'); it comes from the shock of the changing viewpoint, the movement from a sensitive and garrulous author to the bluntness of the shopwoman and the field labourer. The formality of the trial helps too: even the words

[1] *Adam Bede*, ch. 43

'My name is Sarah Stone' hit us with a shock. I do not wish to suggest anything so foolish as that the style of Hemingway is 'better' than that of George Eliot; but if we had been advising the George Eliot of *Adam Bede* how to overcome her natural weaknesses, how to startle the reader with a crude factual power when unfolding Hetty's story, would we not have told her to use the vocabulary of some unreflecting, some simply articulate man like John Olding:

> And just as I was stooping and laying down the stakes, I saw something odd and round and whitish lying on the ground under a nut-bush by the side of me. And I stooped down on hands and knees to pick it up. And I saw it was a little baby's hand.[1]

When we come to Hetty's own version, we are given something more ambitious. Now there is a moral dimension to be introduced: we are to be shown that Hetty was unable to get rid of the clutch of compassion. The George Eliot of *Middlemarch* could—and would —have made this explicit; the George Eliot of *Adam Bede* was wiser to find a symbol, the baby's cry, and to leave out the word itself. When Hetty at last tells her story the simplicity remains, and takes on a further tremor: 'I heard the baby crying, and thought the other folks heard it too, and I went on.' It could be Bunyan now, as well as Hemingway. We get no comment, and need none.

Then finally there is the conversion itself. This is in two parts. The first awakening of Hetty to an outside influence comes near the beginning of her return journey, when she catches sight of Dinah's name in her red-leather case:

> Now for the first time she remembered without indifference the affectionate kindness Dinah had shown her, and those words of Dinah in the bed-chamber—that Hetty must think of her as a friend in trouble. Suppose she were to go to Dinah, and ask her to help her?[2]

This is the first time it occurs to Hetty that another person might have something to say to her, not on her own terms, but on that other person's. What stirs in Hetty's now more accessible mind is

[1] Ibid., ch. 43   [2] Ibid., ch. 37

a memory, the memory of Dinah's visit to her bedroom at the Hall Farm, and her offer of help. If we turn back to that scene (turn back in memory, as readers, or turn back the page, as critics) we are sure to be disappointed: there is nothing in it as vivid as the glance, the 'one, direct, pathetic look', which Mr Tryan gives Janet, nothing more clearly realised than 'Dinah, covered with her long white dress, her pale face full of subdued emotion'. All the vividness of George Eliot's creative sympathy has gone to Hetty's alarm ('there now came a low tap, and Hetty, with a leaping heart, rushed to blow out the candles and throw them into the drawer') and not enough to Dinah's attempts at human contact: so that the scene will not bear the weight it is given in the book and in Hetty's memory.

More important, however, is the second stage in Hetty's conversion: her response to Dinah praying for her in the prison cell. And here George Eliot is explicitly religious in a way she had been careful to avoid in *Janet's Repentance*. In the first place, she says, in her own person:

We are over-hasty to speak, as if God did not manifest Himself by our silent feeling, and make His love felt through ours.[1]

This is surprising enough, from the agnostic George Eliot. It is true that the last sentence was 'But it was born in upon her, as she afterwards said, that she must not hurry God's work—that is, a reflection by Dinah herself, cast in the religious terminology that is inevitable to her; and George Eliot, wanting to agree with Dinah, may have felt it clumsy to shift the vocabulary too suddenly. But this is, at best, an excuse; and indeed, causes us to question the artistic validity of inserting here a later reflection of Dinah's, as if Dinah was the narrator, or a real person known to the narrator —there has been no other hint of this.

And, as we read on, we can be certain that George Eliot did in fact *mean* to adopt a religious vocabulary:

She felt the Divine presence more and more—nay, as if she herself were a part of it, and it was the Divine pity that was beating in her heart, and was willing the rescue of this helpless one.[2]

[1] *Adam Bede*, ch. 45   [2] Ibid., ch. 45

This is almost an exact reversal of the sentence about Divine Pity in *Janet's Repentance*: 'the tale of the Divine Pity was never yet believed from lips that were not felt to be moved by human pity'. In the case of Dinah, we are virtually being told that her human pity was simply a version of the Divine Pity.

And when Dinah finally makes contact with Hetty, it is by praying:

> Come, Lord, and gather of the fruits of Thy travail and Thy pleading; stretch forth Thy hand, Thou who are mighty to save to the uttermost, and rescue this lost one.[1]

This prayer, which is a page long, is in the conventional religious language that Marian Evans' Aunt Samuel (the 'original' of Dinah Morris) might well have used; and it is immediately followed by:

> 'Dinah,' Hetty sobbed out, throwing her arms round Dinah's neck, 'I will speak . . . I will tell . . . I won't hide it any more.'[2]

Surely we have been cheated. The main concern of the novelist in this scene should be the contact between Dinah and Hetty, what it was that enabled Dinah to open Hetty's heart: and that is precisely what we aren't given. George Eliot tells us nothing about the conversion that Dinah could not have told us herself; neither directly, in comment, nor in dialogue or imagery, is there any attempt to show us why Dinah succeeded. The novel has dodged its climax.

One reply to this is sure to occur to many readers: that Dinah succeeds by grace, which it is beyond the power of any writer to demonstrate, or even to understand; so that if I were to insist that grace must be rendered in the scene, not merely asserted, I could be told that I am asking the impossible. What disturbs me about this argument is not merely the fact that George Eliot wouldn't have used it herself, but the fact that it is asking the novelist to abandon his art at the crucial moment. We assume that to create a scene the novelist must understand, be able to express, what is happening between his characters; to exempt him from this is to remove the possibility of fiction being about the real world. And so this argument would be claiming that the climax is incomprehensible, not in the general sense that all human actions have a residue of mystery that will tinge the novelist's style with a sense

---

[1] Ibid., ch. 45   [2] Ibid., ch. 45

of the strangeness of personality, but in a quite special sense that removes it from the sphere of the human. That must remove it from the sphere of the novelist; and will mean that as he reaches the edge of religious experience the novelist must draw back, or abandon his art. There can be novels with religious characters, but no religious novels.

And if it is true that George Eliot loses her grip as a novelist towards the climax of the book, it would fit with what no modern reader of *Adam Bede* can help noticing—the streak of melodrama that begins with Adam's declaration to Mr Massey:—

> I used to be hard sometimes; I'll never be hard again. I'll go, Mr Massey—I'll go with you.—[1]

rises through the 'piercing shriek' that 'rang through the hall' when Hetty hears the verdict, and culminates in the lurid picture of Hetty, on the way to be executed, being rescued by Arthur Donnithorne 'cleaving the crowd at full gallop', looking as if 'his eyes were glazed by madness', and 'carrying in his hand'—yes, reader, you've guessed it—'a hard-won release from death'.

Almost all George Eliot's other novels offer a study in conversion, in most cases at the very centre of the book: Felix Holt's effect on Esther, Dorothea's on Rosamund, Daniel Deronda's on Gwendolen. In all these cases, she works in purely secular terms: not only do they differ from *Adam Bede* in not using Christian language, they differ from *Janet's Repentance* in that the process is not even ostensibly religious.

3 George Eliot's Beliefs

Perhaps it will be best to pause here and document George Eliot's attitude to Christianity from outside the novels. It is not easy to do this, since her personal beliefs differed so markedly from the way she regarded the religious beliefs of others. She herself not only disbelieved in miracles and in immortality, she regarded belief, at any rate in the latter, as actually pernicious. She states this with characteristic wit in her attack on Young's *Night Thoughts*:

> If it were not for the prospect of immortality, he considers it would be wise and agreeable to be indecent, or to murder

---

[1] *Adam Bede*, ch. 42

one's father; and, heaven apart, it would be extremely
irrational in any man not to be a knave.[1]

Morality which is motivated by a wish for reward is egotistical;
and no less so if the reward comes in another world instead of this.
'Young has no concept of religion as anything else than egoism
turned heavenward.' After disposing of Young, she turns to the
positive she wishes to set against his other-worldly cynicism:

> It is conceivable that in some minds the deep pathos lying in
> the thought of human mortality—that we are here for a little
> while and then vanish away, that this earthly life is all that
> is given to our loved ones and to our many suffering fellow-men
> —lies nearer the fountains of moral emotion than the concep-
> tion of extended existence. . . . Because learned gentlemen
> are theological, are we to have no more simple honesty and
> goodwill.[2]

George Eliot's scepticism was not a negative creed, a *pis aller*,
but the first step to an ennobling of humanity. Yet, paradoxically,
she hated to attack religion. 'The bent of my mind,' she wrote to
Clifford Allbutt, 'is conservative rather than destructive, and . . .
denial has been wrung from me by hard experience—not adopted
as a pleasant rebellion.'[3] Her letters are filled with this reluctance
to destroy, this 'reverence for the hard-won inheritance of the ages'.
Thus she wrote to Charles Bray in 1859:

> Let everyone believe—as they will, in spite of your kind
> efforts—*what they like to believe.* . . . I can't tell you how much
> melancholy it causes me that people are, for the most part, so
> incapable of comprehending the state of mind which cares for
> that which is essentially human in all forms of belief, and
> desires to exhibit it under all forms with loving truthfulness.[4]

This places George Eliot in the dilemma of both wishing and not
wishing to attack Christianity. It is a dilemma whose formulation
she was very familiar with, for she translated it. In the last chapter
of *The Life of Jesus*, Strauss discusses the various courses open to

---

[1] 'Worldliness and Other-worldliness' (1857); George Eliot's *Essays*, ed.
Pinney, p. 337
[2] Ibid., p. 375
[3] Letter to Clifford Allbutt, August, 1868
[4] Letter to Charles Bray, 5 July, 1859

B*   41

the speculative theologian—that is, the scholar who has come to interpret the scriptures mythically, and to reject the historical validity of the Incarnation, yet is at the same time a minister of the Christian Church. Since he will not be able to elevate the whole Church to his own austere and sophisticated view, 'the speculative theology threatens us with the distinction of an esoteric and exoteric doctrine, which ill accords with the declaration of Christ, that all shall be taught of God'. Strauss' solution—to adhere to the forms of the popular conception but to strain on every occasion to show their spiritual significance—is no more a solution than dilemmas usually yield, and he admits its instability: such a minister will too easily draw the charge of hypocrisy, and then his own uneasiness will cause it to become true. George Eliot sometimes appears to be in the same dilemma: and in practice her solution was to distinguish exoteric from esoteric doctrine. The religion she is reluctant to attack is that of Dolly Winthrop and Adam Bede: that of simple, unspeculative people. The theological worldliness she denounces is that of Young or of the evangelical writer Dr John Cumming—those who were learned and sought to be influential.

In real life, this can never be more than an awkward compromise: we cannot set our acquaintances an examination before deciding which face to turn to them. But in her novels it led George Eliot to the quite acceptable—indeed profitable—position of valuing religion in so far as it was a metaphor for conduct. For this then divides the dilemma according to the exigencies of literary creation. The truth of a belief is something which concerns the author only beyond the boundaries of his book; what matters artistically is not its truth but its function. Strauss' distinction between two forms of the Higher Criticism—the naturalistic and the mythical—is valuable to the literary sensibility. The efforts of the naturalist to disinter historical fact from a misleading garment of interpretation concern only the scientist, the historian and the believer. The mythical interpreter sees the scriptural record as a whole, as a 'sacred legend', as a record of 'the spirit of a people or a community', in very much the same way we see a work of art as a whole.

George Eliot is in one sense more agnostic than many of the great Victorian agnostics: not only does she refuse to know whether God exists, she refuses to know whether this decision need be taken by everyone. In her impartial regard for human experience, she included the religious: not rejecting Christianity, but treating it as a human phenomenon. Thus her continuing interest in evangelicalism, long after she had left her youthful Methodist phase, was due to her belief that its terminology described, and its influence cultivated, some of the most valuable springs of human action. To believe this it was necessary neither to believe its doctrines, nor to take issue with those who did.

This is most easily seen in *Janet's Repentance*. I have already discussed the means by which Mr Tryan converts Janet, and the fact that he did it in the name of his religion. If now we ask what that religion was like in whose name he acted, we find that George Eliot prefers to describe it with no reference to the Divine.

> The movement, like all other religious 'revivals', had mixed effect.... It may be that some of Mr Tryan's hearers had gained a religious vocabulary rather than religious experience; that here and there a weaver's wife, who, a few months before, had been simply a silly slattern, was converted into that more complex nuisance, a silly and sanctimonious slattern.... Nevertheless, Evangelicalism had brought into palpable existence and operation in Milby society that idea of duty, that recognition of something to be lived for beyond the mere satisfaction of self, which is to the moral life what the addition of a great central ganglion is to animal life. No man can begin to mould himself on a faith or an idea without rising to a higher order of experience: a principle of subordination, of self-mastery, has been introduced into his nature; he is no longer a mere bundle of impressions, desires, and impulses.[1]

Both sides of the case are here set forth in terms of conduct: the behaviouristic simile of the great central ganglion tells us of a way of influencing and controlling what people do. What matters about the 'recognition of something to be lived for beyond the mere satisfaction of self' is not its truth but is function.

Now I have at this point to admit the possibility of a radical Christian attack on what I have been claiming. I can imagine a theist saying that (as one theist did say) all this has been operating with his grandfather's notion of God; that a good deal of modern theology has modified traditional notions of God until they resemble what I have described as the absence of God. I do not know what to do with this objection. I do not want to argue theology: this

---

[1] *Janet's Repentance*, ch. 10

book (as will soon become plain) trespasses enough as it is on fields beyond the edge of literary criticism. And naturally I do not wish to question that right of theologians to tell us what is meant by 'God', or even to tell us that the agnosticism of George Eliot is really a form of Christianity. No revolution in Christian thought, however, can deny what had happened in the past, and a God who exists only as part of our experiences (or whose independent existence can never be known) would not have been called 'God' by most of George Eliot's contemporaries. Since my friend's grandfather may well have been among her readers, I shall have to operate with his notions.

We can illustrate even more particularly George Eliot's view that religion is valuable in so far as it is a metaphor for conduct. Sometimes the status of her religious terminology is explicitly that of a simile. When Jermyn is left alone after his tremendous quarrel with Mrs Transome, he tries to justify himself without taking into account 'the exasperation and loathing excited by his daring to urge the plea of right'.

> A man who has stolen the pyx, and got frightened when justice was at his heels, might feel the sort of penitence which would induce him to run back in the dark, and lay the pyx where the sexton might find it; but if in doing so he whispered to the Blessed Virgin that he was moved by considering the sacredness of all property, and the peculiar sacredness of the pyx, it is not to be believed that she would like him the better for it.[1]

Now this is offered as a parallel case and nothing more: it is not in any sense the type or the origin of offensive self-justifications, merely another example, and the Virgin's reaction is described in language which suggests that she is a woman like Mrs Transome. Perhaps George Eliot's early evangelicalism had clung to this extent, that when looking for a theological case to use in this casual way, she chose a Catholic and not a Methodist one.

Prayer, on such a view, is a form of magic: its true purpose is not to invoke supernatural aid, but to arouse emotion:

> —*I take it much to heart*
> *That other people are worse off than I,—*
> *I ease my soul with praying for them all.*

[1] *Felix Holt*, ch. 42

> *—That is your way of singing, Agatha;*
> *Just as the nightingales pour forth sad songs,*
> *And when they reach men's ears they make men's hearts*
> *Feel the more kindly.*[1]

This appears to be explicitly agnostic. Such a view of prayer could, of course, be held by a Christian who maintained that the use of grace is not to cause miracles in the natural world, but to awaken men's hearts. The two views would differ in their version of the world, but agree about prayer: its function would be very like the function of art, as George Eliot conceived that.

Other religious concepts besides prayer and grace can be given human meaning—immortality, for example. Without personal survival, immortality consists of one's presence in the lives of others:

> *O may I join the choir invisible*
> *Of those immortal dead who live again*
> *In minds made better by their presence: live*
> *In pulses stirred to generosity,*
> *In deeds of daring rectitude, in scorn*
> *For miserable aims that end with self,*
> *In thoughts sublime that pierce the night like stars,*
> *And with their mild persistence urge man's search*
> *To vaster issues.*
> > *So to live is heaven:*
> *To make undying music in the world. . . .*[2]

The idea is common in George Eliot, especially in her poetry: it is one of the few ideas that warms her poems into something more than worthy and intelligent verse:

> *No good is certain, but the steadfast mind,*
> *The undivided will to seek the good:*
> *'Tis that compels the elements and wrings*
> *A human music from the indifferent air.*
> *The greatest gift the hero leaves his race*
> *Is to have been a hero. Say we fail!—*
> *We feed the high tradition of the world,*
> *And leave our spirit in our children's breasts.*[3]

[1] *Agatha* (1869)
[2] 'O May I join the Choir Invisible' (1867); in *Jubal and Other Poems* (1874)
[3] Zarca to Fedalma in *The Spanish Gypsy*

Though the direct statement of this thought, in the last two lines, is no more than a literary gesture groping at the sublime, the lines that work up to it have, surely, a finer quality. Their Miltonic echo when speaking of the steadfast mind, the undivided will, is in the tradition of:

> *Death closes all: but something ere the end,*
> *Some work of noble note, may yet be done,*
> *Not unbecoming men that strove with Gods.*[1]

This Miltonising is common in Romantic poetry, and I find it more genuine than the wide-encroaching Miltonising of the eighteenth century. All nineteenth-century poets were Satanists; and they echoed Milton when praising heroic fortitude, perseverance and the steadfast mind—and echoed him powerfully because they were expressing an emotion both highly poetic and important to them. I will not argue whether this shows the truth of the Satanist view of *Paradise Lost,* or merely explains its popularity.

But (to revert to the quotation from *The Spanish Gypsy*) the most impressive lines in the passage are also (surely) the most anti-religious:

> *Tis that compels the element and wrings*
> *A human music from the indifferent air.*

This (and it is not the only occasion in George Eliot's poetry) could be Wallace Stevens: it ascribes all value to man, and praises man's effort to impose meaning on a world without it, on 'this dividing and indifferent blue'. There are plenty of other examples in George Eliot's poetry of immortality as a human phenomenon: I will quote only one, the remarks of Armgart (the singer) on the now dead composer, who has—George Eliot would have welcomed Auden's phrase—become his admirers:

> *Tell them, Leo, tell them*
> *How I outsang your hope and made you cry*
> *Because Gluck could not hear me. That was folly!*
> *He sang, not listened: every linked note*
> *Was his immortal pulse that stirred in mine,*
> *And all my gladness is but part of him.*[2]

[1] Tennyson: 'Ulysses', ll. 51-3
[2] 'Armgart' (1870), in *Jubal and Other Poems*

4 The Influence of a Noble Nature: 'Felix Holt'

Now if conversion is a human process, what corresponds to grace? The answer to this, given over and over in George Eliot's work, the foundation on which she builds the very structure of some of her novels, is the influence of a nobler nature. 'I begin to think we can only get better,' says Gwendolen Harleth, 'by having people about us who raise good feelings.' Perhaps no moment in *Middlemarch* is more famous—certainly none meant more to the author—than that of Dorothea's influence on Lydgate.

> The presence of a noble nature, generous in its wishes, ardent in its charity, changes the light for us: we begin to see things again in their larger, quieter masses, and to believe that we too can be seen and judged in the wholeness of our character.[1]

What had usually been admitted, in the evangelical view, as a necessary stimulus—the minister whose preaching or conversion first opened the sinner's heart—is here moved to the centre of the process. It need no longer be a minister: but this finer person who catches the imagination of the penitent is now not merely the stimulus to but the cause of the change of heart. This change can be apparent not only in conduct but even in appearance:

> She looked unusually charming today, from the very fact that she was not vividly conscious of anything but of having a mind near her that asked her to be something better than she usually was.[2]

The observation behind this is perfectly true: it is, as we all know, often possible to see that a woman is in love, and aware of the presence of her man. Sexual love is only one form that this influence can take, and is neither a necessary nor a sufficient condition for it. Indeed, in exploring the relation between the two states, George Eliot is at her most subtle. The shadow of sexual love falls on the relationship between Lydgate and Dorothea, and more than the shadow on Gwendolen's regard for Deronda: but Esther Lyon is the only one of George Eliot's 'sinners' who is influenced mainly and directly as a consequence of falling in love with the noble nature. It does not at first seem like this, either to Esther or to Felix Holt. The feeling she is first conscious of is a resentful and puzzled respect:

[1] *Middlemarch*, ch. 76   [2] *Felix Holt*, ch. 24

47

she is drawn to heed his graceless (even rude) manner because he does not seem to be susceptible to her woman's charm. Neither of them realises that he *is* susceptible, and that his bluntness is his way of showing it.

> 'A peacock!' thought Felix. 'I should like to come and scold her every day, and make her cry, and cut her fine hair off.'[1]

This is the shrewdest detail in the whole Felix-Esther story. It makes plain to us what is concealed from Felix himself, that his attraction to Esther is sexual. The mechanism of concealment is to turn the impulse of attraction to a hostile one; and with one of those psychological insights we shall discuss later, George Eliot sees that such a mechanism would produce this startlingly convincing sadistic wish. The same process operates in Felix's soliloquy at the end of the chapter. He is reflecting that he will never marry:

> I'll never marry, though I should have to live on raw turnips to subdue my flesh. I'll never look back and say, 'I had a fine purpose once—I meant to keep my hands clean and my soul upright, and to look truth in the face; but pray excuse me, I have a wife and children—I must lie and simper a little, else they'll starve;' or 'My wife is nice, she must have her bread well buttered, and her feelings will be hurt if she is not thought genteel.' That is the lot Miss Esther is preparing for some man or other. I could grind my teeth at such self-satisfied minxes, who think they can tell everybody what is the correct thing, and the utmost stretch of their ideas will not place them on a level with the intelligent fleas. I should like to see if she could be made ashamed of herself.[2]

Once again, the train of thought reveals more to us than to Felix himself. He believes he has been thinking of his possible marriage in wholly general terms, and so he has during his first example ('pray excuse me, I have a wife and children'); but it is as plain as a pikestaff where the second examples comes from—it is a little sketch of Esther. Since this must be clear even to Felix, he now has to shift to another form of generality: he must tell himself that he is not thinking of his own marriage but of anyone's—'That is the lot Miss Esther is preparing for some man or other'. The displaced sexual feeling then emerges as general indignation at 'such self-satisfied minxes', and at the harm they do, not to Felix Holt, but

---

[1] *Felix Holt*, ch. 5   [2] Ibid., ch. 5

to men. The indignation is of course a projection of his own anger with himself at being attracted. We can only admire the shrewdness of Felix' censor (and of course George Eliot's understanding of it) that so ingeniously conceals from him the fact that he is thinking of marrying Esther.

Yet 'the influence of a noble nature' suggests something rather different from falling in love; and I am sure that George Eliot wants us to believe that the respect and the outspokenness are not merely consequences of their love but also causes, and in Felix' case at least have something of an independent existence. This point is very clear in the case of Lydgate. It is Rosamund with whom he falls in love: it is Dorothea who changes the lights for him. When he gives himself up 'for the first time in his life, to the exquisite sense of leaning entirely on a generous sympathy, without any check of proud reserve', it is a surrender free of all sexual element— as free, that is, as is compatible with the use of words like 'leaning', 'check' or (earlier) 'the searching tenderness of her woman's bones'; with the fact that Lydgate is young and Dorothea impulsive and beautiful; and with our awareness that George Eliot is not evasive on such matters. She knows that a man could not have had this effect on Lydgate; and it is probably intended as a criticism of Lydgate that it did not occur to him to fall in love with Dorothea. The fact that he didn't disappointed many of her contemporary readers (and reviewers), who felt that the hero of a novel, however complex the plot, ought to marry the heroine. George Eliot no doubt knew they would have this expectation, and by thwarting it she directs fresh attention to the 'spots of commonness' in Lydgate's nature: the fact that he could dismiss Dorothea as 'a good creature . . . but a little too earnest', and be captivated by Rosamund's dimples and white neck.

A religious view of conversion has for the writer the great advantage that he can take on trust the source of grace: he does not have to portray God. The novelist could perhaps be as eloquent as Dante if all he had to show was the effect of a noble nature, but he cannot so limit himself. He must depict the noble nature too: must even, probably, make him a central figure, and must therefore step between the devil of making him too genuinely human to seem a sufficient cause for such great effects, and the deep sea of making him too good to be true. The second danger is, alas, very clear in *Felix Holt*.

Let us begin from the scene where Esther, finding that she cannot escape the need to hear Felix and (if necessary) be rebuked by him, calls at his house. The one good thing in this chapter is the account of Esther's vacillation about whether she should call or not:

> Her watch had a long-standing ailment of losing; possibly it wanted cleaning; Felix would tell her if it merely wanted regulating, whereas Mr Prowd might detain it unnecessarily, and cause her useless inconvenience. Or could she not get a valuable hint from Mrs Holt about the home-made bread, which was something as 'sad' as Lyddy herself? Or, if she came home that way at twelve o'clock, Felix might be going out, she might meet him, and not be obliged to call. Or—but it would be very much beneath her to take any steps of this sort.[1]

When she does knock on the Holts' door (for 'at the last moment there is always a reason not existing before—namely, the impossibility of further vacillation') we find Felix binding up the cut finger of Job Trudge, aged five, whom he has taken under his wing, submitting with perfect dignity to his mother's complaints, and reacting with great sensitivity to the obvious fact that Esther did not come merely about her watch. During this scene we see not Esther but Felix: a hopelessly sentimentalised Felix. We find that he is just as perfect as the stung imagination of Esther expected:

> 'This is a hero, Miss Lyon. This is Job Trudge, a bold Briton, whose finger hurts him, but who doesn't mean to cry. Good morning, boys. Don't lose your time. Get out into the air.'[2]

Felix is too good to be true: he is decorated not only with Job, to show his kindness and wisdom, but with six or seven other boys, just about to leave. Esther, we realise, came at the right time: she had to see the boys, to realise how good Felix was to them, but the boys had to be off so that she could see Felix's considerateness for her in private (Job stays, but only to enhance the tender scene —seven boys would have ruined it). I call these boys decoration, and that's all they are: George Eliot has not interested herself in them at all, but has used them to suffuse the scene with a pied-piper glow.

> 'Don't keep Miss Lyon at the door mother; ask her to come in.' said the ringing voice of Felix, surmounting various small shufflings and babbling voices within.[3]

---

[1] *Felix Holt*, ch. 22   [2] Ibid., ch. 22   [3] Ibid., ch. 22

Felix's voice is not 'ringing' because George Eliot wants us to hear it, but because she wants us to feel what a fine fellow he is; and the 'various small shufflings and babbling voices within' are merely coy.

We are only offered one critical remark on Felix. After she has described his opinion of Esther (he believed 'she would utterly scorn him in any other light than that of an acquaintance, and the emotion she had shown today did not change that belief'), George Eliot allows herself to add:

> That was the brief history Felix would have given of his relation to Esther. And he was accustomed to observe himself. But very close and diligent looking at living creatures, even through the best microscope, will leave room for new and contradictory discoveries.[1]

And this is not a critical remark at all—it is simply meant to enhance Felix still further in our eyes. The strong and wise man who knows all about himself except the fact that he is in love with the heroine is a well-tried figure of Victorian fiction: George Eliot's use of it does not really mean that she has stepped back to regard Felix from a distance.

Perhaps there is no other scene in the book where the treatment of Felix goes so visibly soft under our eyes; but there are all too many other touches of idealisation. I mention only one, which follows interestingly from what I have already said about George Eliot's agnosticism. Felix' effect on Esther is so completely secular that we are likely to assume he has no religion; this seems confirmed by his reply when Esther asks why he doesn't go to chapel and read Howe's *Living Temple* and join the church:

> I know why I don't do these things. I distinctly see that I can do something better.[2]

This is the nearest Felix ever comes to expressing unbelief: ought this not, on reflection, to surprise us? Outspokenness is almost his most marked characteristic. When in a perverse mood, he does not hesitate to offend Mr Lyon's deeply held Radical convictions by contending 'that universal suffrage would be equally agreeable to the devil'; he damages his case at the trial, and ensures his own conviction, by going out of his way to assert that he would, on occasion, be prepared to assault a constable; and are we to believe that he would not at any time, in his many arguments, have found

[1] Ibid., ch. 22   [2] Ibid., ch. 10

occasion to denounce Christianity? Radicals did it often enough in real life.

The reason of course is that it would have lowered him in the eyes of his author. George Eliot's too anxious respect for Felix has led her to attribute to him her own dislike for attacking 'the hard-won inheritance of the ages'; and, however ill it may sit with the rest of his character, she has kept him silent about religion, and left us to deduce his agnosticism from occasional hints.

This then is the reason why Felix is perhaps the deadest of all George Eliot's main characters: the author never sees him with her own eyes. She sees his influence upon Esther, she understands how Esther's resistance gradually turns into idealisation—and then she accepts that idealisation as a true version of Felix. It is almost as if her strength involves a weakness. Unless she can manage a sharp change in viewpoint (which here she can't), her understanding of what happens to Esther must lead to a sentimentalising of Felix.

5 *The Influence of a Noble Nature: 'Daniel Deronda'*

I turn now to the most ambitious, and perhaps the finest of all George Eliot's studies in the influence of a noble nature: that of Daniel Deronda on Gwendolen Harleth. The comparison with Hetty and Esther is a good starting-point for discussing the strengths and the weaknesses of this remarkable book.

I suggested that the development of Hetty Sorrel fell into three stages: her hardness, her suffering, her awakening. In *Felix Holt* the second stage was almost entirely omitted: Esther is not prepared by suffering to receive Felix' influence. In *Daniel Deronda* all three are present again, and all are treated with far greater fullness and complexity than anything in *Adam Bede*. Any discussion of this book must seem more schematic, more crudely unjust to the richness of the novel itself, than was the case with *Adam Bede*: but simply to write literary criticism is, after all, to resign oneself to schematisation and to doing injustice, and the better the books one discusses, the truer this is.

The unregenerate Gwendolen appears in Book I, *The Spoiled Child*, and above all in the superb character sketch that makes up Chapter IV. This chapter, which seems to me one of the finest things in English fiction, puts before us a poised, quickwitted, beautiful girl, 'witching the world with her grace on horseback', self-confident and egotistical; and then curves away into a speculation on why she so easily succeeded in commanding the attention and help of others. This was not merely because of her charm:

> If she came into the room on a rainy day when everybody else was flaccid and the use of things in general was not apparent to them, there seemed to be a sudden, sufficient reason for keeping up the forms of life . . .

but mainly because of her ruthlessness: she is one of those people who have:

> a strong determination to have what was pleasant, with a total fearlessness in making themselves disagreeable or dangerous when they did not get it.[1]

Very early on in the portrait of the spoiled child we are shown the vulnerability of her self-sufficiency; and very early on in her sufferings we are shown her first awakening. The stages of her development are not chronologically distinct as they were with Hetty, but constantly interact on each other. This makes Gwendolen more complex, not only than Hetty, but also than Rosamund Vincy. Because Gwendolen is vulnerable from the beginning, the drama of her story lies within her, whereas that of *Middlemarch* lies in the interaction between Rosamund and Lydgate. The chink in Gwendolen's egoism can be seen in her fitful sensitivity to the feelings of others. She is tender to her mother, though always in a way that costs her nothing; she resents and resists the advice and sympathy of Herr Klesmer, but:

> When he had taken up his hat and was going to make his bow, Gwendolen's better self, conscious of an ingratitude which the clear-seeing Klesmer must have penetrated, made a desperate effort to find its way above the stifling layers of egotistic disappointment and irritation.[2]

And above all it can be seen in one desperately moving moment in Chapter VII, when after dismissing with contempt Rex's attempt to propose to her, she suddenly dissolves into violent and helpless weeping:

> I shall never love anybody. I can't love people.
> I hate them.[3]

This burst of self-reproach reveals that she is not yet totally possessed by her egoism.

---

[1] *Daniel Deronda*, ch. 4   [2] Ibid., ch. 23   [3] Ibid., ch. 7

Yet that is to put the point too morally: Gwendolen's vulnerability lies in her imagination. Of course the two are not distinct: all George Eliot's fiction is an attempt to show that the imagination is the instrument of the moral life, that the egoist is he whose imagination is narrow, that to widen the range of feelings is to learn to love others. And as if to reinforce this, George Eliot inserted one episode to show the naked power of imagination in Gwendolen, an episode that seems at the time to have no moral dimension. This is the glimpse of the painting hidden behind the wainscot.

When Mrs Davilow and her daughters first come to Offendene, they find behind a hinged panel in the drawing-room a picture 'of an upturned dead face, from which an obscure figure seems to be fleeing with outstretched arms'. The panel is locked and forgotten about, but a series of coincidences leads to its suddenly flying open when Gwendolen is acting in a tableau, and the effect on her is startling:

> Herr Klesmer, who had been good-natured enough to seat himself at the piano, struck a thunderous chord—but in the same instant, and before Hermione had put forth her foot, the movable panel, which was on a line with the piano, flew open on the right opposite the stage and disclosed the picture of the dead face and the fleeing figure, brought out in pale definiteness by the position of the wax-lights. Everyone was startled, but all eyes in the act of turning towards the opened panel were recalled by a piercing cry from Gwendolen, who stood without change of attitude, but with a change of expression that was terrifying in its terror. She looked like a statue into which a soul of Fear had entered: her pallid lips were parted; her eyes, usually narrowed under their long lashes, were dilated and fixed.[1]

Why did Gwendolen react with such intensity? Perhaps we ought not even to wonder: the excitement of her public appearance, the thunderous chord, the suddenness of the apparition, might have frightened anyone. Yet we are meant to attach a greater significance to the incident than that: Gwendolen's egoism, showing itself in proud self-control, has given way in this instant. It has happened before, but never so humiliatingly.

> She wondered at herself in these occasional experiences, which seemed like a brief remembered madness, an unexplained

Daniel Deronda, ch. 6

exception from her normal life; and in this instance she felt a peculiar vexation that her helpless fear had shown itself, not, as usual, in solitude, but in well-lit company.[1]

I described this imaginative susceptibility as having no moral dimension. The fear that seizes Gwendolen's imagination is as selfish as the proud wish to appear unmoved before others— 'daring in speech and reckless in braving dangers'. It is only for herself that she is afraid: indeed, the fear is so primitive a reaction that it exists below the level at which self-regarding divides from other-regarding. If we turn back to the moment when the painting is first discovered, we can see that George Eliot has planted a hint for us.

'Oh *Gwendolen*!' said the small Isabel, in a tone of astonishment, while she held open a hinged panel of the wainscot at the other end of the room.

Everyone, Gwendolen first, went to look. The opened panel had disclosed the picture of an upturned dead face, from which an obscure figure seemed to be fleeing with outstretched arms. 'How horrible!' said Mrs Davilow, with a look of mere disgust; but Gwendolen shuddered silently, and Isabel, a plain and altogether inconvenient child with an alarming memory, said—

'You will never stay in this room by yourself, Gwendolen.'

'How dare you open things which were meant to be shut up, you perverse little creature?' said Gwendolen, in her angriest tone. Then snatching the panel out of the hand of the culprit, she closed it hastily, saying, 'There is a lock—where is the key? Let the key be found or else let one be made, and let nobody open it again; or rather, let the key be brought to me.'

At this command to everybody in general Gwendolen turned with a face which was flushed in reaction from her chill shudder, and said, 'Let us go up to our own room, mamma'.[2]

This is as shrewd and as economical as anything in that marvellous first book of *Daniel Deronda*. With the child's perfectly realistic exclamation, George Eliot has reminded us in passing of Gwendolen's dominant position in the family, and perhaps has shown that she is present in their feelings in a way they are not in hers (would Gwendolen have called out someone's name if she had found it?). Mrs Davilow's reaction, with its look of mere disgust, is the normal, limited, healthy one: her imagination is proof against such fear as

---

[1] Ibid., ch. 6   [2] Ibid., ch. 3

Gwendolen is already feeling the breath of. The really subtle hint, however, comes through the plain and altogether inconvenient remark of Isabel's: 'You will never stay in this room by yourself, Gwendolen.' Isabel has inconveniently remembered the terror that Gwendolen does not like to show, and Gwendolen's anger is a reaction against this penetration of her dignity. The fear is thus linked in our minds both with Gwendolen's egoism and with the chink in it; and though this is not offered as a cause for her later terror (which is too immediate and violent to need such specific causes), it remains associated with it.

Of course we are to remember this at the end of the book. The picture of the dead face terrifies Gwendolen because it corresponds to a formless fear of her own: it is a projection of something in her stronger than she can control. When Grandcourt drowns, and she rebukes herself as a guilty woman, because she has wished it, she uses a sentence that calls up the same idea: 'I know nothing—I only know that I saw my wish outside me'.

What had George Eliot to learn from psycho-analysis? As a novelist, surely little or nothing. Gwendolen's fear had been so powerful because it had been a reaction from a repressed wish: she had been frightened of destructive powers in herself. When her hatred of Grandcourt takes shape, what frightens her is its intensity: for it has become a focus for these destructive impulses that are now called into consciousness. Her final terrible discovery, in the boat, was that her old fear and her new hatred were the same. She has already more or less found this out, for that old image of fear stays in her imagination, attaching itself to her new fear, of what she might wish to do to her husband.

> Her vision of what she had to dread took more decidedly than ever the form of some fierce impulsive deed, committed as in a dream that she would instantaneously wake from to find the effects real though the images had been false: to find death under her hands, but instead of darkness, daylight; instead of satisfied hatred, the dismay of guilt; instead of freedom, the palsy of a new terror—a white dead face from which she was for ever trying to flee and for ever held back.[1]

But it is not until Grandcourt falls in the water that the discovery hits her with full violence; and after the first moment of horror her

[1] *Daniel Deronda*, ch. 54

reaction is to suppress it (consciously now, not unconsciously) and escape from her new knowledge of herself:

> But he was gone down again, and I had the rope in my hand—no, there he was again—his face above the water—and he cried again—and I held my hand, and my heart said, 'Die!'—and he sank; and I felt, 'It is done—I am wicked, I am lost!'—and I had the rope in my hand—I don't know what I thought—I was leaping away from myself—I would have saved him then. I was leaping from my crime, and there it was—close to me as I fell—there was the dead face—dead, dead.[1]

'I was leaping away from myself': Gwendolen's hysteria when she is brought into land and confesses to Deronda is her recoil from her own identity, as she has how seen it; but it is a therapeutic hysteria, because the repugnance and the struggle are now conscious. The image that has haunted her, and the picture of her drowning husband, now merge; and the dead face on which this passage ends can be either or both—we are for once, surely, not meant to distinguish them.

Such is one glimpse only of the complexity and psychological subtlety with which George Eliot has shown the nature of Gwendolen's egoism. Gradually, as the book proceeds, we see her freeing herself from it, never easily, never with assurance. Deronda is the agent in this process, for she learns to regard him as her own better self. It is a reversal of the process by which the super-ego is formed. As the super-ego grows by the introjection of parental authority that in the process becomes less rational, so he takes on a peculiar moral authority in her eyes as she invests him with sanctions that are too weak to have an independent life in herself—and that become more rational when mediated by his thoughtful bluntness. Her responsiveness to Deronda is something unique in her life. It depends on a rare concourse of circumstances—his initial presumption in returning the necklace she had pawned, and her ability, when alone with him, to avoid triviality and evasiveness:

> The hurried directness with which she spoke—the absence of all her little airs, as if she were only concerned to use the time in getting an answer that would guide her, made her appeal unspeakably touching[2].

Largely this is due to the spell Deronda casts over her (though

---

[1] Ibid., ch. 56   [2] Ibid., ch. 36

'spell' suggests almost the opposite of the directness with which he regularly treats her); but partly too it is due to circumstances, for George Eliot, with complete candour, recognises that the intense impression made by her rare meetings with Deronda owes something to that very rarity, that Gwendolen is helped not hindered to avoid triviality by the snatched brevity of their conversations.

Something is owing to Deronda too: at the few crucial moments he does not hedge or evade:

> She turned her brow to the window again, and said impatiently, 'You must tell me then what to think and what to do; else why did you not let me go on doing as I liked and not minding? If I had gone on gambling I might have won again, and I might have got not to care for anything else. You would not let me do that. Why shouldn't I do as I like, and not mind? Other people do.' Poor Gwendolen's speech expressed nothing very closely except her irritation.
>
> 'I don't believe you would ever get not to mind,' said Deronda, with deep-toned decision. 'If it were true that baseness and cruelty made an escape from pain, what difference would that make to people who can't be quite base or cruel? Idiots escape some pain; but you can't be an idiot. Some may do wrong to another without remorse; but suppose one does feel remorse? I believe you could never lead an injurious life—all reckless lives are injurious, pestilential—without feeling remorse.' Deronda's unconscious fervour had gathered as he went on: he was uttering thoughts which he had used for himself in moments of painful meditation.
>
> 'Then tell me what better I can do,' said Gwendolen insistently.
>
> 'Many things. Look on other lives besides your own. See what their troubles are, and how they are borne. Try to care about something in this vast world besides the gratification of small selfish desires. Try to care for what is best in thought and action—something that is good apart from the accidents of your own lot.'
>
> For an instant or two Gwendolen was mute. Then, again moving her brow from the glass, she said—
>
> 'You mean that I am selfish and ignorant.'
>
> He met her look in silence before he answered firmly—
>
> 'You will not go on being selfish and ignorant.'
>
> She did not turn away her glance or let her eyelids fall, but a change came over her face—that subtle change in nerve and

muscle which will sometimes give a childlike expression even to the elderly: it is the subsidence of self-assertion.[1]

A long quotation, but both the merit of the scene and its importance justify this. We see that George Eliot came very close to spoiling Deronda—to turning him into a wooden figure: his long speech to Gwendolen comes very near to preaching. It is common for critics to assume that she did spoil him, that he is wooden, but I believe if we read carefully we shall see this is oversimplified. What saves the portrait is, first, the exhilaration we feel in the contrast with the brittle self-protective wit that Gwendolen usually speaks in— and how typical this seems of George Eliot's genius, that she can make us delight in the appearance of plain speech, honesty, even fervour, amid all the sophistication. Secondly, there is the fact that Deronda builds the fervour out of his own nervous stresses. It is not enough, of course, merely to be told this, and I shall suggest in a moment how George Eliot shows it too. Most of what Deronda says in this scene we can credit as coming from his own struggle, except perhaps that last sentence, whose very syntax ('all restless lives are injurious . . .') betrays the fact that it is a mere generalisation, based on theory or the wish to moralise. Gwendolen's last remark ('You mean that I am selfish and ignorant') is perfectly in character: is it defensive, even offended, even falsely gay? Or is it a simple question, even a plea for help? No doubt Gwendolen herself was uncertain; and Deronda does her the best service he can by taking from this uncertainty the assumption that she had spoken simply and wanted an honest, not a witty or reassuring reply. So he finds a response that though honest is not crushing; and the result of this—seen briefly but clearly in the 'subtle change in nerve and muscle'—is the crucial moment in Gwendolen's long awakening.

During this slow awakening, Gwendolen needs Deronda, to sustain as well as to cause the process. She needs him; and her conversion is not complete until she has learned to do without him. Just as the patient who has affected a successful transference on to the analyst has to learn to detach himself from this dependence before he is fully cured (and Deronda's relationship with Gwendolen offers plenty of parallels to that of psycho-analyst and patient), so Gwendolen has in the end to face a life in which she can no longer

[1] *Daniel Deronda*, ch. 36

lean on the man whom she had invested with the power of her own super-ego. The one process is as painful as the other.

What above all distinguishes this relationship from the earlier equivalents in George Eliot's novels (from that between Esther and Felix, say) is its instability. We are never allowed to forget how tempting and how easy it would be for Gwendolen to retreat into herself. The very intensity of her relationship with Deronda makes her peculiarly vulnerable to such insinuations as that of her husband, that Mirah is his mistress; and even apart from any loss of faith in Deronda, the sheer difficulty of the effort tempts her constantly to withdraw, to cease the task of using her emotional involvement with someone else to effect a shift in her own personality.

Such is Gwendolen's difficulty; and Deronda is equally tempted to destroy the fragile relationship:

> Without the aid of sacred ceremony or costume, her feelings had turned this man, only a few years older than herself, into a priest; a sort of trust less rare than the fidelity that guards it.[1]

He shows this fidelity; but we are not to feel it was easy. We are continually shown Deronda's occasional resentments, his uneasiness in the role bestowed on him by Gwendolen. Jerome Thale is quite wrong when he makes, rather more wittily than others do, the standard complaint about Deronda:

> Deronda is the well-bred (and very nice) English gentleman as Alyosha. George Eliot assumes that the simplicity and insight of the one are compatible with the ordinary acquired virtues of the other, and she does not see that Deronda's debility of will can be a defect.[2]

Deronda is interesting precisely because he is not Alyosha. George Eliot knows very well that to play the role of saviour or psycho-analyst to even one person is very, very difficult for him, and that his debility of will is a grave defect in doing so; and she demonstrates this at great length. Deronda tries to fight against his role:

> Against his better will, he shrank from the task that was laid on him: he wished, and yet rebuked the wish as cowardly, that she could bury her secrets in her own bosom. He was not a priest.

[1] *Daniel Deronda*, ch. 35   [2] *The Novels of George Eliot* (1959), p. 123

He dreaded the weight of this woman's soul flung upon his own with imploring dependence.[1]

It is not only uncongenial but also difficult to maintain the role: we see this later in the same chapter, after Gwendolen has had one of her rare realisations that her trust is an imposition on Deronda:

> 'What I most desire at this moment is what will most help you. Tell me all you feel it a relief to tell.'
> Devoted as these words were, they widened his spiritual distance from her, and she felt it more difficult to speak: she had a vague need of getting nearer to that compassion which seemed to be regarding her from a halo of superiority, and the need turned into an impulse to humble herself more.[2]

How hard it is for Deronda not to say the wrong thing. He must not talk about himself, but he must not too obviously or too virtuously refrain from doing so. And with a shrewdness that startles, George Eliot reminds us of the accidental advantages that Deronda has:

> 'It could never be my impulse to forsake you,' said Deronda promptly, with that voice which, like his eyes, had the unintentional effect of making his ready sympathy seem more personal and special than it really was.[3]

—though perhaps this is not accidental after all: George Eliot was surely determinist enough to believe that the quality of Deronda's voice was not unconnected with his personality.

Deronda can help Gwendolen because of his own inner distresses (as a good analyst is one who has himself undergone neurotic stress); and by helping her he helps himself:

> Those who trust us educate us. And perhaps in that ideal consecration of Gwendolen's, some education was being prepared for Deronda.[4]

His education was no easier than hers; and that George Eliot never lost her realistic sense of what is hard and what easy can be seen from the thought that comes to Deronda at the very moment he is rising to Gwendolen's need and saying, 'I will not forsake you'.

> And all the while he felt as if he were putting his name to a blank paper which might be filled up terribly.[1]

[1] Ibid., ch. 56 [2] Ibid., ch. 56 [3] Ibid., ch. 57
[4] Ibid., ch. 35 [5] Ibid., ch. 56

It must have cost George Eliot a lot to write that sentence, when her hero was successfully giving himself to the needs of another. There is strong pressure of truth behind it, that shows itself (I hope this is not too far-fetched) in the blunt rhythm, in the naked force of the closing words 'which might be filled up terribly'. No one could say that Deronda is sentimentalised there.

Where does the line run between the good and bad parts of *Daniel Deronda*? It runs not between Gwendolen and Deronda, nor even between Gwendolen's view of Deronda and Deronda himself, but through the character of Deronda. It is in the Jewish theme that George Eliot, the victim of a shrill but (alas) not fully absorbed enthusiasm, gave way to stiffness and melodrama: the lurid scene of Mirah's rescue from drowning, the improbability of Deronda turning out to be so conveniently Jewish, the sentimentalising of Hans Meyrick when he tells Deronda that he is the lucky man, and (worst of all) the impossible figure of Mordecai. Since few readers can ever have admired this part of the book much (in recent times, at any rate: its contemporary reception by Jews was enthusiastic), it would be foolish to dissect it in any detail; I will simply point out the serious invasion that it makes into the character of Deronda.

> 'It is through your inspiration that I have discerned what may be my life's task. It is you who have given shape to what, I believe, was an inherited yearning—the effect of brooding, passionate thoughts in many ancestors. . . . You have said to me—'Our religion united us before it divided us—it made us a people before it made Rabbanites and Karaites.' I mean to try what can be done with that union—I mean to work in your spirit. Failure will not be ignoble, but it would be ignoble for me not to try.[1]

I omit most of this outpouring of Deronda's, which is as stilted and derivative as the opening sentence suggests. It is his final yielding to the enthusiasm of Mordecai, his final submission to the influence of his wild and prophetic Jewish friend. Such a climax of self-surrender is, for George Eliot, a climax of special importance: it is *the* climax in fact, in the development of Deronda's character. And how stiff, how disappointing it is. Deronda's outpouring is simply a piece of Zionist theory attached to a conception of his personal development that has taken no hold on the author's

---

[1] *The Novels of George Eliot* (1959), ch. 63

imagination. It has none of the quality of the corresponding climax of Gwendolen's. And looking at the sentence in which it is analysed, we can surely detect the source of weakness:

> To estimate the effect of this ardent outpouring from Deronda we must remember his former reserve, his careful avoidance of premature assent or delusive encouragement, which gave to this decided pledge of himself a sacramental solemnity, both for his own mind and Mordecai's.[1]

It is not because it is explicit that this is bad: the account of Gwendolen's abandonment before Deronda which concluded Book VII was just as explicit, to say nothing of the superb analysis of her character in Chapter IV. No, this passage is bad because the explicitness is apologetic, a form of self-justification: betraying, as it were, a fear that the reader may not notice the importance of the moment, may not have taken all the hints on earlier pages. And because such a climax is supremely important in a George Eliot novel, we must conclude that the bad half has bitten deep into the person of Deronda, and turned what is in part one of her most triumphant successes into something like failure.

6 The Effects of Conversion: Novel v. Drama

How long does conversion last?

I am not (of course) asking this question about real life: for an answer to that one would go to the psychologists, and perhaps they would not know it. But nor am I asking it of literature in a merely descriptive sense (what has been the practice of writers?) How long ought conversion to last in a work of literature, if we are to be both convinced and aesthetically satisfied? And the answer depends on the literary form.

Does a tragedy need to be a play? Traditional usage has said yes, yet there have been suggestions that this restriction is mere formalism, that now that prose fiction has taken over from drama or poetry as our central form, the best tragedies will be found in novels. The story of Lydgate, for instance, has the classical shape of tragedy. Here is the 'man not eminently good and just, yet whose misfortune is brought about not by vice or depravity, but by some error or frailty', as the Aristotelian formula demands. Lydgate has in his devotion to science the nobility of purpose that raises him

---

[1] Ibid., ch. 63

in our eyes to begin with, and in his 'spots of commonness'—the fact that he does not use the same high standard in the rest of his life—that tragic flaw that causes his downfall. The path of the action is carefully plotted to show us that Lydgate is responsible for his fate; and under the influence of Dorothea he rises at the end to an acceptance of his lot and a wisdom he had not known in prosperity. Does this account distort the story of Lydgate more than so brief a summary necessarily must? Would it not be mere pedantry to see the Duchess of Malfi, say, or Bajazet, as tragic figures, and not the far more interesting Lydgate?

I raise the question because the present discussion suggests at any rate a partial answer; and because the implications of this answer feed back into my argument. What we have been calling 'conversion' is very similar to the purgation of the tragic hero. If we broaden conversion to include any intense emotional experience that causes us to change our views or our conduct, then we can call the climax of most tragedies a conversion. Oedipus learns the truth about his history, and also about his own nature; Othello realises what he has done; Phèdre, Beatrice-Joanna, Miss Julie, above all King Lear, face the truth about themselves—and die. If we think of the tragic climax as a conversion, we can see why the tragic hero has to die: for a conversion is never so perfect as in the moment of its consummation, and to freeze the life of the hero in that one moment is to make it plain wherein the triumph of his story lies. Tragedy is essentially a gesture. There are differences of emphasis, even of opinion, about what it is a gesture of: of man's defiance, or of his acceptance of himself, or of his courage, in facing a truth and managing to change. Only if it is offered as a gesture can this courage be made permanent and accepted unquestioningly: and it can only be a gesture if we never need to see the hero unmake it, or ask how long it will last. If you live on, you have to end your speech and lower your arm.

The assertion of man that tragedy offers us is therefore, in one respect, evasive; it does not ask: What then? This is why tragedy is so much better suited to drama than to the novel: it culminates in a scene, a moment, a climax that becomes larger than life. But the novel does not live in the theatrical: it must curve back into the world of everyday which nourishes it. It must ask: What then?

Adam Bede turns into a play at its climax: we have already seen this, and how disastrous it was. And though there is a long stretch of narrative left, some of it very good, none of it concerns Hetty: we get nothing but a brief mention of her death. In *Daniel Deronda*, as we have seen, the question 'What then?' is being asked all through the book: almost the whole history of Gwendolen's soul lies after her awakening, so we cannot accuse George Eliot of abandoning the meticulous truthfulness of the novel for the grand gesture of tragedy—although when Gwendolen is faced with her final crisis, the need to live without Deronda, we are given nothing but her grief, her hysteria, and her determination to conquer it:

> 'I will try to live. I shall think of you. What good have I been? Only harm. Don't let me be harm to *you*. It shall be the better for me—'[1]

This is perhaps the one false note in the entire portrayal of Gwendolen: the novel has turned into a play.

And Rosamund: here we have a more difficult case. For Rosamund, like any tragic heroine, does not awaken till the last act: in her case the first stage, the hardness, lasts for almost the entire book. Though her sufferings, in one sense, begin when Lydgate gets into financial difficulties, in a more important sense they do not begin until Dorothea finds her flirting with Will, and leaves her to the lash of his tongue. That is the first event that really breaks through the armour of her egoism; and it does not occur until the 78th of the book's 86 chapters. And in the 81st, Rosamund is converted.

Or is 'converted' too large a word? Under the influence of Dorothea, Rosamund blames herself for the flirtation, and speaks of Will in such a way as to bring him and Dorothea together again: a wholly unselfish act, committed under the spell of a greater emotional change than even Dorothea realises:

> She was under the first great shock that had shattered her dreamworld in which she had been easily confident of herself and critical of others.[2]

This 'new crisis' in Rosamund's experience, this 'new movement which gave all things some new, awful, undefined aspect' is presented as meticulously, with the same accuracy of detail, the same scrutinising of phrase and tone, as everything else in the novel.

[1] *Daniel Deronda*, ch. 69   [2] *Middlemarch*, ch. 81

If there is to be a special emotional power at the climax, it is not to be achieved by a change of technique. So for all the enthusiasm she feels—and wishes us to feel—for Dorothea, George Eliot pauses, as she has often done throughout the book, to mention 'her usual tendency to overestimate the good in others' (Dorothea will be discussed more fully in Part II). Rosamund is taken hold of by an emotion stronger than her own, and George Eliot takes the trouble to tell us—in those very words—that this has happened: we the readers are not to be taken hold of by the same transfiguring emotion, or not in the same unreflecting way as we might be in the theatre. And by this reserve we are prepared for asking if the conversion will last, and are not surprised to learn that it doesn't. The short paragraph in the *Finale* that tells the later history of the Lydgates would be impossible in a tragedy: it is a dispassionate account of what happened when Rosamund was herself again. It is true that 'she never uttered a word in depreciation of Dorothea', but though this is evidence of a kind of permanence in the effect, it was not Dorothea's aim to produce *that*: we can even read a final irony into the fact that this totally unselfish act of Dorothea's produced nothing more lasting than a benefit to her own reputation. For the rest, Rosamund is Rosamund still. There is no dramatising of her story, but a relentless answer to the question What then?; and the terrible cool gaze of the novelist is fixed on us as we close the book.

What keeps the novel, then, at its best, from turning to the more imposing mode of tragedy, to the direct impact of heroic gesture, is a scrupulousness that is perhaps inherent in its technique: a meticulous regard for what followed, an inability to be totally swept away, a necessary truthfulness. This brings us to the central point of my argument, prefigured in the title; but before turning to it, I must pause to treat of Lawrence. I shall not show at such length that he is not a religious writer, since the demonstration is essentially the same as that used for George Eliot. A shorter discussion and fewer examples should suffice.

7 *The Absence of God in Lawrence*

Lawrence's famous description of himself as religious occurs in a letter to Edward Garnett, written in 1914, and remarkably prophetic of his later work:

But primarily I am a passionately religious man, and my novels must be written from the depths of my religious experience. That I must keep to, because I can only work like that. And my Cockneyism and commonness are only when the deep feeling doesn't find its way out, and a sort of jeer comes instead, and sentimentality, and purplism. But you should see the religious, earnest, suffering man in me first, and then the flippant or common things after.[1]

Now even in this passage we can see that Lawrence is concerned not with belief but with experience. Being religious is contrasted not with disbelief but with the jeer, sentimentality and purplism of his 'commonness'; and when he writes 'religious, earnest, suffering', as if they were synonyms, we can suspect him of secularising the meaning of the first even more than George Eliot.

A letter to John Middleton Murry a few years later makes his position plainer:

There is no writing and publishing news. Philosophy interests me most now—not novels or stories. I find people ultimately boring: and you can't have fiction without people. So fiction does not, at the bottom, interest me any more. I am weary of humanity, and human things. One is happy in the thoughts only that transcend humanity.[2]

Reading such passages in Lawrence, one has always, first of all, to discount the tone of finality: when he says 'at the bottom' he means 'at the moment'. I would like to know who Lawrence was reading when he wrote this—what philosophers deal in the 'thoughts that transcend humanity'. Whether they are idealists, or metaphysicians, or mystics, or even (improbably) theologians, it is clear that here we have an interest that could be called religious in a very different sense from the concern with experience shown in the other letter. And what matters for our argument is that when Lawrence dwells in such thoughts he loses interest in fiction. Perhaps this passage should remind us to hesitate before applying such 'philosophical' works as *Psychoanalysis and the Unconscious* to his novels.

There is no need, as a matter of fact, to argue so carefully towards establishing what Lawrence meant by calling himself religious, for he tells us. 'Religion', he says in the essay on *New Mexico*:

[1] Letter to Edward Garnett, 22 April, 1914
[2] Letter to J. M. Murry, 23 May, 1917

is an experience, an uncontrollable sensual experience, even more so than love: I use sensual to mean an experience deep down in the senses, inexplicable and inscrutable.[1]

And in another essay, *Education of the People*, he defines the religious faculty as 'the inward worship of the creative life-mystery', and goes on to indicate the place of beliefs in terms ('An *idea* or the *ideal* is only instrumental in the unfolding of the soul of man') that George Eliot could have accepted completely. She would have liked his eloquence, too, for once:

> Our sophistry has intervened like a lamp between us and the slow-stepping stars, we have turned our cheap lanterns on the dark and wizard face of Galileo.[2]

That letter to Edward Garnett, then, does not show Lawrence to have been religious in any sense that disturbs the argument of this chapter: none the less the depth of religious experience which it mentions is the most important thing in Lawrence, and must now occupy us. The letter accompanied the manuscript of *The Rainbow* (then called *The Wedding Ring*) and is about that book. Now in *The Rainbow* there is certainly a level of experience that lies below the everyday, that reveals the deepest feelings of an earnest, suffering man. Take for example the scene in which Tom Brangwen asks the Polish lady to marry him:

> 'No,' she said, not of herself. 'No I don't know.'
> He felt the tension breaking up in him, his fists slackened, he was unable to move. He stood there looking at her, helpless in his vague collapse. For the moment she had become unreal to him. Then he saw her come to him curiously direct and as if without movement, in a sudden flow. She put her hand to his coat.
> 'Yes, I want to,' she said, impersonally, looking at him with wide, candid, newly-opened eyes, opened now with supreme truth. He went very white as he stood, and did not move, only his eyes were held by hers, and he suffered. She seemed to see him with her newly-opened, wide eyes almost of a child, and with a strange movement, that was agony to him, she reached slowly forward her dark face and her breast to him, with a slow insinuation of a kiss that made something break in his brain, and it was darkness over him for a few moments. . . .[3]

[1] 'New Mexico' (1931); *Phoenix*, p. 144
[2] 'Education of the People' § 8; *Phoenix*, p. 35
[3] *The Rainbow*, ch. 1

In the case of Lawrence (this had better be said at once) quotation is even more difficult than with the other two authors, since his effects so often build up slowly, by repetition of phrase and by a cumulative rhythm that might last several pages while the action pauses. These two paragraphs are the beginning of a page or two of description that ought not really to be split up, and that I must ask the reader to look at: for my comment is about the whole.

The most important word in the passage is 'impersonally'. Lydia and Tom are here making contact on a level which lies below the distinctions of the individual personality. It is by breaking through to this that Lydia can learn her own true wish; it is from his contact with her on this impersonal level that Tom comes to realise the new birth in him ('Aerial and light everything was, new as a morning, fresh and newly begun'). To find the vocabulary for dealing with such experience is extremely difficult, even self-defeating: most images would be too specific, too lacking in the sense of 'darkest sleep, utter, extreme oblivion'. It is Lawrence's strength and weakness as a novelist that he is constantly trying to describe experience on this level. Inevitably, it produces false notes, such as Lydia's eyes, 'opened now with supreme truth'.

I don't know if it has been remarked that one of Lawrence's favourite words is 'something'. There is an instance in the passage above; and every book can supply others.

—And the youth went home with the stars in heaven whirling fiercely about the blackness of his head, and his heart fierce, insistent, but fierce as if he felt something baulking him.[1]

—It was a shock for the young officer. He felt something sink deeper into his soul, where nothing had ever gone before.[2]

—They were silent. And immediately the strange thrill of secrecy was between them. Something had gone beyond sadness into another, secret, thrilling communion, which she would never admit.[3]

This sense of groping seems the necessary result of Lawrence's quest for 'the fecund darkness'; and it is his triumph that so often we feel he is not groping, but showing us what he knows. This

[1] Ibid., ch. 4
[2] 'The Prussian Officer', § 1; Phoenix edition of the Short Stories, vol. 1, p. 97
[3] 'The Ladybird'; Phoenix edition of the Short Novels, vol. 2, p. 26

is true of a great deal of *The Rainbow*, of the love between Will and Anna even more than of that between Tom and Lydia. If Lawrence is to be called religious, it is because of his wild bold exploration of this dark region of the personality: he explores it direct during most of *The Rainbow*, and the direct rendering of Lydia's love for her husband, Will's for his daughter, seems to take us further into the fecund darkness than the vaguely splendid symbols of the horses and the rainbow that impose themselves on the ending.

Lawrence himself, in an even more famous letter, described what he was doing in The *Rainbow*:

> You mustn't look in my novel for the old stable *ego* of the character. There is another *ego*, according to whose action the individual is unrecognisable, and passes through, as it were, allotropic states which it needs a deeper sense than any we've been used to exercise, to discover are states of the same single radically unchanged element. (Like as diamond and coal are the same pure single element of carbon. The ordinary novel would trace the history of the diamond—but I say, 'Diamond, what! This is carbon.' And my diamond might be coal or soot, and my theme is carbon.)[1]

This passage should be printed as an epigraph to every edition of *The Rainbow*: no critic can improve on its clarity, its eloquence, its crisp certainty of tone. It describes with classic accuracy the centre of interest of that book, indeed the central aim of Lawrence's fiction: the aim that makes him one of the major writers of our century.

8 *The Carbon of the Unconscious*

It would be almost (but not quite) accurate to paraphrase this statement of Lawrence's as a claim that his theme is the unconscious. The 'carbon' which Lawrence is after, the 'radically unchanged element', is impersonal: it is the same from one individual to another. Now the unconscious mental life is in one sense highly personal: it contains the permanent traces of intense emotional experiences that, more than anything, we are told, have shaped the personality of the adult. Yet it is not too wild a paradox to say that the most personal parts of our lives are also the most imper-

[1] Letter to Edward Garnett, 5 June, 1914

sonal. It is easier to classify neurosis than it is to classify casual traits of normal behaviour. We have learned from Freud that even casual behaviour is determined: the determining factors that interest us most are those that plunge deep into the mental life, and the symptoms most rewarding to classify are those whose causes lie beneath the surface, imperceptible to ordinary observation. The unconscious speaks the most universal language, but speaks it from the individual's heart. And Lawrence's metaphor of carbon is therefore doubly appropriate for the unconscious: carbon is found everywhere, as the unconscious speaks to us all, and carbon is unchanging, as are the basic unconscious symbols.

Yet we must hesitate to say that either Lawrence or any other novelist takes the unconscious for his theme. The reason for this concerns Lawrence less than it concerns the concept of the unconscious itself. It is very difficult for the layman, reading Freud and the Freudians, to decide how inaccessible the unconscious is, and how complete is the division between it and the conscious mental life. We are told that the unconscious is simply the conscious mental life of the first five years of childhood; that neuroses only result from conflicts and repressions if the material repressed attaches itself to an earlier, childhood repression; and that the unconscious is often totally impervious to influence, and quite independent of the conscious mind—only deep therapy can give access to it. Now if all this is true, the novelist can only conclude that the unconscious is not his concern. For how can he regard the environment of the adult (indeed, of the child older than six) as having only a superficial influence on character? And how can he concern himself with an area of mental life that is inaccessible to him?

But Freudian theory is elusive on this point: the inaccessibility of the unconscious seems to grow and shrink at different points in the theory, or in its exposition. When Freud paid tribute, on his seventieth birthday, to the great poets and novelists who had discovered the unconscious before him, he did not mean that they had used psycho-analysis, or interested themselves only in the early childhood of their characters. Although he maintains that long and patient exploration is needed for the full explanation of a dream (though even this varies from dream to dream), he is content to offer very simple explanations for some of the slips and errors of everyday life. And some of the modifications of psycho-analytic theory, for purposes of experiment or briefer therapy, even claim to set up (and cure) micro-neuroses by methods that pierce only just beneath the surface.

The conclusion which the novelist is entitled to draw is encouraging. It is the more technical aspects of the concept of the unconscious—those which bind it most closely to the details of psychoanalytic theory—which tell us that it is inaccessible. Since there is precedent for disbelieving in its inaccessibility, we have reason to try and detach the concept from its more technical and limiting aspects. To read Freud's case histories is to confirm this conclusion. They are so full of evidence, and none of it is crucial: every layman who reads them must feel that the theory has elaborated itself with a precision that far outruns any ability to handle the material itself. The more fascinating the interpretations, the more arbitrary.

The conclusion is irresistible. Let the novelist take, and use, the most central, the most generalised concepts of psycho-analysis; if he uses them non-technically, they may help him to speak about non-clinical situations. That there is an unconscious mental life; that its operations are sometimes charged with intense emotion; that it expresses itself in symbols; that we project on to other people or situations impulses that were originally directed at ourselves; that material (from adult as well as childhood life) can be repressed, and that repression produces resistance and rationalisation—this is what the novelist wants to know. He will use it without (for example) asking himself whether the repression of recent experience is only important because it attached itself to a childhood trauma that the analyst would unearth during therapy, or whether the link between the two is established rather than discovered by the analysis. He will use the concept of rationalisation without asking whether all reasoning is really rationalisation. He will trust his own intuition to work out symbolic patterns, avoiding the too great precision and the too great vagueness that have alike made symbol-hunting ridiculous at times. And he need not feel so uneasy about leaving so many questions unanswered; psycho-analysis does not answer them either.

We can therefore say that in a general—almost (but not quite) a non-technical sense—the novelist does deal with the unconscious. In pre-Freudian writers it must of course be completely non-technical, nothing more than an awareness that we have thoughts and feelings we do not know about. Even Jane Austen is aware of the unconscious in this sense: Emma discovers the love she has long felt for Mr Knightley, and to put it that way is to say she had been unconscious of that love:

> Emma's eyes were instantly withdrawn; and she sat silently meditating in a fixed attitude for a few minutes. A few minutes were sufficient for making her acquainted with her own heart. A mind like hers, once opening to suspicion, made rapid progress; she touched, she admitted, she acknowledged the whole truth. Why was it so much worse that Harriet should be in love with Mr Knightley than with Frank Churchill? Why was the evil so dreadfully increased by Harriet's having some hope of a return? It darted through her with the speed of an arrow that Mr Knightley must marry no one but herself![1]

In describing the discovery, Jane Austen directs no attention to what the earlier experience of being in love without knowing it had been like; nor does she find it puzzling that Emma should be able to make a discovery like this about herself. Jane Austen is not puzzled, because it was a well-known phenomenon, and her mind was conventional enough to accept things not because they were clear, but because they were familiar. We however, who have read Freud, can observe that Jane Austen's account is at odds with itself: did Emma make the discovery through steady reasoning, or did it appear in her consciousness with the suddenness with which something darts up from the unconscious? We are told on the one hand that it took 'a few minutes', and Emma is given what looks like a reasoning process ('Why was it so much worse . . . ?') through which she moves to her conclusion; yet in the final phrase, 'it darted through her with the speed of an arrow' we seem to have a different, an incompatible and (we now see) a much truer version of what happened.

Yet even this apparent contradiction is interesting. Jane Austen is here running together two different processes which she is not yet in a position to sort out. One is the instantaneous process, quite different from deduction, by which a particular memory or realisation that had long been present in the unconscious finds its way into consciousness; the other is the deductive process by which we satisfy ourselves of the existence of the unconscious. For there is a resemblance between these thoughts of Emma's and what Freud describes in his paper on *The Unconscious*:

[1] *Emma*, ch. 47

That another man possess consciousness is a conclusion drawn by analogy from the utterances and actions we perceive him to make, and it is drawn in order that this behaviour of his may become intelligible to us. . . . Now psycho-analysis demands nothing more than that we should apply this method of inference to ourselves also. . . . If we do this, we must say that all the acts and manifestations which I notice in myself and do not know how to link up with the rest of my mental life must be judged as if they belonged to someone else and are to be explained by the mental life ascribed to that person.[1]

Is this not what Emma is doing? If only Jane Austen had *known* more, she could have sorted it all out. It is a moment, after all, to apply such a purely cognitive criterion: Jane Austen has paused to offer us an analysis of her heroine's thoughts. If she had been able to sort out the experience itself from the analysis thereof, she would have seemed to be on the edge of the idea of the unconscious. She would then have told us that Emma discovered her love instantaneously; and that 'a few minutes were sufficient for making her acquainted' with the train of thought and feeling that had brought that love to consciousness.

George Eliot is on that edge. There is, as it happens, an episode in her work very similar to this: Mirah's discovery of her love for Daniel Deronda. Just as Emma's discovery is sparked off by perceiving that Harriet loves Mr Knightley and thinks that love returned, so Mirah's is sparked off by the news of Grandcourt's death, and Hans' remark (which she agrees with) that now Deronda will be able to marry Mrs Grandcourt. But Mirah's love is expressed before she is aware of it—it comes out first as anger with Hans. 'She was pressed upon,' writes George Eliot,

by a crowd of thoughts thrusting themselves forward as interpreters of that consciousness which still remained unuttered to herself.[2]

George Eliot tries to mention explicitly what Jane Austen had simply shown in action—the state of being motivated by an unconscious sentiment. In George Eliot it is not the woman herself who first realises what this sentiment is—far more plausibly it is Hans, rendered sensitive by his own love for Mirah:

[1] 'The Unconscious' (1915); *Collected Papers* (International Psycho-analytical Library), IV, p. 101
[2] *Daniel Deronda*, ch. 61

Hans, on his side, had a mind equally busy. Mirah's anger had waked in him a new perception, and with it the unpleasant sense that he was a dolt not to have had it before.[1]

A few pages later, George Eliot gives us the very moment that corresponds to Emma's discovery: presenting it not nearly so dramatically, without any of that sense of shock which Jane Austen renders so convincingly, in which what we have just discovered and what we have always known turn out to be the same. What George Eliot captures, however is (through her image) something of the feel of the thought process itself:

> But in the still, quick action of her consciousness, thoughts went on like changing states of sensation unbroken by her habitual acts; and this inward language soon said distinctly that the mortal repugnance would remain even if Ezra were secured from loss.[2]

By sheer reflection, George Eliot taught herself a good deal of what psycho-analysis has since discovered; and though she formulated it in general terms, this is (as I have been trying to suggest) as much of an advantage as otherwise, when compared with the technical detail of Freudian theory. *Daniel Deronda*, her last novel and (from this point of view) her most interesting, was written when Freud was still at school.

> The thought of his dying would not subsist: it turned as with a dream change into the terror that she should die with his throttling fingers on her neck avenging that thought. Fantasies moved within her like ghosts, making no break in her more acknowledged consciousness and finding no obstruction in it: dark rays doing their work invisibly in the broad light.[3]

This brilliant sentence concludes an analysis of Gwendolen's fear and hatred of her husband, from whom she is now totally alienated in sympathy. Are these fantasies conscious or unconscious? Certainty 'the terror that she should die with his throttling fingers on her neck' is conscious; and one would therefore suppose that the next sentence is describing a double consciousness, that 'acknowledged' means 'acknowledged publicly' and 'invisibly' means 'invisibly to others'—all of which would be psychological observation of the greatest acuteness. Yet how tempting it is to take it as

[1] Ibid., ch. 61   [2] Ibid., ch. 61   [3] Ibid., ch. 48

an account of unconscious fantasies, to ascribe to 'acknowledged' and 'invisibly' the meanings we would more naturally give them today. And perhaps we need not resist this temptation. Perhaps George Eliot (consciously? unconsciously? half-consciously?) wrote the passage so that it could refer to the fantasies and terrors of whose existence she was only gropingly aware, and Gwendolen not at all. She spoke after all (in *The Spanish Gypsy*) of 'reasons deep below the reach of thought'.

And perhaps her awareness was not altogether groping. Here is the epigraph to an earlier chapter:

> Men, like planets, have both a visible and an invisible history. The astronomer threads the darkness with strict deduction, accounting so for every visible arc in the wanderer's orbit; and the narrator of human actions, if he did his work with the same completeness, would have to thread the hidden pathways of feeling and thought which lead up to every moment of action, and to those moments of intense suffering which take the quality of action—like the cry of Prometheus, whose chained anguish seems a greater energy than the sea and sky he invokes and the deity he defies.[1]

Again we want to ask, Invisible to whom? To others? Is she just saying that the narrator must explore the minds of his characters? Or is she going further: that he must explore what is invisible to the characters themselves? George Eliot is very close here to saying that the consciousness we possess is 'drawn by analogy from the utterances and actions we perceive . . . and it is drawn that behaviour may become intelligible to us', and she is saying it in an image that seems to point to the second half of Freud's analogy, the postulating of our own unconscious. Surely she would have welcomed the formulation, by Freud, of so much that she was on the verge of. This seems one of those moments (rare, but most important) when literature could learn from science: here is a novelist straining to go beyond the psychology she had been provided with. Perhaps those moments only come when science is on the verge of learning from literature.

And, taking a deep breath, we can carry this speculation further; and ask in what sense the novelist can—and must—tell us about the human mind. If we feel no pressure in a novelist to understand

[1] *Daniel Deronda*, ch. 16

his fellow-men, we can grant him only the limited interest we give to a good craftsman or a lively storyteller. The great novel is that which understands, whose vision of man speaks to us with the insistence of truth. Yet we also feel that it is impossibly difficult for any novelist to read up his knowledge of man and then apply what he has read by telling an anecdote, or constructing a plot. So clearcut a distinction between knowledge and illustration seems to make impossible the imaginative fusion that unifies a book's vision and so constitutes the integrity of art. The artist's emotion must permeate his insights and his episodes alike: if we feel he learned the one, then coolly paused to choose the other, this will surely be evidence that such fusion has not taken place.

What then is the novelist to do? He must want to know as much as possible about human motives and behaviour: this will make him avidly curious about psychology. But he must arrive at the knowledge by a process not too different from the creative process that sees the characters and makes up the story: by reflection on his own creations, rather than by pausing in his story and sitting at the feet of professor or doctor. If he picks up any knowledge in this academic way, he will have to labour long and wisely to absorb it into his way of seeing people, killing all that was merely theoretical in it.

And so it will be an enormous advantage to the novelist not to be born too late. He should live at a time when psychology has not specialised itself too clearly away from the traditional line of moral speculation about man. Since no aspect of the human mind fascinates the novelist more than the distinction between conscious and unconscious, we can be even more definite. The great novelist should be born late enough for the concept of the unconscious to be hovering on the edge of European thought: it must be there for him to find if he is thoughtful enough. But it must not have received so much formulation by experts that to read about it he will have to transform himself from novelist into science student. This is why all the great European novels—almost all of them— were written between, say, 1747 (the date of *Clarissa*) and 1924 (Proust was still working on *A la recherche du temps perdu* when he died). I do not want to join the chorus of glib obituary on the novel: it is always easy to see it dying. But at least the growth of psychology has set the novelist a new problem.

That is the corollary we can draw from one relation between

literature and psychology. Another and very different relation will concern us later.

9 Lawrence's Carbon

It is not impossible for a novelist to learn something from experts and then go back and rediscover it as a version of experience: but it must be very difficult indeed. Lawrence is a writer who tried to work out his own psychology, but he did so at a time when there were technical psychologies about him. He did not have to discover the unconscious: the term was given to him, from outside. It should follow from my argument that this was not altogether an advantage to him.

Compare, for instance, these two passages:

It is like a lovely, suave, fluid, *creative* electricity that flows in a circuit between the great nerve-centres in mother and child. The electricity of the universe is a sundering force. But this lovely polarised vitalism is creative. It passes in a circuit between the two poles of the passional unconscious in the two now separated beings. It establishes in each that first primal consciousness which is the sacred, all-containing head-stream of all our consciousness.[1]

From the first the baby stirred in the young father a deep, strong emotion he dared scarcely acknowledge, it was so strong and came out of the dark of him. When he heard the child cry, a terror possessed him, because of the answering echo from the unfathomed distances in himself. Must he know in himself such distances, perilous and imminent?[2]

The first is Lawrence's account of mother-love, from a theoretical work; the second his expression of father-love, from a novel. Because it is Lawrence, the style and approach are barely different, but what difference there is is most revealing. What has it helped the first passage that Lawrence can use the terms 'conscious' and 'unconscious'? It has not lessened the dependence on metaphor, almost on invocation; nor has it disciplined the thought. It is not clear how seriously we are to take 'establishes' (similar, that, to

[1] *Psycho-analysis and the Unconscious*, § 3
[2] *The Rainbow*, ch. 8

Freud's too-ready belief that he knows which way causation works); and I can attach little meaning to 'the electricity of the universe is a sundering force'.

Now the second passage is not only much more compelling, the whole paragraph having a rhythmic shape and the ring of genuine emotion: it is also written with more clarity. The unfathomed distances are clearer to us than the 'passional unconscious': there is no pretence in this passage of greater precision than the writer can command. Instead of the pretentious vocabulary of the 'lovely polarised vitalism', there is a willingness to say only what he knows, rendering the emotion even if the psychology is guesswork.

Lawrence did not go beneath the surface of consciousness as thoughtfully as George Eliot, but he went further, and more often. She may describe the structure of carbon with more care, but there is far more of it in his books than in hers. In this, he is a modern: just as the gropings I have quoted from her work make her, typical Victorian as she is, a proto-modern.

What makes a writer modern need not be what makes him good; and it is not easy to be sure how far Lawrence's interest in carbon is a source of strength to his novels, and how far of weakness. A good test case is the superb thirteenth chapter of *The Rainbow*, the account of Ursula's spell of teaching in a slum school. The scene I want to discuss is (once more) too long to quote, and I must fob off the reader with a summary and a plea that he turn it up. It is the scene in which Mr Harby, the Headmaster, passes her classroom and hears the jeering note in the voices of the boys as (against the rules) they call out their answers.

At that moment Mr Harby was passing.

'Stand up, Hill!' he called, in a big voice.

Everybody started. Ursula watched the boy. He was evidently poor, and rather cunning. A stiff bit of hair stood straight off his forehead, and the rest fitted close to his meagre head. He was pale and colourless.

'Who told you to call out?' thundered Mr Harby.

'Please sir, I was answering,' he replied, with the same humble insolence.

'Go to my desk.'

The boy set off down the room, the big black jacket hanging in dejected folds about him, his thin legs, rather knocked at the knees, going already with the pauper's crawl, his feet in their big boots scarcely lifted. Ursula watched him in his crawling, slinking progress down the room. He was one of *her* boys!

Mr Harby then stays for a few minutes to examine the class.

'What is your composition about?' asked the Headmaster. Every hand shot up. 'The —' stuttered some voice in its eagerness to answer.

'I wouldn't advise you to call out,' said Mr Harby. He would have a pleasant voice, full and musical, but for the detestable menace that always tailed in it. He stood unmoved, his eyes twinkling under his bushy black eyebrows, watching the class. There was something fascinating in him, as he stood, and again she wanted to scream. She was all jarred, she did not know what she felt.

'Well, Alice?' he said.

'The rabbit,' piped a girl's voice.

'A very easy subject for Standard Five.'[1]

Ursula, stuck among the back forms, can do nothing but listen. She finds herself disliking Mr Harby for his bullying, the aggressive imposing of his cheap authority; yet at the same time she finds him an attractive man, 'with strength and male power and a certain blind, native beauty'. While she is reflecting on this contradiction— puzzled, humiliated, resentful—Mr Harby goes to his desk and beats Hill, who comes 'crawling back, blubbering piteously'. His misery does not last as long as her shame; and in the end the lesson returns to normal—or the nearest Ursula can ever come to normal.

This is one of Lawrence's great scenes, unforgettably true and powerful. It is the work of someone who has seen and heard with vivid accuracy, and whose details are arresting in their realism— the 'big voice' with which Mr Harby calls out, the boys 'cunning, cynical reserve', and above all (an objective image for Ursula's whole complex reaction of shame, dislike and pity) the superbly rendered walk, the 'pauper's crawl' with which Hill goes to Mr Harby's desk, leaving Ursula doubly ashamed, that Hill should represent her before Mr Harby, and that she should have got Hill into trouble. Lawrence can catch an overtone in a phrase: 'a very easy subject for Standard Five' captures exactly the tone in which Mr Harby would rebuke Ursula under the guise of rebuking her

[1] *The Rainbow*, ch. 13

class. Lawrence is writing here with the steady eye and keen observation of one of the great realists—Zola, say, or Arnold Bennett.

Yet Bennett could not have written this scene. Perhaps there is no detail, in the parts I have quoted, altogether out of the range of Bennett's realism, though he seldom scores so many bullseyes together; but the long paragraph analysing Ursula's feelings towards Mr Harby is quite foreign to the world of *The Old Wives' Tale* and *Riceyman Steps*. In part, it is a reflection on the pointlessness of authority:

> He had a decent, powerful, rude soul. What did he care about the composition on 'The Rabbit'? Yet his will kept him there before the class, threshing the trivial subject. It was habit with him now, to be so little and vulgar, out of place. She saw the shamefulness of his position, felt the fettered wickedness in him which would blaze out into evil rage in the long run, so that he was like a persistent, strong creature tethered. It was really intolerable. The jarring was torture to her.[1]

There is a great deal more like this, in a paragraph almost as long as the rest of the scene. It is an exploring of the edge of consciousness. Ursula is conscious of most (perhaps not quite all) of this train of thought; but the part of Mr Harby's nature she is pondering is largely unconscious. She is distressed above all by his 'blind, dogged, wholesale, will'.

'Will' is one of the commonest and most puzzling of Lawrence's psychological terms. It usually means an intense determination to act that is not based on the 'candle flame, forever upright and flowing' which represents his ideal of the whole man. It is always a derogatory term. The result of this violence of will in Mr Harby is 'the fettered wickedness in him which would blaze out into evil rage in the long run'. Here we are beyond the personality of Mr Harby, on the edge of meeting something very like an account of repression. This is not diamond, but carbon.

It is Lawrence's interest in the general (including the unconscious) operation of psychic forces ('Diamond, what! This is carbon') that takes him beyond the range of a realist like Bennett. Lawrence is able to render the surface of this scene with such superb truth because he is sensitive to what goes on beneath the surface. We

[1] Ibid., ch. 13

praise Bennett for his honesty: for the human warmth without idealisation that can portray (say) the relationship between Violet and Elsie in *Riceyman Steps*. But Lawrence is so much more honest —he gets in so much more of the irritations, the exact intonations of malice, shame or love—that after reading him we can never feel quite the same about Bennett. Bennett seems to touch us on the quick when he writes about domestic tensions and resentment; but compared to Lawrence he is always slightly reserved.

And so we can say that if Lawrence had not been able to write that exploring paragraph in which Ursula analyses Mr Harby, he would not have been able to employ that hypersensitive eye and ear, and would not have caught the realistic details of speech and crawl so vividly: by transcending realism, he becomes greater than the realists at their own method. This is true: but it is also true that the long paragraph of analysis is a flaw. Many readers must wish it away; almost all readers must wish it shorter. Only by quoting it all can one convey the repetitiveness, the wearisome, almost pedantic repetitiveness, that dilutes and hinders its impact; and there are details which can be seen in quotation. How slovenly, for instance, is the adjective 'wholesale', when Lawrence writes of Mr Harby's 'blind, dogged, wholesale will'. And after the powerful sentence about the 'fettered wickedness in him', Lawrence descends with shocking insensitivity to 'It was really intolerable'. There was not a single false note in the dramatic rendering of the scene itself, but Lawrence loses all that perfect control when he turns to deal with what lies beneath the surface.

We can see the same thing on a larger scale by comparing *The Old Wives' Tale* with *The Lost Girl*. Lawrence may have written his novel in imitation of Bennett—certainly there can be no doubt of the influence. The first third or so of *The Lost Girl* is as vivid and powerful as Bennett (it seems to me the one Lawrence novel that his admirers underrate), and its occasional sense of the depths that lurk beneath what is observed make it in many ways greater; but there is nothing in *The Old Wives' Tale* as tedious as the Natcha-Kee Tawaras, nor any character as pretentiously created as Cicio.

Lawrence's description of himself as 'religious', we may then conclude, though it is misleading, points to something of great importance in his work, perhaps the most important quality of all, his interest in carbon. It is this that makes him modern, and it is this that makes him great; but this is also the source of his stridency, tediousness and vagueness. Later, we shall see at greater length how close is the connexion between Lawrence's greatness and his faults.

10 Telling the Truth

I can now formulate the main point of this first part. Speaking of George Eliot, I remarked on her cool gaze, her determination to sacrifice not only the expectations of the Victorian public but also the gesture of tragedy, for the common trudge of truth; speaking of Lawrence, I have come to see the strength of his realism in its yield of truth, the strength of his concern with a further dimension of character in what it opens up of a deeper honesty—just as its danger is its possible dishonesty. What I have now reached the edge of saying (and it is as true of Jane Austen) is that the main strength of these novelists is that they tell the truth.

To see religious experience as a human phenomenon, to use religion as a metaphor for conduct, can only be truthtelling to the irreligious: or to those whose religion has rejected a transcendent for an immanent God. Since this is the way George Eliot sees religious experience, and since she weakens her grip as a novelist when she ceases to see it this way; since the same is true of Jane Austen and of Lawrence; and since I believe one could demonstrate the same point of all the great 'religious' novelists—Dostoyevsky, Bernanos, Mauriac, Greene—it would seem that the novel, on my view, is a kind of confirmation of agnosticism. On the whole, I believe this; but since this is a work of literary criticism and not of open apologetics, I must make the point only to run away from it: admitting it, then hoping that it will pay off in the course of actual criticism.

And now, to conclude this argument, I shall illustrate, from George Eliot and Jane Austen, the nature, the importance and the artistic function of some of the truths they tell. I begin with a very particular truth: George Eliot's opinion that money matters—that the whole material basis of life is far more important than is easily admitted by those who never need worry about it.

Nicole bought from a great list that ran two pages, and bought the things in the windows besides. Everything she liked that she couldn't possibly use herself, she bought as a present for a friend. She bought coloured beads, folding beach cushions, artificial flowers, honey, a guest bed, bags, scarfs, love birds, miniatures for a doll's house, and three yards of some new cloth the colour of prawns. . . . Nicole was the product of much ingenuity and toil. For her sake trains began their run at Chicago and traversed the round belly of the continent to California; chicle factories fumed and link belts grew link by link in factories; men mixed toothpaste in vats and drew mouthwash out of copper hogsheads. . . —these were some of the people who gave a tithe to Nicole, and, as the whole system swayed and thundered onward, it lent a feverish bloom to such processes of hers as wholesale buying, like the flush of a fireman's face holding his post before a spreading blaze.[1]

Good society has its claret and its velvet carpets, its dinner-engagements six weeks deep, its opera and its faery ballrooms; rides off its ennui on thoroughbred horses, lounges at the club, has to keep clear of crinoline vortices, gets its science done by Faraday, and its religion by the superior clergy who are to be met in the best houses: how should it have time or need for belief and emphasis? But good society, floated on gossamer wings of light irony, is of very expensive production; requiring nothing less than a wide and arduous national life condensed in unfragrant, deafening factories, cramping itself in mines, sweating at furnaces, grinding, hammering, weaving under more or less oppression of carbonic acid—or else, spread over sheepwalks, and scattered in lonely houses and huts on the clayey or chalky cornlands, where the rainy days look dreary.[2]

Scott Fitzgerald is not an author one readily compares with George Eliot, though they have a good deal in common. Here we see how interested they both were in the means of production, and how aware that it determines spending habits and social preference. Such phrasing suggests Marxism; and perhaps George Eliot's way of describing the economic basis of culture is actually nearer to Marxism than Fitzgerald's. Where he sees the glamour, she sees the unfairness. Even in this shortened quotation, Fitzgerald's fascination with the colour and luxury of Nicole's shopping is evident; and we can see the same romantic lure in his account of the 'ingenuity and toil' that 'drew mouthwash out of copper hogsheads'—interesting, unusual, but not, as he describes it, arduous. There is, except for that final, haunting, perhaps sinister

[1] F. Scott Fitzgerald: *Tender is the Night*, Bk. II, ch. 13
[2] *The Mill on the Floss*, Bk. IV, ch. 3

image, no revolutionary material here. But George Eliot has not
bothered with ingenuity or romance: she writes with a firm cumulative anger of 'sweating at furnaces, grinding, hammering, weaving
under more or less oppression of carbonic acid'. And if this is near-
Marxism, there is one sentence in *Middlemarch* which should make
George Eliot acceptable to the strictest party line—the curt reference to:

> those philanthropic models who make a profit out of poison-
> ous pickles to support themselves while they are exposing adul-
> teration, or hold shares in a gambling-hell that they may have
> leisure to represent the cause of public morality.[1]

A few years earlier she had writen in the *Westminster Review*:

> How little the real characteristics of the working-classes are
> known to those who are outside them, how little their natural
> history has been studied, is sufficiently disclosed by our Art
> as well as by our political and social theories.[2]

In her essay on Riehl, author of two books on the German people,
she sets against the traditional idylls of the merry peasantry what
she considers the much harsher truth:

> The slow gaze, in which no sense of beauty beams, no humour
> twinkles,—the slow utterance, and the heavy slouching walk,
> remind one rather of that melancholy animal the camel, than
> of the sturdy countryman, with striped stockings, red waist-
> coat, and hat aside, who represents the traditional English
> peasant. . . . That delicious effervescence of the mind which we
> call fun, has no equivalent for the northern peasant, except
> tipsy revelry; the only realm of fancy and imagination for the
> English clown exists at the bottom of the third quart-pot.[3]

This is harsher than anything in her novels: what could Felix Holt
do, talking to these? But though her mood grew softer, her gaze
did not cloud, and she never ceased (as Barbara Hardy very well
puts it[4]) to 'place her sympathetic plea outside her characters, showing them realistically as too dumb to plead or too charmless to

---

[1] *Middlemarch*, ch. 15
[2] 'The Natural History of German Life' (1856); George Eliot's *Essays*, ed.
Pinney, p. 268
[3] Ibid., p. 269
[4] Barbara Hardy, *The Novels of George Eliot* (1959), pp. 16-17

attract'. Mrs Hardy contrasts this favourably with Dickens, who depicts the social horrors, but somehow exempts his appealing heroines and victims from having suffered any effects from this; and she is able to quote, in support of her preference, a sentence from this very essay on Riehl, rebuking Dickens for entertaining—or almost entertaining—'the miserable fallacy that high morality and refined sentiment can grow out of harsh social relations, ignorance and want'.

All this is familiar, and has been praised in George Eliot. I want to add that the same materialism is found on the level of the individual. George Eliot knows not only that morality and leisure rest on an economic basis (there must be a leisured and a moralising class), but also that the individual is free to devote his attention to them in proportion as his wants are taken care of. 'Eats first, morals after,' as Brecht has it. It's hard to imagine Marian Evans putting it quite that way, but she essentially agreed.

To read her letters is to be struck by her steady and open concern with money. She was not grasping—she was even generous—but she clearly prided herself on her frankness. A touching mixture of worldliness and unworldliness emerges sometimes from her remarks on her own earnings:

> You see, I speak to you without circumlocution, and I am sure you will like that best. You know how important this money question is to me. I don't want the world to give me anything for my books except money enough to save me from the temptation to write *only* for money.[1]

George Eliot learned the value of money from Marian Evans; and there are several examples in her books of those who do not realise the value of money because they have always had it. Daniel Deronda passes through a stage common in 'the young man of our day':

> that of questioning whether it were worth while to take part in the battle of the world: I mean, of course, the young men in whom the unproductive labour of questioning is sustained by three or five per cent on capital which someone else has battled for.[2]

[1] Letter to John Blackwood, 13 September, 1859
[2] *Daniel Deronda*, ch. 17

The most celebrated example is Lydgate, who:

> did not mean to think of furniture at present; but whenever he did so, it was to be feared that neither biology nor schemes of reform would lift him above the vulgarity of feeling that there would be an incompatibility in his furniture not being of the best.[1]

Lydgate does not consider money important, because he has never had to: he buys a dinner service, not because he can afford to, but because he hates ugly crockery and happens to see this one. 'It was expensive, but that might be in the nature of dinner services.' Marian Evans once wrote to Blackwood, 'I care a great deal for money, as I suppose all anxious minds do that love independence'. Lydgate loved independence, but his mind was not anxious enough.

11 Exposing Self-deception

The lesson which Lydgate learns about money can be seen as one application of a much larger lesson: the need to free oneself from self-deception. This is the kind of truthtelling that will engage the novelist more than any other. George Eliot's letters and journals are studded with remarks on how literature produces its effect by enlarging our sympathies and opening our imagination:

> My function is that of the *aesthetic* not the doctrinal teacher— the rousing of the nobler emotions . . . not the prescribing of special measures.[2]

> If art does not enlarge our sympathies, it does nothing morally, I have heart-cutting experiences that *opinions* are a poor cement between human souls: and the only effect I ardently long to produce by my writing is, that those who read them should be better able to imagine and to *feel* the pains and the joys of those who differ from themselves in everything but the broad fact of being struggling, erring, human creatures.[3]

If we accept this, it follows that the only truths which the novelist really needs to tell are those which his readers will resist: those it would enlarge their sympathies to accept. The truths we resist are

[1] *Middlemarch*, ch. 15
[2] Letter to Mrs Peter Taylor, 18 July 1878
[3] Letter to Charles Bray, 5 July 1859

those we have trained ourselves to ignore or disbelieve; and the novelist, describing these, is describing the way we deceive ourselves. That is why self-deception is of such tremendous interest to the novelist. Because our wishes are so strong, we easily persuade ourselves that what we wish to be so, is so—or soon will be. The wish may not always be pleasant, for the super-ego has wishes too, and the 'facts' that we believe against all probability may be unpleasant ones with which we punish ourselves. I say 'ourselves' but the novelist, of course, does not know us: the only self-deceptions he can show are those of his characters. He does not even need to murmur 'if the cap fits'—that can be left to the reader. To discuss the varieties of self-deception will therefore be to discuss the kinds of self-deceiving characters the novelist creates. Let us (laying Lawrence aside for the moment, since he does not treat self-deception so neatly) consider some of its varieties in Jane Austen and George Eliot.

Though really the starting-point might have been Dickens. We can always trust Dickens to offer us a psychological process at its simplest and most universal, and the most famous case of self-deception in English literature is probably Mr Micawber's conviction that something will turn up. *Sanditon* has a Micawber, in the person of Mr Parker, who has set his heart on making the town into a fashionable holiday resort, and therefore believes that no person can be really well 'without spending at least six weeks by the sea every year'. He is tireless in finding reasons why Sanditon is more suitable than any other place; and in finding evidence that the world is at last taking his advice and coming there:

'Civilisation, civilisation indeed!' cried Mr Parker, delighted. Look, my dear Mary—look at William Healey's windows. Blue shoes and nankin boots!'[1]

The comic incongruity here lies between what Mr Parker sees and his ingenuity in interpreting it to feed his illusion, between the blue shoes and the amazing season—and, since illusions about Sanditon are never as interesting as illusions about oneself, between the blue shoe and his conclusion: 'Well, I think I *have* done something in my day'.

We do not often deceive ourselves with quite this openness: and the novelist can seldom expose quite so simply, if he is concerned at

[1] *Sanditon*, ch. 4

all with verisimilitude. Mr Craig, the gardener in *Adam Bede*, however, is almost as simple:

> 'Pee-ee-eh!' said Mr Craig. 'A man doesna want to see fur to
> know as the English 'ull beat the French. Why, I know upo'
> good authority as it's a big Frenchman as reaches five foot high,
> an' they live upo' spoon-meat mostly. I knew a man as his
> father had a particular knowledge o' the French.'[1]

Since Mr Craig is not talking of himself or his own doings, we might
feel that this is not self-deception but merely ignorance; and that
by laughing at it George Eliot is forsaking her role as novelist for
that of raconteur—even that she is being patronising, looking
down on the uneducated. But this would be unfair: Mr Craig *is*
talking about himself, for his general intent is always to cut a
figure as a knowledgeable man. Details like 'Why, I know upo' good
authority' or (earlier) 'Well, you mark my words' are therefore
central to the effect: indeed, as we read over his speeches, we can
see that the very rhythm of his sentences serves to create his
picture of himself as knowing everything a bit better than everyone else:

> And how are *you*, Mrs Poyser?—thinking o' gathering' the red
> currants soon, I reckon. You'd a deal better gether 'em afore
> they're over-ripe, wi' such weather as we've got to look forward
> to.[2]

Before he came out with the advice in his second sentence, had he
not revealed in the first his intention to give it?

What we are offered in Mr Parker and Mr Craig is the immediate
laughter of caricature: the incongruity between what is and what is
seen is funny because it is so obvious. Perhaps the only book of
Jane Austen's which remains wholly on this level is *Northanger
Abbey*, the slightest and most immature of them all. What is it
that makes self-deception more complex, more moving, more disturbing, more significant than this?

Neither Mr Craig, nor Mr Parker, nor Catherine Morland, do any
serious harm to themselves or others. If they did, our response
could not remain that of being merely amused. It could change in
two ways. If the emphasis were placed on the danger to others, our
reaction would include fear of the self-deceiver; if it were placed on

---

[1] *Adam Bede*, ch. 18   [2] Ibid., ch. 18

the harm done to oneself, it would include grief for him. There are in *Adam Bede* two studies of self-deception far more serious than Mr Craig, Hetty and Arthur. Hetty deceives herself with day-dreams:

> Oh yes! she was very pretty: Captain Donnithorne thought so . . . And Hetty looked at herself tonight with quite a different sensation from what she had ever felt before; there was an invisible spectator whose eye rested on her like morning on the flowers. His soft voice was saying over and over again those pretty things she had heard in the wood; his arm was round her, and the delicate rose-scent of his hair was with her still.[1]

Arthur too had his daydreams, of the figure he will cut as squire. His capacity to shut out reality is less than Hetty's (for in her case it is almost total), yet we see that egoism always finds an ultimate barricade—always finds an argument to convince itself that un-pleasant truths, however much territory they conquer, will leave the last refuge of self still safe:

> It was an unfortunate business altogether, but there was no use making it worse than it was, by imaginary exaggerations and forebodings of evil that might never come. The temporary sadness for Hetty was the worst consequence; he resolutely turned away his eyes from any bad consequence that was not demonstrably inevitable. But—but Hetty might have had the trouble in some other way if not in this. And perhaps hereafter he might be able to do a great deal for her, and make up to her for all the tears she would shed about him. She would owe the advantage of his care for her in future years to the sorrow she had incurred now. *So* good comes out of evil. Such is the beauti-ful arrangement of things![2]

In both these cases, we have entered a realm of experience in which the simple amusement caused by Mr Parker is no longer possible. In Hetty we are shown the danger of self-deception to oneself, in Arthur to others. I have already discussed the terrible consequences of Hetty's folly, and the way George Eliot invests her novel with something of tragic dignity in the account of Hetty's journey to Windsor and back. Nothing in Arthur's story, and nothing in the earlier part of Hetty's story, is written with quite this power, and to ask why is to gain some insight into the limitations of the early George Eliot.

[1] *Adam Bede*, ch. 15   [2] Ibid., ch. 29

Much of the portrayal of Arthur is highly effective: its weakness is **very** clear if we continue the last quotation a little further.

> Are you inclined to ask whether this can be the same Arthur who, two months ago, had that freshness of feeling, that delicate honour which shrinks from wounding even a sentiment? . . . The same, I assure you, only under different conditions.[1]

The tone towards the reader has now changed: we are being badgered. Our most simple-minded objections are being anxiously, insistently refuted. And if we continue the quotation about Hetty's daydreams, we shall find very much the same:

> It was very much in this way that our friend Adam Bede thought about Hetty; only he put his thoughts into different words. If ever she behaved with cold vanity towards him he said to himself, it is only because she doesn't love me well enough; and he was sure that her love, whenever she gave it, would be the most precious thing a man would possess on earth. Before you despise Adam as deficient in penetration, pray ask yourself if you were ever predisposed to believe evil of any pretty woman—if you ever *could*, without hard head-breaking demonstration, believe evil of the *one* supremely pretty woman who had bewitched you. No: people who love downy peaches are apt not to think of the stone, and sometimes jar their teeth terribly against it.[2]

'People who love downy peaches are apt not to think of the stone.' If only George Eliot had left it at that. Here is her terse proverbial style at something like its best, but she will not leave it alone (or, since this is her first full-length novel, perhaps we should say she has not isolated it yet). That initial 'No' weakens the effect; so does the dotting of the i's as she continues, and above all her schoolmarmish 'terribly'. And the preceding sentences are never wholly at ease, never quite free from patronising touches ('our friend Adam Bede' or the heavy-handed italicising—almost a wink —of the '*one* supremely pretty woman who had bewitched you').

To expose self-deception is to point out an incongruity: between true and false versions of the world or the self, between what is seen and what is. In *Adam Bede* George Eliot shows one-half of the incongruity (what is seen) with consummate skill: in Hetty's daydreams, in Arthur's reassurances to himself ('No! I'm a devil of a fellow for getting myself into a scrape, but I always take care the load shall fall on my own shoulders'). The failure comes in her rendering of the other half: for she sometimes *tells* us what is, at effusive, even embarrassing length, and with a frequent betrayal of uncertainty. Her eye strays from the object, and her attention strays to whether she has made her point clearly enough, or whether the reader will be enlightened enough to believe it. The result is the sarcasms, reproaches and italics that betray her art.

When she tried again at Arthur Donnithorne, twenty years later, she did much better.

> Fred Vincy, we have seen, had a debt on his mind, and though no such immaterial burden could depress that buoyant-hearted young gentleman for many hours together, there were circumstances connected with this debt which made the thought of it unusually importunate. . . . Fred had felt confident that he should meet the bill himself, having ample funds at his disposal in his own hopefulness. You will hardly demand that his confidence should have a basis in external facts; such confidence, we know, is something less coarse and materialistic. . . . Fred felt sure that he should have a present from his uncle, that he should have a run of luck, that by dint of 'swapping' he should gradually metamorphose a horse worth forty pounds into a horse that would fetch a hundred at any moment—'judgement' being equivalent to an unspecified sum in hard cash.[1]

Fred, like Arthur, is an optimist because he has been spoilt: never having been in real difficulties, he cannot believe that he will ever be—or that anyone else ever will be. He is so like Arthur, and is portrayed with such similar means, that I find it hard to say why his portrait is the more successful—hard but important: if we can draw this distinction, which is purely one of quality and not one of intention, we shall have gone a long way towards describing George Eliot's growth as an artist.

The success of the irony in this passage is largely a matter of tone. Fred is not being crushed or triumphed over by the author. She sees without blinking the incongruity between his wishes and the truth, but does not gloat or make easy verbal points. Because the tone establishes our trust in the author, we are all the more affected by the extent of the self-deception she shows. 'Fred had

---

[1] *Middlemarch*, ch. 23

felt confident that he should meet the bill himself, having ample funds at his disposal in his own hopefulness.' This begins as a cool paraphrase of Fred's own thoughts, and the last four words make their ironic point without breaking the surface of the prose. The next sentence ('You will hardly demand . . .') could have come from *Adam Bede*, and the tone of 'coarse and materialistic' is perhaps a shade lofty, the point too easy; but in *Adam Bede* we could not have gone on to the brilliant matter-of-fact account of the actual ways he might make money, where the cool accuracy of the analysis contrasts with the vagueness of Fred's own thoughts. The style is tauter, less dilute, the author more detached than in *Adam Bede*: we are shown the same traits of character, but more powerfully now. There is a truer objectivity (as in the account of swapping, surely beyond the range of the earlier book); and an assurance of tone that makes it safe to use irony.

I take the last example from *Theophrastus Such*.

We are led by a tradition about ourselves, so that long after a man has practically departed from a rule or principle, he continues innocently to state it as a true description of his practice—just as he has a long tradition that he is not an old gentleman, and is startled when he is seventy at over-hearing himself called by an epithet which he has only applied to others.

'A person with your tendency of constitution should take as little sugar as possible,' said Pilulus to Bovis somewhere in the darker decades of this century. 'It has made a great difference to Avis since he took my advice in that matter: he used to consume half a pound a day.'

'God bless me!' cries Bovis. 'I take very little sugar myself.'

'Twenty-six large lumps every day of your life, Mr Bovis,' says his wife.

'No such thing!' exclaims Bovis.

'You drop them into your tea, coffee and whisky yourself, my dear, and I count them.'

'Nonsense!' laughs Bovis, turning to Pilulus, that they may exchange a glance of mutual amusement at a woman's inaccuracy.

But she happened to be right. Bovis has never said inwardly that he would take a large allowance of sugar, and he had the tradition about himself that he was a man of the most moderate habits; hence, with his conviction, he was naturally disgusted at the saccharine excesses of Avis.

The author is totally absent from the snatch of dialogue, and even from the sentence 'But she happened to be right', which is not comment but summarised narrative. The opening sentence, though it tells, not shows, is scarcely less objective. There is no anger in 'innocently': it is pure observation. The last sentence strikes one false note—the ponderous sarcasm of 'saccharine excesses'—but apart from that it continues the even tone that shows George Eliot complete master of her material. Of course the material is less powerful and less complex than was Fred Vincy.

The next paragraph is even more interesting:

> I have sometimes thought that this facility of men in believing that they are still what they once meant to be—this undisturbed appropriation of a traditional character which is often but a melancholy relic of early resolutions, like the worn and soiled testimony to soberness and honesty carried in the pocket of a tippler whom the need of a dram has driven into peculation—may sometimes diminish the turpitude of what seems a flat, barefaced falsehood. It is notorious that a man may go on uttering false assertions about his own acts till he at last believes in them: is it not possible that sometimes in the very first utterance there may be a shade of creed-reciting belief, a reproduction of a traditional self which is clung to against all evidence? There is no knowing all the disguises of the lying serpent.[1]

The objectivity so well caught in the dialogue has not been lost: though now represented only by the calm tone of the writing, and the sombre simile of the testimonial. But there has been a change: the man we are hearing of is no longer simply amusing in a way Mr Parker was amusing, he is a sufferer. He clings against all evidence because it is the only way he can reach to his own sad fate; and grief is increased by our realisation that it is a reaction of pure evasion, making things worse. For a moment we glimpse the George Eliot who created Dunstan Cass and Tommy Trounsem.

With each of these examples we have glimpsed the two directions in which we can be taken when the self-deception is no longer merely amusing. Arthur does harm chiefly to others, and excites our anger; the anonymous subject of the last paragraph amuses, but also wrings for a moment from us the grief of sympathy.

---

[1] 'How we come to give ourselves false testimonials and believe in them', *Theophrastus Such*, § 13

Now these reactions can suggest one generalisation: for they seem to be the responses appropriate to three principal literary genres. That which amuses is comedy; that which moves to anger, fear or indignation is satire; and that which moves us because we identify with the hero who destroys himself is surely tragedy. In all the welter of discussion on how to distinguish genres, here perhaps is one principle as helpful as any other single criterion. Ignoring structural criteria for the moment, may we not offer this difference of response as a distinguishing factor?

And we can go further. We have also seen what responses are appropriate to the failure of the last two genres. I suggested that the satiric portrait of Arthur failed when George Eliot could not find an objective bodying forth of both halves of the incongruity: when she tells us that there is incongruity and that she is indignant about it, protesting too much as she does this. When this happens, satire has turned into denunciation; and we no longer have the sense of being shown a truth that arouses genuine literary anger. Similarly one way in which tragedy can go wrong is for us not to feel sufficiently convinced that the harm done to himself by the self-deceiver is really bodied forth in the literary work: then the tragic figure will be amusing, or nasty.

And finally, since this classification of responses does not square with the usual classification of genres, we can wonder if the latter ought to be tinkered with. When our attention is concentrated on the viciousness and danger of the self-deceiver, then the result is satiric: but when we are shown the grief of the victims, our response becomes a blend of hostile awe in one direction, sympathetic grief in the other. This is more like a tragic than a satiric response, but perhaps it is not really like either. *Brittanicus, Sejanus, Hedda Gabler* are not tragedies in the usual sense. They may be constructed like tragedies, but the response they arouse is the one I am here describing.

The disadvantage of distinguishing genres by response rather than structure is that works then shift so uncomfortably from one to the other, as we change our minds about their interpretation. This has a corresponding advantage, however: it reminds us that no work has really come into being until we have fully responded to it. And since we are distinguishing attitudes and not plots, the same structure must hold the possibility of being treated comically, satirically or tragically. Will this mean that in any satire, there is a potential comedy and a potential tragedy—and so for the other two?

Usually we shall not feel this very strongly, for the depicting of a character is impregnated with the author's attitude: that determines not only the tone but also the selection of what facts to give us. But there will be rare examples where the author seems to have walked right round his character: a character so many-sided and so real that it contains the possibility of arousing a whole range of attitudes, and the author knows it. This would seem (in the terms of my Introduction) to be the attaining of the dramatic extreme. The effect can be even more startling, and more exhilarating, when it is felt in a thoroughly committed author. The one supreme example of this is Mr Casaubon. When we first see him he is the object of grave satire, though we are constantly aware that he could be comic; when later he becomes a tragic figure, the satiric view is not forgotten.

12 'Emma', or 'The Match-maker'

But is not all this unfair to comedy? I seem to have suggested that it is the most trivial of the genres: the presentation of incongruity for its own sake, the effect merely amusing. Certainly the self-deceiver can cause us mere amusement, and such works are certainly comic. But is there not a fuller, a richer response than is still comic? To show that there is, I turn to *Emma*. If any work belongs unequivocally to any genre, *Emma* is a comedy. And it is certainly about self-deception. Before drawing any conclusions, let us pause to examine it.

Perhaps we can designate its theme even more narrowly: we can say it is about match-making. On her first appearance in the book, Emma comes before us as a match-maker. She claims the credit for having brought Mr Weston and Miss Taylor together. Since all her other attempts are so disastrous, we are perhaps inclined to agree with Mr Knightley's scepticism about this one: 'Your making the match, as you call it, means only your planning it, your saying to yourself one idle day, "I think it would be a very good thing for Miss Taylor if Mr Weston were to marry".' But as the story proceeds Emma is very much more active than this, and she mismatches almost every couple of social standing in Highbury. And when the story is over, and everybody, despite Emma's efforts, has married the right person, and she has seen the error of her ways, there is still a furtive delight to be taken in the birth of Mrs Weston's daughter. Emma

> had been decided in wishing for a Miss Weston. She would not acknowledge that it was with any view of making a match for her, hereafter, with either of Isabella's sons; but she was convinced that a daughter would suit both father and mother best.[1]

If the story of Anne Elliott could be called *Persuasion*, that of Emma Woodhouse has a fair claim to being named *The Match-maker*.

Match-making is a way of managing the lives of others: it is a comic version of the exercise of power. Comic, because to be married is not, after all, a calamity. The scheming of Emma is a parallel to the scheming of Iago, but Iago's aims are calamitious, so the effect can no longer be comic. Emma makes innumerable mistakes in the course of the book, but her principal mismatchings are three: Harriet and Mr Elton, herself and Frank Churchill, Harriet and Frank Churchill.

The Harriet- Mr Elton match forms a kinds of prelude: it is over, and Emma has repented, before the end of Book I. The comedy of course lies in the contrast between what we know and what Emma sees: this incongruity is clearest on a second reading, but the perceptive reader may enjoy a good deal of the joke immediately. Noticing that Mr Elton is really courting Emma and not Harriet, we admire the skill with which Jane Austen has happened to make him do so in terms that Emma can misinterpret; and we delight both in the author's technical skill, and in our superiority to Emma's limited insight.

> 'I think your manners to him encouraging. I speak as a friend, Emma. You had better look about you, and ascertain what you do, and what you mean to do.'

> 'I thank you; but I assure you, you are quite mistaken. Mr Elton and I are very good friends, and nothing more;' and she walked on, amusing herself in the consideration of the blunders which often arise from a partial knowledge of the circumstances, of the mistakes which people of high pretensions to judgement are for ever falling into; and not very well pleased with her brother for imagining her blind and ignorant, and in want of counsel.[2]

[1] *Emma.*, ch. 53   [2] Ibid., ch. 13

Every detail of Emma's reflection on her brother-in-law is turned against her by the reader. Emma has high pretensions to judgement, and is mistaken; and Emma's self-deception causes us just the same amusement that John Knightley here causes her.

This first mistake leads to a first awakening:

> It was foolish, it was wrong, to take so active a part in bringing any two people together. It was adventuring too far, assuming too much, making light of what ought to be serious—a trick of what ought to be simple. She was quite concerned and ashamed, and resolved to do such things no more.[1]

In itself, this passage contains no direct suggestion that Emma's repentance is partial or insincere; though the re-reader may observe that it has none of the force and eloquence of her later awakening:

> With insufferable vanity had she believed herself in the secret of everybody's feelings; with unpardonable arrogance proposed to arrange everyone's destiny. She was proved to have been universally mistaken; and she had not quite done nothing—for she had done mischief. She had brought evil on Harriet, on herself, and, she too much feared, on Mr Knightley.[2]

Perhaps the only hint in the earlier passage of such a contrast is the (presumably) limiting 'quite' of 'quite concerned and ashamed'; and perhaps it would be richer if it did hint more directly. But it is not long, as we read on, before we realise that this first self-discovery of Emma's is very partial. She has not learned to cease managing others: she has merely decided to tread more carefully in future. The point is neatly (too neatly?) made as we juxtapose in memory Mr Knightley's remark 'You have been no friend to Harriet Smith, Emma', with Emma's own 'I have been but half a friend to her. She has but half awakened.'

Now come Emma's two serious mistakes: both of them involving Frank Churchill. Though one follows the other (she obviously cannot marry him to Harriet until she had refused him herself), they are closely interrelated. The second goes ingeniously wrong: believing she is encouraging Harriet to think seriously of Frank Churchill, she is in fact encouraging her to think of Mr Knightley. It is by discovering this mistake that she discovers her own love for Mr Knightley. For a while Emma believes she has awoken to

---

[1] *Emma*, ch. 16   [2] Ibid., ch. 47

the truth too late, and has nothing left to her but a Stoic dignity in self-knowledge; but we are by then sufficiently adjusted to the comic tone to feel confident, even on a first reading, that all will come well. It is not until after this that Emma discovers her earlier mistake: that the affection which Frank Churchill had felt for her, and that she had refused to respond to, had never existed. And in depicting this situation Jane Austen uses her gayest and most complex irony:

> There was nothing to denote him unworthy of the distin-
> guished honour which her imagination had given him; the
> honour, if not of being in love with her, of being at least very
> near it, and saved only by her own indifference—(for still her
> resolution held of never marrying)—the honour, in short, of
> being marked out for her by all their joint acquaintance.[1]

The joke here consists in the exquisite skill with which Emma is drawing distinctions of feeling within a non-existent situation. Once we know that Frank Churchill feels none of the interest she credits him with, we can see that hers is a parody of skill, a discrimination among shadows.

Emma's shadow-scrupulousness grows even nicer as she proceeds:

> 'I do not find myself making any use of the word *sacrifice*,'
> said she. 'In not one of all my clever replies, my delicate
> negatives, is there any allusion to making a sacrifice. I do
> suspect that he is not really necessary to my happiness. So
> much the better. I certainly will not persuade myself to feel
> more than I do. I am quite enough in love. I should be very
> sorry to be more.'[2]

By now she is talking about her own feelings. This is not because she has ceased to manipulate Frank's: on the contrary, she is now so confident that she knows the exact shade of his, that she can transfer her attention to deciding what her own proper reaction should be. It is not difficult for us to realise that she is in a shadow world: the whole basis of her discrimination is wrong, and we must at least suspect that her own feelings are no more genuine than those she attributes to Frank Churchill. Once we see what her feelings are, as her love for Mr Knightley awakens, this suspicion is con-

[1] Ibid., ch. 25   [2] Ibid., ch. 31

firmed. Emma is not in all this romancing discovering anything about her own true emotions: she is dealing only in the conveniently postulated emotions that the match-maker thinks he perceives. She is manipulating herself.

All is now prepared for the awakening that forms the climax of the book. Emma's explosion of self-knowledge is convincing because it has been prepared for both technically and psychologically. Technically, in being anticipated by her half-awakening at the end of Book I; psychologically because Emma's egoism is never closed, never impenetrable, like that of Mrs Elton. Jane Austen is very careful in the way she plays off Emma against Mrs Elton:

> 'Well,' said she, 'and you soon silenced Mr Cole I suppose.'
> 'Yes, very soon. He gave me a quiet hint; I told him he was mistaken; he asked my pardon, and said no more. Cole does not want to be wiser and wittier than his neighbours.'
> 'In that respect how unlike dear Mrs Elton, who wants to be wiser and wittier than all the world.'[1]

—and how unlike dear Miss Woodhouse! At this point there is a clear irony at Emma's expense, and a reminder by Jane Austen that she is like Mrs Elton, whom she detests. For Mrs Elton too is a manipulator; she too enjoys arranging the lives of others, and does it entirely to satisfy her own ego, not out of a true interest in them. Emma must go to Bath: 'a line from me would bring you a little host of acquaintance'. When Mr Knightley has guests at his home, she insists 'Oh leave all that to me—Only give me a carte blanche—I am Lady Patroness, you know'. Most mischievous, Jane Fairfax must accept the place as a governess that she has found for her; no refusal will be tolerated; she insists 'on being authorised to write an acquiescence by the morrow's post'. It is Emma's behaviour written larger, in grosser letters.

But though Jane Austen insists on the resemblance, she also insists on the difference. There is no doubt that the letters are grosser, and, in case there was, Jane Austen is careful to follow this conversation by one between Emma and Jane Fairfax, in which Jane announces that she wishes to slip home, and Emma insists on offering her carriage—will not take no for an answer, until Jane says

[1] *Emma*, ch. 33

'I am fatigued; but it is not the sort of fatigue—quick walking will refresh me. Miss Woodhouse, we all know at times what it is to be wearied in spirits. Mine, I confess, are exhausted. The kindness you can show me will be to let me have my own way, and only say that I am gone when it is necessary.'

Emma had not another word to oppose. She saw it all; and entering into her feelings, promoted her quitting the house immediately, and watched her safely off with the zeal of a friend.[1]

Mrs Elton's insistence is so fresh in memory, that we cannot help noticing the difference: Mrs Elton would not have left off at that point, and so could never have deserved such a phrase as 'the zeal of a friend'.

There are other ways in which Emma's self-regard is shown as imperfect and therefore capable of cure: most obvious is her treatment of her father. Mr Woodhouse has the function in this book of Mrs Davilow in *Daniel Deronda:* the self-centred heroine has the habit of effacing herself for a parent (Gwendolen less thoroughly, for her ego has a longer road to travel), and so has shown us from the beginning that she is not impervious to others.

Emma is a very warm and a very sharp book: that is, it arouses a good deal of the response appropriate to tragedy, and that appropriate to satire. Yet it remains unequivocally a comedy. The treatment of Mrs Elton is pure satire, but Emma, as I have said, is carefully distinguished from Mrs Elton. There is a good deal of satire lurking elsewhere, too. We must be careful not to get too cross with old Mr Woodhouse (when, for instance, he does poor Mrs Bates out of her sweetbread and asparagus), or we shall begin to react to him as to a figure of satire. Perhaps the ideal reader of *Emma* has not got an aged parent. This may be good for us: to keep the book as comedy, we have to surpass John Knightley in forbearance. There is much less danger of taking any of the book as tragic, and yet there is a good deal of sympathy and even grief in it. For three-quarters of the story, there is no one character on whom our sympathy can focus: it floats loosely. Emma may engage our emotions completely after her awakening, but until then identification with her is impossible. The ironic gaze is so persistent (and most of the ironies scored off Emma are by no means to her credit),

[1] *Emma,* ch. 42

that we must feel detached. Jane Fairfax and Mr Knightley, the two best characters morally, are firmly seen from the outside: to take us inside Jane Fairfax's thoughts would not only let the secret of the plot out, it would also undermine Emma's position as heroine. As for Frank Churchill, our strong moral disapproval is played off against the delight we take—and he takes—and despite herself Jane Austen takes—in his skilful managing. Somehow or other he manages to see Jane every day without anyone suspecting that he has arranged it. He is a much better Iago than Emma; and the joke on her, of course, is that when she thinks she is managing she is really being managed.

Since for three-quarters of the book there is no one person whose point of view we share and with whom we also sympathise totally, and since the book is infused with a warmth, a joy in human relationships, the pressure that builds up towards our final identification with Emma is very strong. It comes out in odd and surprising places before then—Mrs Weston, Mr Knightley, even Miss Bates, may suddenly at a chapter's end become the focus for an impulse of delight that is warmer than mere amusement.

In the end, I can only fall back on a formula. *Emma* is a full and rich and human book, all the responses it arouses dig deep into warmth and anger, grief and fear. But in no situation does any of these emotions take charge. The author's eye is fixed so steadily on the contrast between what is and what is believed, that however powerfully we are moved by one or other half, we remain aware of the whole as a balanced situation. The harm and grief are never violent enough to run away with our attention. The richer the human material, the harder it will be for the author to maintain the judicious, amused balance of comedy: to be amusing is always easier when one is merely amusing. Perhaps *Emma* is as profound as pure comedy can be.

13 Consequences of Truthtelling

What do we imply when we praise a novelist for telling the truth? We imply that his work contains a kind of knowledge; and we therefore raise the possibility—and even the need—of measuring his work against more systematic forms of knowledge. We also make it difficult to censure him when he pauses in his narrative to tell us his truths, straight out. The remainder of this first part will be concerned with these two issues; and I begin with the latter and lesser one.

Few technical devices have been so attacked, in our own day, as the habit of stating explicitly whatever general reflection the situation has suggested to the author—has suggested, or has even been invented to illustrate. It has become the creed of one school of criticism (and of several novelists) that the author must never intervene in his own person to draw conclusions. George Eliot has naturally been a victim of such a creed, though it is a stick that can be used on almost any pre-Jamesian novelist. Lawrence is a transgressor too, but his detractors have found so many other sticks that they haven't used this one very much. Jane Austen is usually forgiven for her elegance, or for being so very old-fashioned. We touch here on a wider issue (it has become the central question in much discussion of technique): how much should the author claim to know, how much should he tell us? This book is not about technique, except indirectly, and I do not wish to mix into the argument about point of view. The several kinds of author-ial comment are distinguished and described with great lucidity by (for example) Wayne Booth, in *The Rhetoric of Fiction*, and of the seven kinds he lists I am only concerned with the one he rightly describes as the most extreme of all. Comments which summarise narrative, heighten significance or manipulate mood (some of Booth's headings) could in theory have been recast in some other form; but to offer a general truth based on, or explaining, the par-ticular instance of the story must require an explicit statement of that truth.

Both Jane Austen and George Eliot are fond of doing this, and sometimes they state the same truth.

It is a truth universally acknowledged, that a single man in possession of a good fortune must be in want of a wife.

However little known the feelings or views of such a man may be on his first entering a neighbourhood, this truth is so well fixed in the minds of the surrounding families, that he is con-sidered as the rightful property of some one or other of their daughters.[1]

Some readers of this history will doubtless regard it as incred-ible that people should construct matrimonial prospects on the mere report that a bachelor of good fortune and possibilities

[1] *Pride and Prejudice*, ch. 1

was coming within reach, and will reject the statement as a
mere outflow of gall; they will aver that neither they nor their
first cousins have minds so unbridled; and that in fact this is not
human nature, which would know that such speculations might
turn out to be fallacious, and would therefore not entertain
them. But, let it be observed, nothing is here narrated of human
nature generally; the history in its present stage concerns only
a few people in a corner of Wessex,—whose reputation, however, was unimpeached, and who, I am in the proud position of
being able to state, were all on visiting terms with persons of
rank.[1]

Jane Austen is neater, more epigrammatic, more elegant; George
Eliot more ponderous, longer (often much longer), more involved—
more elephantine, even—sometimes (as here) not quite happy in
her tone: but at her best more profound. Jane Austen's generalisations are free from the apologetic note that so disfigures those of
Adam Bede: she does not seem to concern herself about whether
the reader will believe her, or bother to insist that her remarks are
not mere outflow of gall.

George Eliot wrote to Blackwood in 1873 that:

I have always exercised a severe watch against anything that
could be called preaching, and if I have ever allowed myself
in dissertation or in dialogue anything which is not part of the
structure of my books, I have there sinned against my own
laws.[2]

As it stands, this could fit Hemingway: but it is clear that we must
not read it in the light of the extreme rejection of authorial comment
that has taken place since. George Eliot must be referring to those
comments whose tone preaches, rather than to comment, generalisation, or 'dissertation' as such (though her contrast with 'structure'
perhaps obscures this point); and she would probably not have
considered the passage just quoted from *Daniel Deronda* to be a
transgression of her precept. But there is no conceivable definition
of 'preaching' that would not include this:

Love of this sort is hardly distinguishable from religious
feeling. What deep and worthy love is so? Whether of woman or
child, or art or music. Our caresses, our tender words, our still
rapture under the influence of autumn sunsets, or pillared

---

[1] *Daniel Deronda*, ch. 9
[2] Letter to John Blackwood, 12 November, 1873

vistas, or calm majestic statues, or Beethoven symphonies, all bring with them the consciousness that they are mere waves and ripples in an unfathomable ocean of love and beauty.[1]

Perhaps we wince at this more than we ought: it is uplift, certainly, and too earnestly Victorian for us, but the really serious blemish of the Victorian novelists is not uplift, or earnestness, but coyness. All the same, it is hard to feel that the passage has either pressure of experience or any grace of style; if we turn from it to a Jane Austen epigram:

> Human nature is so well disposed towards those who are in interesting situations, that a young person, who either marries or dies, is sure of being kindly spoken of. . . .[2]

there is no doubt who comes best out of the comparison.

Adam Bede is an early work, and we can hope that kindly oblivion had enfolded such passages in George Eliot's mind when she wrote that letter fifteen years later. In *Daniel Deronda*, which she had not yet begun, there are aphorisms as pithy as Jane Austen, and far more profound. She speaks of 'that want of perceived leisure which belongs to lives where there is no work to mark off intervals', and we see how tight is the limitation of the satiric glance that Jane Austen throws on society, for we could never imagine her attaining this reach of social insight; or she speaks of 'that rashness of indignation or resentment which has an unpleasant likeness to the love of punishing', and one has to remind onself that she had not read modern psychology.

Praising a novel for telling the truth does not imply that a novel is no different from an essay; but it does suggest some overlap, and makes it difficult for us to be too purist about aphorisms. 'It is notorious,' wrote George Eliot in *Theophrastus Such*, 'that a man may go on uttering false assertions about his own acts till he at last believes in them.' 'We have all of us,' she had written twenty years earlier:

> considerable regard for our past self, and are not fond of casting reflections on that respected individual by a total negation of his opinions.[3]

The first of these is from a book of essays, the second from a novel: this means (presumably) that in the first case the generalisation is

---

[1] *Adam Bede*, ch. 3   [2] *Emma*, ch. 22
[3] *Janet's Repentance*, ch. 12

the aim of the essay, and any incidents narrated are simply illus-
trative; whereas in the second, the generalisation is there to enable
us to reach a fuller understanding of the story. But we surely could
not tell this merely from reading the two sentences; and there are
incidents in *Theophrastus Such* that we could easily mistake for
moments from a George Eliot novel. This makes it quite clear that
we are on common ground between the two forms: and this lends
ammunition to the purist, who can complain that novels which
employ such digressions turn into essays.

Aphorisms and generalisations are only one manifestation of a
larger claim. To praise a novelist for truthtelling is to imply a
cognitive view of literature. Now the contrast between emotive
and cognitive views is an old and complex issue of literary theory:
all the cards are on the side of the emotive view (it recognises what
literature *is*, and how it differs from other things), but cognitive
theories obstinately refuse to die: we continue to praise the insight,
wisdom and truth of great writers. If we really grew convinced that
works of literature contain only pseudo-statements, that they
convey experiences but not knowledge, then we might be in a
position to construct an impregnable theory of poetics, but we
would cease to read—and the writers would cease to write. In
this work I am not much concerned with the theoretical implications of the more or less cognitive view I am advancing: but I will
say that our persistence in finding insight, truthfulness or wisdom
in literature varies with the literary kind: it is strongest in the
novel, weakest in the lyric. If we arrange the arts on a scale according to their cognitive element, we shall have Music—Sculpture—
Painting—Lyric Poetry—Narrative Poetry and Drama—Novel
—and then (continuing the list beyond the borders of art)—Essay
—Treatise. The essay and the treatise (the less and the more systematic discussion of man and society) share a wide overlap with the
novel: and it is into this area of overlap that the authorial generalisation steps.

We can now ask what sort of treatise comes at the end of this
scale. If the novel contains a good deal of unsystematic knowledge,
what systematic discipline does it overlap with? Here we have to
give a fourfold answer, before turning to deal in some detail with
the most interesting of the four.

Every novel has a centre and a setting: it portrays the life of a
particular time and place, and then tells the story of a number of

individuals living there. The systematic students of society are the historian and the sociologist; of the individual, the biographer and the psychologist. To be too lucid here is to oversimplify: these studies overlap among themselves, and the social psychologist is perhaps not (as my scheme implied) identical with the sociologist. None the less, we can perhaps describe the pair of contrasts (historian and sociologist, biographer and psychologist) by calling the first in each pair non-experimental and the second—as far as their subject-matter permits—experimental. To limit the discussion, I will turn to the second pair. Now the methods of the biographer certainly have more resemblance to the novelist's art than have those of the psychologist. Yet—and partly for this reason—to compare the novelist's portrayal of individuals with biography does not seem very illuminating. Biography (except in the most superficial sense) has no methodology of its own; it has not even—like history—an achieved body of work, forming a whole discipline of study. The really radical comparison to draw would be the more far-fetched one with psychology. Is there any sense in which the knowledge offered by the novel resembles 'real' knowledge—the empirical knowledge offered us by psychologists?

14 Literature and Psychology

There is no shortage nowadays of discussions of the relations between literature and psychology: yet most of them have not quite asked the question we are here asking. It is common to ask whether literary criticism can learn from psychology. To probe the motivations and the creative process in the mind of the writer, or to uncover in the literary work meanings that may need the technical vocabulary of psycho-analysis for their formulation, is to bring psychology to the aid of the critic. In a world in which psychologists and literary critics are cooled by the same winters and warmed by the same salary cheques, this is not surprising; but I want here to turn to the other possible relation between the two disciplines, that in which psychologist and writer are not researcher and subject, but allies.

Psychology, as much as literary criticism, has its schools and its factions; how is the poor writer, looking for a few tips to stimulate his thinking about human nature, to choose amongst them? This is the question I want now to turn to, but it presupposes a full and expert exposition of what these schools are, which I cannot here give. What I can do however is point to, and contrast, two of its extreme forms, which have battled against each other with almost literary fury. At the one extreme is psycho-analysis, with its theories (?its mythology) of id, ego and super-ego, its mechanisms of projection, introjection and regression, its topography of the conscious, the preconscious and the unconscious mind. When psycho-analysis first appeared, it was greeted with horror as a cynical undermining of much that the writer (like anyone else) believed about human nature. Today it has become common to see psycho-analysis as the useful friend of literature, and I largely assumed this view when discussing the growth of the idea of the unconscious. Psycho-analysis is congenial to the traditionalist because of the elaborate system of inner entities which it postulates, even believes in. At the opposite extreme, then, will stand that school which denies all inner entities, and all inner causes, refusing to postulate anything but responses (dependent variables) and stimuli, or independent variables in the environment that bring them about. This is behaviourism.

> States of consciousness like the so called phenomena of spiritualism are not objectively verifiable, and for that reason can never become data for science. . . . The behaviourist finds no evidence for 'mental existences' or 'mental processes' of any kind.[1]

Thus J. B. Watson, the founder of behaviourism; and there are plenty of equally aggressive statements. Watson had none of the tact that many scientists find useful to conceal the radical implications of their work, and many contemporary psychologists prefer to disclaim or at least ignore his shrill insistences, and to describe themselves as (for instance) operational behaviourists, leaving aside any subersive philosophical implications. Tact is not one of literature's favourite qualities, and I will therefore take as the spokesman of contemporary behaviourism a psychologist who is quite as outspoken and (I suppose) quite as well hated, B. F. Skinner. Skinner too is fond of taking the implications of his work into other disciplines (law, economics, sociology, education, even religion and the arts), and using them to undermine traditional concepts of man.

[1] J. B. Watson, quoted by Keller, *The Definition of Psychology*, ch. 4

Skinnerian behaviourism, according to my layman's understanding of it, attempts to remove from psychology all concepts that describe what takes place within an organism. Psychology is the study of behaviour, and it must not be distracted into dealing with mental or even with physiological states. Physiological states can be left to the physiologist: they do not tell us about behaviour. Nor do mental states, but there is no scientist to whom *they* can be left, and they had better be removed from scientific vocabulary altogether:

> The fictional nature of this form of inner cause is shown by the ease with which the mental process is discovered to have just the properties needed to account for the behaviour. . . . In all this it is obvious that the mind and the ideas, together with their special characteristics, are being invented on the spot to provide spurious explanations. A science of behaviour can hope to gain very little from so cavalier a practice.[1]

The inner states there are 'mind' and 'ideas'; Skinner is just as stern with states that don't seem mental at all, such as hunger:

> When we are told that a man stole a loaf of bread because 'he was hungry', we have still to learn of the external conditions responsible for the 'hunger'. These conditions would have sufficed to explain the theft.[2]

Even 'drive'—a term beloved of the most hard-headed of psychologists—is viewed with scepticism, since it might be set up as an explanatory fiction:

> All these examples could be described by reference to 'drives'. We could say that the eating of salty hors d'œuvres makes a guest thirsty and that his thirst drives him to drink. It is simpler in both theory and practice, to restrict ourselves to the fact that consuming salty hors d'œuvres leads to drinking.[3]

This example makes it clear why Skinner wants to reject inner states: the analysis he seeks is one in terms of causes ('independent variables') outside the organism, and the danger of paying attention to what goes on within it is that it may be used as an excuse for not fully studying the external causes:

[1] Skinner, *Science and Human Behaviour*, p. 30
[2] Ibid., p. 35   [3] Ibid., p. 147

One who readily engages in a particular activity is not showing an interest, he is showing the effect of reinforcement. We do not give a man a sense of achievement, we reinforce a particular action. To become discouraged is simply to fail to respond because reinforcement has not been forthcoming. Our problem is simply to account for probability of response in terms of a history of reinforcement and extinction.[1]

This imposes on Skinner an enormous task of translation: the traditional explanatory fictions must be translated into functional terms, so that wishes, hatreds and motives become probabilities of response and schedules of reinforcement. An emotion is viewed as a probability of certain forms of behaviour. It is (alas) not true, as Skinner claims, that the result is simpler than the use of the traditional terms: until one has grown used to the new language (which I for one never did) the result is bewilderingly difficult to read. Of course it is simpler in terms of the analyses that Skinner wishes to give, but that is a kind of tautology. There is (there must be) a huge circular argument justifying the use of functional terminology: it was designed to suggest methods of investigating the effect of independent variables on behaviour; it is more acceptable because it describes such effects.

Functional analyses of behaviour cannot directly answer any of the traditional questions. Attacking the concepts of 'thinking' and 'reasoning' as 'fictional processes', Skinner declares: 'A functional analysis removes much of the mystery which surrounds these terms'. This is exactly what it does: instead of solving mysteries, it removes them. Whether this will, in the end, indirectly answer any of our traditional questions (or show them to have been unnecessary) no reader of this book will live long enough to know.

I do not intend (or even wish) to make an amateur attack on behaviourism: only to describe it in such a way as to bring out certain literary parallels. Two points in Skinner's work will have to detain us slightly longer. One is his study of language, called *Verbal Behaviour* (the phrase has a slightly wider meaning than 'language'), which contains some fascinating 'translations' of traditional terminology. It restates, for instance, the question of the effects of language on thought:

[1] Skinner, *Science and Human Behaviour*, p. 72

If it is 'impossible to express a given idea' in a given language because a necessary term is lacking, we have only (*sic*) to say that the contingencies arranged by a given verbal community fail to respect a possible variable. If it is difficult 'to express the same idea in two languages', we have merely to say that the reinforcing practices of two verbal communities differ. . . . There is *indescribable* beauty in the sense that contingencies in a nonverbal environment generate behaviour which has no parallel among verbal responses.[1]

The explanatory fiction which *Verbal Behaviour* aims to eliminate is 'meaning'. Skinner will not even allow meaning an 'as if' status.

We seek 'causes' of behaviour which have an acceptable scientific status and which, with luck, will be susceptible to measurement and manipulation. To say that these are 'all that is meant by' ideas or meanings is to misrepresent the traditional *practice*.[2]

Of course, if you give a traditional practice a bad name (if you do not allow it to grow and modify) then it is easy to hang it.

The other detail in Skinner's work I want to mention is his critique of psycho-analysis. He appears to have a great respect for Freud's discoveries, and for much of the content of his theories: what he objects to is the use of 'explanatory fiction' in their formulation—of a mental apparatus which stole the show and distracted attention from behaviour.

The cogency of the (environmental) variables was frequently missed because the variables were transformed and obscured in the course of being represented in mental life.[3]

When Skinner adds 'what has survived through the years is not aggression and guilt, later to be manifested in behaviour, but rather patterns of behaviour themselves' he is once more arguing for his own terminology. Whether or not we accept this, we can see the value of his criticism: it is a complaint that our attention has been distracted from what actually happened. By introducing the middle term (anxiety, or guilt) between the childhood situation and the adult behaviour being studied, we obscure a number of specific

[1] Skinner, *Verbal Behaviour*, p. 451
[2] Ibid., p. 10
[3] Skinner: 'A Critique of Psycho-analytic Concepts and Theories', *Cumulative Record*, p. 189

resemblances between them. The metapsychology gets in the way. Who has not felt the same on reading Freud?

What now is the reaction of the literary man to all this? Often enough his first reaction is to recoil in horror. Anything seems better than that man is an organism with nothing inside him; and so he flees to the now friendly bosom of psycho-analysis, that gives him back his guilts, his repressions, his hidden hatreds, his incestuous longings, all that makes him human.

What is the difference between the literary and the scientific mind? Above all, surely, it is the fact that the scientist is able to restrain curiosity. In any concrete situation, there is a rich variety of questions that thrust themselves on our attention—all, we feel, interrelated, if we could but find the threads. In a human situation, the range is virtually infinite. The most trivial action (why did he hear this word and not that? Why did he forget this, remember that?) can open out into an answer that involves the whole personality of the subject. The literary mind is constantly pursuing such answers: it cannot be patient with less. The more widely an answer ranges, and the more it seems to open out into a picture of the man's whole personality, the more exciting it will seem. Any attempt to bracket off one small area of behaviour, to lose interest in the rest, will seem to the literary mind merely unimaginative and trivial. Is that not why the thinkers who represent modern thought to the man of letters (Kierkegaard, Nietzsche, Freud—especially the later Freud—Jung, Frazer) all have this in common, that they did not perform experiments: it is difficult to imagine them ceasing to think for long enough to do so. But empirical investigation is only possible if you take a very small step each time, pushing aside the wider and vaguer interrelations of an event in order to isolate what can be accurately measured and compared.

I neither deny nor disapprove all this: literature will always live a long way from experiments. But I want to assert that on second thoughts we can have another reaction. Behaviourism may be quite as anti-literary as I have suggested, but there is another way in which it is highly congenial to the literary mind. I want to point this out (it is the one point this discussion is designed to make) partly because it fascinates me, and partly for a more practical and urgent reason. If the literary sensibility takes up its anti-behaviourist position with too much assurance, scientists accuse literature of being anti-scientific. Now literature is and will remain unscientific, but ought never to become anti-scientific. The unscientific man is he who persists in reckless curiosity about questions which science will not be ready to answer for another few hundred (or few hundred thousand) years. The anti-scientific is he who believes in doctrines which science had disproved; who persists in preferring the scientists of yesteryear, defending them with arguments that contain bad science; who is eager to teach the scientist, but unwilling to learn from him. Theology, during the great controversies of the mid-nineteenth-century, was anti-scientific; since then it has learned, painfully, to be unscientific. I would not like to see literature having to learn the same lesson.

I cannot here redraw the shape of literature's interest in psychology: it needs doing, but it is a vast task. But in order to give that interest a little push in the right direction, I want to suggest one respect at any rate in which there is a natural alliance between behaviourism and literature: whether this alliance contrasts them both with psycho-analysis I must leave it to the behaviourists to claim and the psycho-analysts, if they think it worth the trouble, to deny. I am not, I hope, trying to change the nature of the literary sensibility in doing this, but merely pointing to an element in it that is not always remembered. The alliance is based on the fact that both parties are interested in behaviour.

I begin (to show that I really am not trying to change anything) with a point that is unimpeachably literary. It concerns *Tess of the D'Urbervilles*, and I brush psychology aside for the moment to discuss the book as a novel.

15 'Tess of the D'Urbervilles'

What is wrong with *Tess*? It is almost one of the great English novels, and perhaps Hardy's masterpiece: there can be few novels in which theme and setting blend so perfectly. The rich earth, the intense productive life of Talbothays, is splendidly created, and with it the haze of absorption that takes hold of the consciousness of those who work there. Hardy's genius for descriptive writing, for rendering the landscape without ceasing to be a novelist, is never better seen than in this book. The sight and feel of early morning milking is caught with a poet's reaction, yet we never digress into poetry: every detail is seen as part of a productive process and the life of the community, or as part of the sensibility of those taking part. Balanced against the fertility of Talbothays, and the genuine community it gives rise to, are the harsh earth and mean manners of Flintcombe Ash. Tess's fortunes move on a path that literally and symbolically takes her from one to the other. Yet one hesitates to use the word 'symbolic' of anything in this book, the two farms are so utterly real in their rich particularity.

Into this setting are fitted some of Hardy's finest individual studies. Angel Clare is a success because Hardy had just enough natural sympathy with him to take him seriously, without ceasing to be bitter at what he did to Tess; the Durbeyfield parents are in Hardy's best vein, and illustrate (but, once again, not 'symbolically') his constant theme of a changing rural society; and Tess herself must be Hardy's most-loved heroine. Yet almost every admirer of the book feels that something is wrong, something in the book's very conception.

It has something to do with Tess herself: masterly though the picture is, there remains something unachieved in it. Why did Hardy feel it necessary to call her 'a pure woman' on the title page? Is he protesting too much? Is he uneasily, aggressively, asking for our support on what he feels to be a weakness? Tess bears an illegitimate child to Alec D'Urberville; later, after her marriage, she goes back to live with him; when Angel turns up, she kills him: yet she is pure. This is not an impossible paradox, but by setting it to himself as a theme the novelist incurs obligations. He must present with special care those actions which appear impure; those moments of decision when Tess seems to weaken, to lose her purity, must be given us with a vividness and clarity that will convince us that the world has judged wrongly. And this is just what Hardy has failed to do.

Take the rape of Tess. I say 'rape', but I do not know whether Tess was raped or seduced. Chapters X and XI are so vivid that it seems churlish to complain of what they don't say; but in the context of the whole book it is a complaint we must make. Late on a Saturday night Tess, tired, cold, hungry, having waited for hours to have the company of her fellow-workpeople home from market, finds herself in a quarrel with them, victim of the drunken jealousy of Alec D'Urberville's ex-mistresses. At this point Alec comes up on horseback, and in unthinking relief she leaps up behind him. He rides round with her until they are lost in the wood, winning her goodwill at one moment, losing it the next, as her relief alternates with her distrust, his kindness with his clear intentions. Eventually he leaves her lying among the leaves while he walks off to see where they are. When he comes back, she is asleep. At this point Hardy slips into a touch of his cosmic irony ('where was Tess's guardian angel?'), and then continues:

> Why it was that upon this beautiful feminine tissue, sensitive as gossamer, and practically blank as snow yet, there should have been traced such a coarse pattern as it was doomed to receive; why so often the coarse appropriates the finer thus, the wrong man the woman, the wrong woman the man, many thousand years of analytical philosophy have failed to explain to our sense of order. One may, indeed, admit the possibility of a retribution lurking in the present catastrophe. Doubtless some of Tess D'Urberville's mailed ancestors rollicking home from a fray had dealt the same measure even more ruthlessly towards peasant girls of their time.[1]

This reads like rape. Tess is asleep, and Alec does not appear to wake her. All their conversation has been rendered so vividly, and the change of style is so marked, that he must mean us to think there is no more talk between them. And Tess's mailed ancestors would not have troubled to persuade the peasant girls. At this moment Hardy is concerned to present Tess entirely as a victim—trapped, helpless, unconsenting: he has been building up to that for two chapters. Yet in the very next chapter we are given pause. A few weeks have passed, and Tess is on her way home. We presume (though even this is not absolutely clear) that she has been Alec's mistress all these weeks. And now Tess talks as if she had been seduced.

> If I had sincerely loved you, if I loved you still, I should not so loathe and hate myself for my weakness as I do now! . . . My eyes were dazed by you for a little, and that was all.[2]

And when she comes home and rebukes her mother for not warning her, she once again talks as if seduced:

> Oh mother, my mother!' cried the agonised girl, turning passionately upon her parent as if her poor heart would break, 'How could I be expected to know? I was a child when I left this house four months ago. Why didn't you tell me there was

---

[1] *Tess of the D'Urbervilles*, ch. 11   [2] Ibid., ch. 12

danger in men-folk? Why didn't you warn me? Ladies know what to fend hands against, because they read novels that tell them of these tricks; but I never had the chance o' learning in that way, and you did not help me.'[1]

Now what exactly happened? Did she yield to Alec because of her fear and weariness and the impulse of kindness she felt when he told her of the horse he had given her father? Or did she wake up to find herself ruined? Months later, when the baby is born, Tess is working in the fields, and some of her fellow-labourers discuss her case during the dinner-break. Says one:

'A little more than persuading had to do wi' the coming o't, I reckon. There were they that heard a sobbing one night last year in The Chase; and it mid ha' gone hard wi' a certain party if folks had come along.'[2]

Perhaps this is the most improbable detail in a novelful of improbabilities. Darkness and an hour's riding and all Hardy's descriptive powers had hidden Alex and Tess in the huge wood, their bearings lost and no one near; now suddenly a witness has appeared! A very shrewd witness too, who identified the sobbing, reconstructed what had happened, and was able to gossip all the way back to Marlott, which we have been told is a world cut off from Trantridge. There can only be one explanation for this gross implausibility—that Hardy has a bad conscience about what he had done to Tess. Uneasily realising that he may have let Alec seduce her, he cooks up this story in her defence. It might have been better if he had restored the use of spirits Alec dosed her with in the first draft: a clumsy seducer is preferable to a clumsy author.

Why did Tess leave Alec when she did? Here too there is uncertainty.

'Well, you are absurdly melancholy, Tess. I have no reason for flattering you now, and I can say plainly that you need not be so sad. You can hold your own for beauty against any woman of these parts, gentle or simple; I say it to you as a practical man and a well-wisher. If you are wise you will show it to the world more than you do before it fades. . . . And yet, Tess, will you come back to me? Upon my soul I don't like to let you go like this!'
    'Never, never! I made up my mind as soon as I saw—what I ought to have seen sooner; and I won't come.'[3]

[1] *Tess of the D'Urbervilles*, ch. 12   [2] Ibid., ch. 14   [3] Ibid., ch. 12

Alec's dialogue could not be improved on: the blend of selfishness, rather hearty apology, good advice and waning fascination with Tess shows a realism that Hardy did not often attain to with his wealthy characters—and did not always maintain with Alec. But this dialogue sets up an expectation of realism, so that we want to know what Tess means by her reply. Did she leave when she saw that she didn't love him? Or when she realised how she had fallen below her ideal of herself? Or when she realised that she was pregnant? Is any reader sure?

Why these restless, niggling questions? Because Hardy began them: it was he who called Tess a pure woman, going out of his way (title page, President of the Immortals, and all) to thrust it in front of us. Now it would be possible to make a case for Tess's purity if she was raped; or (though a different case) if she was seduced. And (of course) there are intermediate possibilities. But no case of any sort can be made out if we don't know what happened. We want to feel that the author at any rate knows what case he is making.

It is often said that Hardy was unfortunate in his reviewers, and that the reception of *Jude* stopped him writing novels. Reviewers are no nearer perfection than the rest of us, and there was a good deal of spleen in some of the notices of *Tess*; but there was a good deal of sense too. *The Nation* (New York) considered it 'as profoundly immoral a book as the "young person" can easily lay her hands on', and the reviewer's evident sympathy with Angel Clare's actions carries him to lengths that must make us wince. Yet he has a point:

> When Angel Clare, in the pasture, makes a surreptitious dash at the 'desire of his eyes', she yields to his embrace 'with unreflecting inevitableness'. Again by his phrase is the author's argument eternally pulverized. 'Unreflecting inevitableness' in such a position may be a misfortune; it is not purity. In the crises of existence what one is—one's essential being— expresses itself in action. A greater than Mr Hardy said that conviction is worthless till it convert itself into conduct. He was not deaf to the cry of human nature, but he dared to distinguish between a genuine cry and a sentimental scream.[1]

'In the crises of existence what one is—one's essential being— expresses itself in action.' That is pure Conrad. *Lord Jim* is (like

[1] Review of *Tess* in *The Nation* (New York), 28 April, 1892

Tess) a study of how a single moment of decision can determine a life. But Conrad realises that the moment is important because it undoes character, or betrays that it was already undone. Conrad, so far from using 'unreflecting inevitableness' as an excuse, uses the unreflecting action as evidence, as a fact which any subsequent estimate of Jim's character (including his own) must reckon with.

Now we have, as it happens, Hardy's answer to this point. An interview with Thomas Hardy by one Raymond Blaythwayt appeared in a magazine called *Black and White* not long after *Tess* was published. We have no way of knowing if this (one of the earliest literary interviews, surely) was more or less unreliable than we now know interviews to be. I can only proceed on the assumption (a reasonable one when one reads it through) that it does represent Hardy's views. The interviewer said at one point 'I have to quarrel seriously with you for your deliberate description of Tess as a *pure woman*'. He set forth his objections (they were the usual reviewer's objections), and Hardy replied:

> Very well, but I still maintain that her innate purity remained intact to the very last; though I frankly own that a certain outward purity left her on last fall. I regarded her then as being in the hands of circumstances, not morally responsible, a mere corpse drifting in the current to her end.[1]

Once again, unreflecting inevitableness is used to exempt from the necessity of moral action. One can understand why the reviewer of *The Literary World* (Boston) wrote indignantly:

> We can only repeat that it is the sub-title which renders Mr Hardy's novel presumptuous and profoundly immoral, in implying the inability and consequent blamelessness of the human will against adverse conditions.[2]

It is not necessary to endorse the smug tone of this to agree that Hardy does seem to be denying the very existence of choice, and therefore of morality. For Hardy to claim forgiveness for Tess is one thing (most readers even in his own time would probably have granted it freely); to claim that she was not responsible for her

[1] 'A Chat with the Author of *Tess*', by Raymond Blaythwayt, *Black and White*, 27 August, 1892; reprinted in *Thomas Hardy and his Readers*, ed, Lerner and Holmstrom

[2] Review of *Tess* in *The Literary World*, 4 June, 1892

actions because she was swept away is quite another. It is at least arguable that those who seem swept away have had less to contend with than those who have struggled, so that it is the latter who most deserve pardon. But such discussions are impossible, really: Hardy had adopted a view that would turn pardon, responsibility, guilt and innocence into meaningless concepts—and purity too.

'Her innate purity remained intact to the very last; though I frankly own that a certain outward purity left her on her last fall'. What is this inner purity? Lord Jim had believed that he was brave and responsible; he leapt out of the *Patna* and found that he wasn't—or, at any rate, that he had now to live with a disturbing piece of evidence that suggested he wasn't. How easy for him—and how strong the temptation—to treat his own action as indulgently as Hardy treats those of Tess, to believe that his action, and the verdict of the court of inquiry, simply took from him a certain outward bravery and responsibility. Of course Tess never treats herself with this indulgence, and Hardy, when writing dramatically (as he does most of the time), keeps on her the ruthless gaze of truth. But, whenever he intrudes into the story with his own judgement (and he does this in many ways, not only by his own comments, but in his weighting of the story against her, his manipulation of events to show how fate and society had it in for her, his naïvely moving but ultimately crude cosmic asides) then we can see the contrast recurring between the outer, that hardly matters, and the inner. Some of Conrad's finest writing went into showing us that Jim was too honest for this: his vision of himself was persistent enough to go on haunting him until he at last (for a while) made it square with reality at Patusan; but it was never strong enough to persuade him that it had all along maintained an unbroken existence as 'inner bravery'.

For that way lies Antinomianism: the doctrine that despises the moral law, yet claims to remain a moral doctrine. If faith alone is necessary for salvation it is possible to conclude (as certain antinomian sects did) not only that it does not matter how wickedly you behave, but that wicked behaviour is a positive advantage, since if you can be wicked while remaining pure in heart, you must be saved indeed. Perhaps the most colourful of all antinomian sects were the rather amorphous Ranters, of England's mad decade, the 1650s. 'At this time,' wrote one Laurence Claxton, describing his days as a Ranter, 'my judgement was this, that there was no man could be freed from sin, till he had acted that so-called sin, as no sin.' He preached on the text that 'there is nothing unclean but as man esteems it':

> unfolding that was intended all acts, as well as meats and drinks, and therefore till you can lie with all women as one woman, and not judge it sin, you can do nothing but sin.[1]

Though Claxton slept with any woman in his flock who was willing (and spent some time persuading those who weren't!), he declared to the magistrate when arrested, 'I never lay with any woman but my own wife'. In his pamphlet he justifies this by remarking, 'I say I lie with none but my wife according to the Law, though in the unity of the Spirit I lie with all creation'.

Hardy is not Claxton, nor very far along this road; and, of course, *Tess* is a much finer and more scrupulous book than his remarks in the interview would suggest. But I cite this lurid exaggeration to show what seem to me the implications of a view that is certainly present in the book, even if not as prominent as its misguided author suggested. The answer to this view is, that pure is as pure does.

There is one obvious reply that a modern admirer of Hardy is likely to make. This is that the book was published in 1892, and there was a limit to what an author could then say. Hardy could only have made clear what happened by being much more explicit than convention then allowed. Having decided to deal directly with a theme generally avoided in Victorian fiction, he had already gone further towards defying conventions than the public and the critics found acceptable. Is it not unreasonable to expect him to have gone even further?

It is always unreasonable to expect an author to write a master-piece, or to maintain complete integrity. But the fact that most books are flawed does not explain the flaws away. Hardy was not the first to find that the penalty of defying convention is to find that you have not defied it enough—nor was Tess the last occasion on which this happened to him. *Jude the Obscure*, which is more outspoken than *Tess*, which was received with more hostility, and which attacks the sexual code more directly, is also more seriously flawed by Hardy's unwillingness (or inability) to say just what he thinks about Sue. Similarly, the very outspokenness of *Tess* raises

---

[1] *The Lost Sheep Found*, by Laurence Claxton, 1660

expectations that a more discreet book would not have raised. The realism of Car Queen of Spades, and of the whole coarse episode from which Tess is rescued by Alec, as well as the realism with which Alec is treated, are too rudely forced by the retreat into poetic imagery that Hardy so suddenly allows himself. Contemporary conventions may explain the weakness of *Tess*, but cannot disguise it as strength.

16 The Unobservant Angels

I have tried in this discussion to analyse a literary weakness that manifests itself in occasional touches of evasiveness or stridency. I have tried to analyse it in literary terms, but also in terms which make the psychological parallel clear. Pure is as pure does: it is a behaviourist's point. The only acceptable kind of evidence for an inner state is that it is, somehow, manifested in behaviour. What is not observable ('inner purity') does not, for others, exist.

It is not hard to imagine the violence with which Skinner's view of man (or rather his refusal to have a view of man) would have been greeted by Lawrence; yet I can enlist even so unlikely an ally into this discussion. I turn to his essay 'Why the Novel Matters'. It is one of the best of all modern statements of the literary view of man.

> Now I absolutely flatly deny that I am a soul, or a body, or a mind, or an intelligence, or a brain, or a nervous system, or a bunch of glands, or any of the rest of these bits of me. The whole is greater than the part. And therefore, I, who am man alive, am greater than my soul, or body, or mind, or consciousness, or anything else that is merely a part of me. I am a man, and alive. I am a man alive, and as long as I can, I intend to go on being man alive.[1]

On this claim, Lawrence bases his assertion of the importance of the novel:

> For this reason I am a novelist. And being a novelist, I consider myself superior to the saint, the scientist, the philosopher, and the poet, who are all great masters of different bits of man alive, but never get the whole hog.[2]

[1] 'Why the Novel Matters'; *Phoenix*, p. 535
[2] Ibid., p. 535

'The whole hog': that was what Watson was after. Watson's view of the difference between the physiologist and the psychologist is that the former is concerned with specific functions, the latter 'works with the whole body in action'. Behaviour is something done by the whole man; both Watson and Lawrence are interested in behaviour.

Of course, Lawrence is out of date in his strictures on philosophers:

> These damned philosophers, they talk as if they suddenly went off in steam, and were then much more important than they are when they're in their shirts. It is nonsense. Every man, philosopher included, ends in his own finger tips.[1]

The belief that we suddenly go off in steam has, by now, had more ill treatment from philosophers than from anyone else.

> 'The problem of the relation between body and mind' is a bogus problem which cannot be stated without making a false assumption. What is assumed is that man is partly body and partly mind. On this assumption questions arise about the relations between the two parts; and these prove unanswerable. For man's body and man's mind are not two different things. They are one and the same thing, man himself, as known in two different ways.[2]

Not, as one might think, Gilbert Ryle, but Collingwood in *The New Leviathan*. It is easy enough to match it from Ryle:

> 'Mental' does not denote a status, such that one can sensibly ask of a given thing or event whether it is mental or physical, 'in the mind' or 'in the outer world'. To talk of a person's mind is not to talk of a repository which is permitted to house objects that something called 'the physical world' is forbidden to house; it is to talk of the person's abilities, liabilities and inclination to do and undergo certain sorts of things, and of the doing and undergoing of these things in the ordinary world.[3]

Ryle is the philosopher who spells out in elegantly everyday language a good deal of the methodology of behaviourism:

[1] 'Why the Novel Matters'; *Phoenix*, p. 534
[2] *The New Leviathan*, II, 14
[3] Ryle, *The Concept of Mind*, ch. 9, § 1

When we describe people as exercising qualities of mind, we are not referring to occult episodes of which their overt acts and utterances are effects; we are referring to those overt acts and utterances themselves.[1]

Ryle has lost patience with Plato and Descartes, dividing man into two and sending one-half up in steam; Skinner has lost patience with inner states of consciousness to be reached by introspection; Lawrence has lost patience with the priest, the scientist (the natural scientist, that is) the saint and the poet for their segmentation of man. Three intellectually irritable men in agreement: it seems odd company for Lawrence, but he belongs to it.

I do not lay any emphasis on the fact that Skinner has written a novel. It has no literary merit, and is not meant to have: it is a tendentious statement of what a conditioning process based on reinforcement theory could do for a human community, and it was written to convert, or shock, or both. If we are to see traces of the novelist's way of thinking in Skinner, it will not be in *Walden Two* but in his scientific work—in, for example, this:

> Staying at a single letter in the Allport and Odbert list (a list of words which refer to more or less enduring traits of human behaviour), a biographer might describe the behaviour of a subject as follows: 'There was a remarkable change in his behaviour. Where he had been *happy-go-lucky*, he grew *hesitant* and *heavy-handed*. His natural *humility* gave way to a sustained *haughtiness*. Once the most *helpful* of men, he became *heedless* and *hard-hearted*. A sort of *histrionic horseplay* was all that remained of his fine sense of *humour*.'[2]

What would our reaction be if we met this in a novel? Getting over our puzzled delight at the alliteration, we would feel it might be a very perceptive account of an interesting person: but we would not be sure, until the real description came. What did he *do* during his histrionic horseplay? What did he *say* that was both haughty and hesitant? Only when some of this was offered to us, could we be sure that the writer wasn't simply playing with a dictionary. I cannot put all this better than Skinner himself does:

> A passage of this sort tells us something important. . . . But it may come as something of a surprise to discover that no behaviour has actually been described. Not a single action has

[1] Ibid., ch. 2, § 1   [2] Skinner, *Science and Human Behaviour*, p. 194

been mentioned. The passage might be describing a series of letters—of a colleague or business acquaintance, perhaps. On the other hand, it might be describing a wholly nonverbal scene from a ballet. It might concern a shopkeeper, a plant foreman, a salesman, a diplomat, a schoolboy—in short, any one of dozens of different kinds of people whose behaviour would have nothing in common except those aspects to which the passage refers.[1]

Words without observation are a fraud. A charming fraud (I shall always dream delightedly about that histrionic horseplay), but they tell us nothing about man and the world. They please but do not instruct.

Thus the psychologist. Next, Gilbert Ryle, the philosopher of behaviourism. I have already suggested that the theory of *The Concept of Mind* can fit itself to what literature does: it may seem far-fetched to suggest that the book itself is literary, yet in one sense even this is true. It is a work that has been extravagantly praised and derided by philosophers: praised for its lucidity, its lack of nonsense, and (of course) its behaviourism, derided for its uncuriosity, its reliance on ordinary language, even for the limited range of experience its examples are taken from. I have never heard it called poetic, in either praise or blame. There is no fine writing in it, no concrete richness of examples imagined and described as they might be by a novelist. But Ryle's loving reliance on ordinary speech, his scrupulous and careful sifting of the meanings of words, make one see him as a poet manqué: an elegant, Augustan, fastidious poet:

> Hobbies are not the same sort of thing as habits, and both are different from skills, from mannerisms, from fashions, from phobias and from trades. Nest building is a different sort of property from being feathered, and being a conductor of electricity from being elastic.[2]

I am not the first to say that Ryle's central belief—that what we are is how we behave—is also the novelist's central belief. It has been said by Ryle:

> Novelists, dramatists and biographers had always been satisfied to exhibit people's motives, thoughts, perturbations and

---

[1] Skinner, *Science and Human Behaviour*, p. 195
[2] Ryle, *The Concept of Mind*, ch. 5, § 1

habits by describing their doings, sayings and imaginings, their grimaces, gestures and tones of voice. In concentrating on what Jane Austen concentrated on, psychologists began to find that these were, after all, the stuff and not the mere trappings of their subject.[1]

And next, a novelist. I began by quoting Lawrence, but will choose George Eliot as the quarry for more sustained examples: she is as behaviouristic as any novelist, and in her case too we can begin with theory. Though she wrote no essay like 'Why the Novel Matters', she did write a splendid piece called 'Only Temper', which is pertinent here. It is George Eliot at her most un-Lawrentian—dry, shrewd, ponderously urbane in its irony. It is an attack on the habit of attributing to temper (and so excusing) the way a man actually behaves.

> If a man frequently passes unjust judgements, takes up false attitudes, intermits his acts of kindness with rude behaviour or cruel words, and falls into the consequent vulgar error of supposing that he can make amends by laboured agreeableness, I cannot consider such courses any the less ugly because they are ascribed to 'temper'. Especially I object to the assumption that his having a fundamentally good disposition is either an apology or a compensation for his bad behaviour.[2]

'Disposition' and 'behaviour': it is very like Ryle's contrast between the 'repository' and the 'doing and undergoing of these things in the ordinary world'—or Hardy's between inner and outer purity. George Eliot has found a simile for this way of thinking that Ryle must envy:

> We are in danger of having among us a number of virtuous persons who conduct themselves detestably, just as we have hysterical patients who, with sound organs, are apparently labouring under many sorts of organic disease.[3]

The contrast between this reassuring 'inner goodness' and the bad behaviour which is 'only temper' is really a contrast between potential and actual behaviour. And what might be ought not to be given the same status as what is:

> A man who uses his balmorals to tread on your toes with much frequency and an unmistakable emphasis may prove a fast

---

[1] Ibid., ch. 10, § 2   [2] 'Only Temper', *Theophrastus Such*, § 6   [3] Ibid.

friend in adversity, but meanwhile your adversity has not arrived and your toes are tender.[1]

Even the phrase 'potential behaviour' may not be justified. The 'virtue' of the man with temper may not be potential in any sense the psychologist can recognise: its likelihood may not depend on such evidence as tender toes, but merely on the wishful thinking of the man's friends.

When we turn to George Eliot's novels, we find that no belief runs more firmly through them than the belief that we are what our deeds make us, that handsome is as handsome does. Arthur Donnithorne would gladly have written off his behaviour as 'only temper', or more accurately 'only weakness' or 'only flirting', but his author will not allow it. The eroding of Tito's inner nature by his outward actions is the main theme of *Romola*. In *The Mill on the Floss* she once pauses to make explicitly the same point as she makes in 'Only Temper'. Mr Tulliver, on his way to see his sister, rides through the village of Basset and looks around in disgust:

> Basset had a poor soil, poor roads, a poor non-resident landlord, a poor non-resident vicar, and rather less than half a curate, also poor. If any one strongly impressed with the power of the human mind to triumph over circumstances, will contend that the parishioners of Basset might none the less have been a very superior class of people, I have nothing to urge against the abstract proposition; I only know that, in point of fact, the Basset mind was in strict keeping with its circumstances.[2]

'The power of the human mind to triumph over circumstances.' Few readers nowadays accuse George Eliot of taking too low a view of human nature (though her contemporaries did); but we can see that the ready optimism of this doctrine is, for her, a rationalisation of our habit of ignoring what is, in order to fix our attention on what might be.

When Mr Tulliver reaches his sister's home, and finds in himself a struggle between his anger with Moss and his affection for her, his need of the money he has lent them and his realisation that they need it even more, this struggle is presented, for moments, entirely in external details. 'If a man means to be hard, let him

---

[1] 'Only Temper', *Theophrastus Such*, § 6   [2] *The Mill on the Floss*, Bk. I, ch. 8

keep in the saddle and speak from that height, above the level of pleading eyes, and with the command of a distant horizon.' The scene is too long to quote: its pathos derives much of its force from the translation of Mr Tulliver's feelings into his behaviour.

An example from *Middlemarch* will confirm the point, and may throw some light on the book as well:

'Is there anyone else coming to dine besides Mr Casaubon?'
'Not that I know of.'
'I hope there is someone else. Then I shall not hear him eat his soup so.'
'What is there remarkable about his soup eating?'
'Really, Dodo, can't you hear how he scrapes his spoon? And he always blinks before he speaks. I don't know whether Locke blinked, but I'm sure I am sorry for those who sat opposite him if he did.'
'Celia,' said Dorothea, with emphatic gravity, 'pray don't make any more observations of that kind.'
'Why not? They are quite true,' returned Celia, who had her reasons for persevering, though she was beginning to be a little afraid.
'Many things are true which only the commonest minds observe.'
'Then I think the commonest minds must be rather useful. I think it is a pity Mr Casaubon's mother had not a commoner mind: she might have taught him better.'[1]

Since George Eliot is so often accused of partiality towards Dorothea, it is worth observing how objective she here is. The scene loses a good deal out of its context, for we need to remember not only details like the earlier comparison with Locke, but also that Dorothea is engaged to Mr Casaubon: knowing this from the beginning, we can read with something like her own agitation as Celia makes her disastrous remark. If it was not for this knowledge, and this agitation, would we not assume that the sympathy lay with Celia? It is she who, like the author, actually sees what is in front of her eyes. Like the novelist and the experimental psychologist, she has a common mind.

When Dorothea eventually tells Celia the truth, poor Celia is dumb and pale with horror and remorse: shocked at the news, but wanting to suppress her shock:

[1] *Middlemarch*, ch. 5

Perhaps Celia had never turned so pale before. The paper man she was making would have had his leg injured but for her habitual care of whatever she held in her hands. She laid the fragile figure down at once, and sat perfectly still for a few moments. When she spoke there was a tear gathering.[1]

'Horror, remorse, shock': the words are mine, not George Eliot's. In the novel they are given 'meaning': that is, they become scrupulous, accurate (shall we say Ryle-like) observation of what Celia does. Only after that does George Eliot write 'her fears were the fears of affection', or use the phrase 'subdued astonishment'.

Daniel Deronda is perhaps the richest of all George Eliot's novels in observed behaviour. When Gwendolen, in great agitation, calls on Mirah to find out if she is Deronda's mistress, she:

began to unbutton her gloves that she might button them again, and bite her lips over the pretended difficulty.[2]

A longer passage suggests a more complex comment, and then a generalisation:

While Hans was answering Mirah slipped away to her own room; but not to indulge in any outburst of the passion within her. If the angels once supposed to watch the toilet of women had entered the little chamber with her and let her shut the door behind them, they would only have seen her take off her hat, sit down and press her hands against her temples as if she had suddenly reflected that her head ached; then rise to dash cold water on her eyes and brow and hair till her backward curls were full of crystal beads, while she had dried her brow and looked out like a freshly opened flower from among the dewy tresses of the woodland; then give deep sighs of relief, and putting on her little slippers, sit still after that action for a couple of minutes, which seemed to her so long, so full of things to come, that she rose with an air of recollection, and went down to make tea.[3]

There is one hasty conclusion which this whole argument might seem to lead towards, and which I emphatically do not want to draw. The contrast between behaviour and mental entities is very similar to that between dramatisation and commentary; and I might therefore seem to be suggesting that the novelist must only 'show' and never 'tell'. Nobody could say this and go on drawing

---

[1] *Middlemarch*, ch. 5   [2] *Daniel Deronda*, ch. 48   [3] Ibid., ch. 61

examples from George Eliot, the most explicit of all the great novelists; and I must therefore pause to withdraw this radical and (to
some, perhaps) obvious corollary of my argument. In this passage,
for instance, there is plenty of behaviour: Mirah takes off her hat,
sits down, presses her hands against her temples, and so on. But all
these details are introduced by 'the angels . . . would only have
seen'. The other half of that only-clause is not supplied, but if it
were it would clearly be that these actions alone might not reveal to
the angels (whose names are Skinner and Watson) the full richness
of the inner life they express. Mirah presses her hands against her
temples *as if* she had suddenly reflected that her head ached: but
her head does not ache, or if it does the fact is trivial as an explanation. The intensity of Mirah's suppressed but now conscious love is
determining behaviour that in itself does not bear the full stamp of
its cause. That 'only' is the traditional 'only' of the novelist's
prejudice: that externals are not enough, and must be explained in
the light of postulated inner states, which will have to be told to us.

I seem to have got into a contradiction, and I do not want to
pretend there is an easy way out. We must say that the power of a
novelist consists in the skill and assurance with which he moves from
one kind of terminology to the other. Of course we cannot manage
without words like love and hate, fear and guilt, and (nowadays)
conscious and unconscious: they are the only vocabulary we have
for organising the behaviour we observe into a meaningful pattern,
and they will long remain so. But we must ask of the novelist
that he use them to organise and interpret what he observes, to
classify his responses to what his common mind sees. Once we
suspect that they have become an alternative to this, an easy way
out, a method for the imperceptive novelist to deploy counters
that he does not understand, then we will surely place his novels
with the histrionic horseplay of those who indulge in heavy-handed,
hesitant and happy-go-lucky games with adjectives. Terms like
love and fear must be earned.

We can see this in *Daniel Deronda*. When Gwendolen, by her
reaction to the news of Rex's fall, shows his father that she is not
in love with him, she shows, too, something of her own character:

'Rex has had a fall,' said Mr Gascoigne curtly, throwing himself into an armchair, resting his elbows and fitting his palms
and fingers together, while he closed his lips and looked at
Gwendolen who said,

E   129

'Oh, poor fellow! He is not hurt, I hope?' with a correct look of anxiety such as elated mortals try to superinduce when their pulses are all the while quick with triumph.[1]

The common prejudice against behaviourism believes that it is somehow insensitive to subtle feelings, that it describes the surface and ignores the hidden life below. There is nothing in its theory to make this so, though Skinner does recognise the difficulty of fitting purely private events (toothache or dreams) into a public science. That difficulty is not only the scientist's: if the toothache is purely private, it is hidden from the novelist as well. The novelist is the watcher who watches very carefully, until he is sure that you really have got toothache. The charge of insensitivity should be reversed. To be truly sensitive to the hidden life, to the emotions which are not apparent, is, as these last passages so well show, to be able to spot the less obtrusive forms of behaviour in which they manifest themselves. Both Mr Gascoigne and George Eliot are better observers than those angels; if they had been watching her really carefully, they would have seen that Mirah did not have a headache. The tone of careful observation in which George Eliot writes is meant to imply that she (and we) have better eyes than angels.

One last objection: an attractive one, which we can take from *Middlemarch* itself. Some readers might suggest that the real behaviourist of this book is Rosamund Vincy. It is Rosamund's pride that her conduct is impeccable; it is her hollowness that she does not care about what is within, perhaps does not believe in it:

> Rosamund said in her silvery neutral way, 'Here is your tea, Tertius,' setting it on the small table by his side, and then moved back to her place without looking at him. . . . Her impression now was one of offence and repulsion. But then, Rosamund had no scowls and had never raised her voice: she was quite sure that no one could justly find fault with her.[2]

Rosamund, it appears, believes that nothing matters except behaviour that can be observed by others:

> But the door opened and Rosamund re-entered. She carried the leather box containing the amethysts, and a tiny ornamental

---

[1] *Daniel Deronda*, ch. 7   [2] *Middlemarch*, ch. 58

basket which contained other boxes, and laying them on the chair where she had been sitting, she said, with perfect propriety in her air,

'This is all the jewellery you ever gave me. You can return what you like of it, and the plate also. You will not, of course, expect me to stay at home tomorrow. I shall go to papa's . . .' Rosamund was convinced that no woman could behave more irreproachably than she was behaving; and she went to sit down at her worktable.[1]

If Rosamund could have conquered her feeling that his books were horrid, would she not have found support in Skinner for her conviction?

Yet she would have been wrong. The trouble with Rosamund is precisely that her hollowness does show. To perceive her egoism, we need not ignore what she says and does in order to postulate a shadow self within: we need to attend more carefully. Lydgate is hurt by Rosamund precisely because he is attending:

'Try not to grieve, darling,' said Lydgate, turning his eyes up towards her. That she had chosen to move away from him in this moment of her trouble made everything harder to say, but he must absolutely go on.[2]

The difference between appealing from observation to shadows, and appealing to more careful observation, is made clear by a famous paragraph in the same chapter:

'What can *I* do, Tertius?' said Rosamund, turning her eyes on him again. That little speech of four words, like so many others in all languages, is capable by varied vocal inflections of expressing all states of mind from helpless dimness to exhaustive argumentative perception, from the completest self-devoting fellowship to the most neutral aloofness. Rosamund's thin utterance threw into the words 'What can *I* do?' as much neutrality as they could hold. They fell like a mortal chill on Lydgate's roused tenderness.[3]

This passage has sometimes been taken as evidence that George Eliot was not a true novelist, for she did not trust dialogue. Supplementing her dialogue with explanatory comments she moves, it is claimed, from showing to theorising. In truth, it proves just the

[1] Ibid., ch. 58   [2] Ibid., ch. 58   [3] Ibid., ch. 58

opposite: it shows how fine her ear was, and how thoroughly she respected what she heard. It was not words alone that she heard; and she felt she had to record (let us drop into jargon a moment) the total act of verbal communication. The appeal is not from what happened to a disposition or repository that explains it away, but from a vague to a precise rendering of what happened. It is this scrupulousness which permits her to end on the cliché of 'mortal chill': she has worked for it.

Rosamund is just not a very good behaviourist.

Finally, a modern example: perhaps the pithiest of all. It is from Virginia Woolf: Lily Briscoe, in *To the Lighthouse*, is reflecting on the emotional life of old Mr Carmichael as he lies asleep in the sun.

> When he had heard of Andrew Ramsay's death . . . Mr Carmichael had 'lost all interest in life'. What did it mean—that? she wondered. Had he marched through Trafalgar Square grasping a big stick? Had he turned pages over and over, without reading them, sitting in his room in St John's Wood, alone?[1]

Skinner is wrong if he believes that traditional terminology cannot adapt to his operational definitions. For this is what Virginia Woolf is here doing: she is reversing commonsense. 'What did it mean, the way he sat turning pages over and over?' we usually ask; and we are told 'It meant he had lost all interest in life'. But Virginia Woolf, with the observer's eye, is not satisfied with phrases that have no functional meaning. She is, I suppose, using the James-Lange theory of emotion: that an emotion does not cause but is the bodily changes involved. The theory is a natural for novelists, and it is disappointing that psychology has now rejected it: though since it was always able to handle the coarser emotions better than the finer ones, our regret may be proportional to the writers we are thinking of.

I have to end with another concession. I described the scientist as the man who can restrain curiosity sufficiently to look at one small unit at a time; I quoted the behaviourists as saying that psychology is the study of the whole organism and not of separate parts. To resolve this apparent contradiction, we must distinguish between dividing the organism into parts, and dividing its be-

[1] *To the Lighthouse*, III, § 12

haviour into parts. The natural scientist (for instance, the physiologist) does the former; each small parcel of behaviour that the experimental psychologist studies is behaviour by the whole organism. Now the concession I have to make is that these parts of behaviour appear to the novelist very small pieces indeed: it will be a long, long, time before the experimentalists have moved from rats and pigeons or even from language learning to the full complexity of one total human act. In the meantime, we have to go on living, using terms like love, wish, hate, motive, meaning and even drive, and getting our pre-scientific knowledge of human nature from the common mind and eye of the novelist.

So that all I have really done in this long discussion is to point to an analogy. Novelists are in one important respect like behaviourists, but this does not mean (or does not yet mean) that they are very much help to each other. Of the interest which literature has shown in psycho-analysis, we can at least say that the writers used what they found. I have hardly ever come across an experimental finding in psychology that looked as if it would be much use to a novelist (surprisingly, it may be more use to poets). Perhaps we need to wait a few hundred years for this. And by that time the psychologists may have put the cognitive function of literature out of business. They may have put literature out of business. They or someone else.

PART TWO

IMPULSE AND CONTROL

I. JANE AUSTEN

1 'A Child should be of the Party'

WHAT Jane Austen most admired was the ability to resist impulse; what Lawrence most admired was surrender to it. George Eliot was a Romantic: she did not believe there was a clear opposition between impulse and reason.

That is my argument. It will need qualifying of course: qualifying in a way that will make the three writers more complex and more interesting than this bald summary suggests, but not (I think) less committed or less disturbing. It will also need a good deal of documenting: I shall treat of Jane Austen first, and I begin with a comparison between her and George Eliot.

'On every formal visit,' says Jane Austen, her commentary sparkling with gay malice as Lady Middleton introduces her eldest child, 'a child ought to be of the party, by way of provision for discourse.' Of course the child does not actually speak: he is asked questions, but his mother answers them, 'while he hung about her and held down his head, to the great surprise of her ladyship, who wondered at his being so shy before company, as he could make noise enough at home'. This has the ring of knowledge: the well-bred old maid must have endured in silence the introduction by many smug mothers of their children into the party. In a novel, she must have been tempted to conclude, a child ought to be of the party, by way of provision for satire. Hence, later in *Sense and Sensibility*, one of her most deadly scenes:

Fortunately for those who pay their court through such foibles, a fond mother, though, in pursuit of praise for her child, the most rapacious of human beings, is likewise the most credulous; her demands are exorbitant; but she will swallow anything; and the excessive affection and endurance of the Miss Steeles towards her offspring, were viewed by Lady Middleton without the smallest surprise or distrust. She saw with maternal complacency all the impertinent incroachments and mischievous tricks to which her cousins submitted. She saw their sashes untied, their hair pulled about their ears, their work-bags searched, and their knives and scissors stolen away, and felt no doubts of its being a reciprocal enjoyment. It suggested no other surprise than that Elinor and Marianne should sit so composedly by without claiming a share in what was passing.

'John is in such spirits today!' said she, on his taking Miss Steele's pocket-handkerchief, and throwing it out of the window. 'He is full of monkey-tricks.'

And soon afterwards, on the second boy's violently pinching one of the same lady's fingers, she fondly observed, 'How playful William is!'

'And here is my sweet little Annamaria,' she added, tenderly caressing a little girl of three years old, who had not made a noise for the last two minutes. 'And she is always so gentle and quiet—never was there such a quiet little thing!'

But unfortunately, in bestowing these embraces, a pin in her ladyship's head-dress slightly scratching the child's neck, produced from this pattern of gentleness such violent screams as could hardly be outdone by any creature professedly noisy. The mother's consternation was excessive; but it could not surpass the alarm of the Miss Steeles, and everything was done by all three, in so critical an emergency, which affection could suggest as likely to assuage the agonies of the little sufferer. She was seated in her mother's lap, covered with kisses, her wound bathed with lavender-water by one of the Miss Steeles, who was on her knees to attend her, and her mouth stuffed with sugar-plums by the other. With such a reward for her tears, the child was too wise to cease crying. She still screamed and sobbed lustily, kicked her two brothers for offering to touch her, and all their united soothings were ineffectual till Lady Middleton luckily remembering that in a scene of similar distress, last week, some apricot marmalade had been successfully applied for a bruised temple, the same remedy was eagerly proposed for this unfortunate scratch, and a slight intermission of screams in the young lady on hearing it, gave them reason to hope that it would not be rejected.[1]

Mainly, of course, Jane Austen is interested in the effect of the children on grown-ups: but she has views, too, on the children themselves. 'With such a reward for her tears, the child was too wise to cease crying': how ironical is the word 'wise' here? Is it just children's wisdom—a view of immediate not of long-term self-interest? Even if this is so, the implication is that bringing up

---

[1] *Sense and Sensibility*, ch. 21

children will be like a battle: their immediate interest versus their long-term and our immediate interests (and what guarantee that these two latter will always be allies?). But if by 'wise' Jane Austen really *meant* wise, then she has let the cat out of the bag: she views the struggle between child and adult as a type of the struggle between people; everyone wants what he can get, and we must be careful not to offer free gifts to anybody, child and adult alike.

The satire here is principally directed, however, not against the children, but against the adults. And on them her view is simple. Mothers introduce their children into adult company through vanity; other women admire them through flattery. Elinor and Marianne (behaving alike for once!) are commended for 'sitting so composedly by'; the Miss Steeles' indulgence is at best foolish, at worst sycophantic. Tactfully, their reaction to John and William's monkey-tricks is not mentioned: if they had smiled and shown no annoyance, it would have been hard for the reader not to give them some sort of commendation.

There is a similar scene, with a similar child, in *Felix Holt*:

Between (Esther) and little Harry there was an extraordinary fascination. . . . No sooner had she sat down on the sofa in the library than he climbed up to her, and began to treat her as an attractive object in natural history, snatched up her curls with his brown fist, and, discovering that there was a little ear under them, pinched it and blew into it, pulled at her coronet of plaits, and seemed to discover with satisfaction that it did not grow at the summit of her head, but could be dragged down and altogether undone. Then, finding that she laughed, tossed him back, kissed, and pretended to bite him—in fact, was an animal that understood fun—he rushed off and made Dominic bring a small menagerie of white-mice, squirrels, and birds, with Moro, the black spaniel, to make her acquaintance. Whomsoever Harry liked, it followed that Mr Transome must like: 'Gappa', along with Nimrod the retriever, was part of the menagerie, and perhaps endured more than all the other live creatures in the way of being tumbled about. Seeing that Esther bore having her hair pulled down quite merrily, and that she was willing to be harnessed and beaten, the old man began to confide to her, in his feeble, smiling, and rather jerking fashion, Harry's remarkable feats: how he had one day, when Gappa was asleep, unpinned a whole drawerful of beetles, to see if they would fly away; then, disgusted with their stupidity, was about to throw them all on the ground and stamp on them, when Dominic came in and rescued these valuable specimens; also how he had subtly watched Mrs Transome at the cabinet where she kept her medicines, and, when she had left it for a while without locking it, had gone to the drawers and scattered half the contents on the floor. But what old Mr Transome thought the most wonderful proof of an almost preternatural cleverness was, that Harry would hardly ever talk, but preferred making inarticulate noises, or combining syllables after a method of his own.

'He can talk well enough if he likes,' said Gappa, evidently thinking that Harry, like the monkeys, had deep reasons for his reticence.[1]

Esther reacts like the Misses Steele: instead of sitting by composedly, she bears it all, she is 'willing to be harnessed and beaten'. Her behaviour is the same, but her motives different: for her reaction is positive, is the result of genuinely entering into the child's game, and is directed at the child, not obliquely at the mother. Hence she bears it merrily; hence she 'laughed, tossed him back: kissed and pretended to bite him' (Lucy Steele would not have pretended to bite).

The appropriate comparison is, no doubt, between the Misses Steele and Esther; but the revealing one is between them and Gappa. The old man submits completely, and is ruled by the child: the Misses Steele showed 'excessive affection and endurance' in front of the Middleton children; old Mr Transome 'endured more than all the other live creatures'. When Jane Austen used the word ('endurance') it was so without irony that we can call it querulous; finding it in George Eliot, we ask if it is ironical in this case. The answer seems to be, yes and no. It is unironic in that little Harry behaved quite as tyrrannically as John Middleton: for George Eliot sees all that Jane Austen saw, and there is the material in her scene for satire quite as sharp as that of *Sense and Sensibility* (even John Middleton never got round to those butterflies . . .). Yet so different is the lesson drawn that we must say Gappa did not really 'endure': for he was the better for it. The child had opened up to him the possibilities of a self-forgetting happiness that Jane Austen is not interested in finding in her adults who sport with children. 'He can talk well enough if he likes,' says the old man;

[1] *Felix Holt,* ch. 40

the very words of the complaining governess, refusing to be deceived by any child's 'nonsense'. It is not nonsense to Gappa, but a mark of strange and imposing cleverness.

And is he deceived? Is he a pathetic old man, happy because he is feeble and never going to be disillusioned, or is there something to his blissful wonder at Harry? What, in other words, is George Eliot's view of the child itself? There is no simple answer to this, for she is herself hesitating between an old-maidish clarity and being 'deceived'. George Eliot gives Gappa's account of Harry's pranks not in reported but in summarised speech: the thoughts are the old man's, the words are the authors.' Harry's feats are 'remarkable'; Harry was 'disgusted with the stupidity' of the dead beetles; he watched 'subtly'; he shows 'preternatural cleverness'. Now Harry *is* clever, subtle, remarkable: he is exploring the world, by imposing himself on it. What Gappa can best perceive in an exaggerated case like this, George Eliot can perceive in all human activity: that the line between aggressiveness and curiosity, between selfishness and the acquiring of experience, between dominating and controlling the world, is a delicate one. If we adopt Jane Austen's merely moral attitude to children (she surely believed they should be seen and not heard) it must blind us to the immense human possibilities that a child's selfishness only slightly parodies.

The treatment of Harry is more complex than anything comparable in *Adam Bede*. Although there is no scene in *Adam Bede* which makes such a convenient contrast with the Middletons and the Steeles, the treatment of children in that book points up more clearly, and more crudely, the difference between the two authors. For whereas the Middleton children are a touchstone for folly and flattery, Totty is almost the reverse. In Chapter XIV George Eliot uses Totty as a moral norm: it is Totty who sees clearly the difference between Dinah's love and Hetty's indifference and (with a child's privilege, allowed her both by her mother and her author) expresses what she sees by slapping Hetty. It is a crude scene, making its point with less subtlety—and less ruthless clarity of gaze—than that in *Felix Holt*:

> 'Wilt go to cousin Hetty, my dilling, while mother gets ready to go to bed? Then Totty shall go into mother's bed, and sleep there all night.'
> Before her mother had done speaking, Totty had given her answer in an unmistakable manner, by knitting her brow,

setting her tiny teeth against her under-lip, and leaning forward to slap Hetty on the arm with her utmost force. Then, without speaking, she nestled to her mother again.

'Hey, hey', said Mr Poyser, while Hetty stood without moving, 'not go to cousin Hetty? That's like a baby: Totty's a little woman, an' not a baby.'

'It's no use trying to persuade her,' said Mrs Poyser. 'She allays takes against Hetty when she isn't well. Happen she'll go to Dinah.'

Dinah, having taken off her bonnet and shawl, had hitherto kept quietly seated in the background, not liking to thrust herself between Hetty and what was considered Hetty's proper work. But now she came forward and putting out her arms, said, 'Come, Totty, come and let Dinah carry her up-stairs along with mother: poor, poor mother! she's so tired—she wants to go to bed.'

Totty turned her face toward Dinah, and looked at her an instant, then lifted herself up, put out her little arms, and let Dinah lift her from her mother's lap.[1]

This is effective enough in its negative part—the slapping of Hetty, which is well visualised. The readiness with which Totty goes to Dinah seems less convincing and less clearly seen. But at the end of the chapter there is a subtler version of this positive.

'You may make the door fast now, Poyser: Alick's been come in this long while,' said Mrs Poyser, rising with an appearance of relief from her low chair. 'Get me the matches down, Hetty, for I must have the rush-light burning i' my room. Come, father.'

The heavy wooden bolts began to roll in the house doors, and old Martin prepared to move, by gathering up his blue handkerchief, and reaching his bright knobbed walnut-tree stick from the corner. Mrs Poyser then led the way out of the kitchen, followed by the grandfather, and Dinah with Totty in her arms—all going to bed by twilight, like the birds. Mrs Poyser, on her way, peeped into the room where her two boys lay, just to see their ruddy round cheeks on the pillow, and to hear for a moment their light regular breathing.

'Come, Hetty, get to bed,' said Mr Poyser, in a soothing tone, as he himself turned to go up-stairs. 'You didna mean to be late, I'll be bound, but your aunt's been worried today. Goodnight, my wench, good-night.'[2]

[1] *Adam Bede*, ch. 14   [2] Ibid., ch. 14

In the matter-of-factness of these details there is a sense of the day's ending, of squabbling being over and the family settling to the peace of the night. The hint of reconciliation comes, surely, through George Eliot's use of the very old and the very young. Old Martin Poyser brings the slight softening into Mrs Poyser's voice when she says 'Come, father'; the two young boys, suggesting peacefulness by their light regular breathing, continue the influence, and lead to the final friendly remark to Hetty. It is delicately done, since the old man and the children themselves remain quite passive.

And to round off the contrast, let us return to Jane Austen.

Another minute brought another addition. The younger boy, a remarkable stout, forward child, of two years old, having got the door opened for him by some one without, made his determined appearance among them, and went straight to the sofa to see what was going on, and put in his claim to anything good that might be giving away.

There being nothing to eat, he could only have some play; and as his aunt would not let him teaze his sick brother, he began to fasten himself upon her, as she knelt, in such a way that, busy as she was about Charles, she could not shake him off. She spoke to him—ordered, intreated, and insisted in vain. Once she did contrive to push him away, but the boy had the greater pleasure in getting upon her back again directly.

'Walter,' said she, 'get down this moment. You are extremely troublesome. I am very angry with you.'

'Walter,' cried Charles Hayter, 'why do you not do as you are bid? Do not you hear your aunt speak? Come to me Walter, come to cousin Charles.'

But not a bit did Walter stir.

In another moment, however, she found herself in the state of being released from him; some one was taking him from her, though he had bent down her head so much, that his little sturdy hands were unfastened from around her neck, and he was resolutely borne away, before she knew that Captain Wentworth had done it.[1]

Here the child is a test: but in the opposite sense from Totty. It is not by responding to a child but by combating it that Captain Wentworth proves his worth. The quiet authority that Jane Austen wishes us to value so much (Captain Wentworth is a sailor, we

[1] *Persuasion*, ch. 9

must remember) is shown in his ability to handle Walter with firmness and severity. Children must be kept down.

2 'Facts are such horrid things'

Children are the extreme example of those who act on impulse: and the contrast we have just seen can be followed far into Jane Austen's work. If there is a key moment in all her fiction, it is surely that moment on Box Hill when Emma insults Miss Bates. It is important to the plot, for it precipitates a frankness between her and Mr Knightley that leads to the acknowledgement of their love; but far more than that it is important to the moral scheme of the novel. Though *Emma* is a social comedy, not a moral allegory, we can see its action as a battle (or the comic analogue thereof) for the heroine's soul: we watch her constantly yielding ground to her egoism and her love of power, then regaining it through her warmth of heart or the influence of Mr Knightley (the good angel). This is the moment in the story when she yields most, when her behaviour is nearest to sheer malice:

> 'I am ordered by Miss Woodhouse to say, that . . . she only de-
> mands from each of you, either one thing very clever, be it
> prose or verse, original or repeated; or two things moderately
> clever; or three things very dull indeed; and she engages to laugh
> heartily at them all.'
> 'Oh! very well,' exclaimed Miss Bates; 'then I need not be
> uneasy. "Three things very dull indeed." That will just do for
> me, you know. I shall be sure to say three dull things as soon
> as ever I open my mouth, shan't I?' (looking round with the
> most good-humoured dependence on everybody's assent). 'Do
> you not think I shall?'
> Emma could not resist.
> 'Ah! ma'am, but there may be a difficulty. Pardon me, but
> you will be limited as to number—only three at once.'[1]

Miss Bates does not understand at first; but when she does, we are left in no doubt that she is hurt. The brittle conversation, how-ever, does not stop for her: Mr Weston makes up a feeble and exces-sively inappropriate conundrum in praise of Emma, Mrs Elton is as catty as ever, Frank Churchill's good humour rises almost to hysteria. The sense of unease is brilliantly rendered, and it is no

[1] *Emma*, ch. 43

real surprise when we have **Mr Knightley's** rebuke **and Emma's** remorse, though even then, with the same ruthless realism, we are shown how remorse has to fight its way to the surface through the impulse to laugh it off. But by the time Emma is seated in her carriage there is no doubt of her feelings:

> Time did not compose her. As she reflected more, she seemed but to feel it more. She never had been so depressed. Happily it was not necessary to speak. There was only Harriet, who seemed not in spirits herself, fagged, and very willing to be silent; and Emma felt the tears running down her cheeks almost all the way home, without being at any trouble to check them, extraordinary as they were.[1]

This is one of the most intense moments in the whole of Jane Austen. Usually she avoids scenes of intensity, reporting them briefly and with prim wit ('What did she say? Just what she ought, of course. A lady always does'), but there is no evasion here.

And now what happened at this so important moment on Box Hill? 'Emma could not resist,' we are told: she yielded to impulse. She behaved, in fact, like Mrs Elton, who always feels, and never resists, the impulse of self-assertion. It is Miss Bates and **Mr** Knightley who keep silent, Emma and Mrs Elton who let themselves go. There is no struggle in Emma between two impulses, one to insult, one to cherish Miss Bates (let alone between the impulse to cherish and a restraining convention). Impulse dictates, quite simply, an aggressive egoism: and it must be restrained by Principle.

There is plenty of testimony to Jane Austen's belief in Principle, and her admiration for restraint. It is the whole theme of *Sense and Sensibility* and of *Mansfield Park*; and it emerges constantly from the details of all her books. She believed that high principles (the only moral which her nephew could find in her books was 'the superiority of high over low principles') not only make for virtue, they bring happiness. Julia Bertram, chafing to find herself in the company of two old women when she wants to be with Henry Crawford, is miserable because of 'the want of that higher species of self-command, that just consideration of others, that knowledge of her own heart, that principle of right which had not formed any essential part of her education'. No suggestion that the way to

[1] Ibid., ch. 43

avoid misery would have been to respond more warmly to Mrs
Rushworth and Mrs Norris, for it is not warmth which is needed
(warmth and responsiveness has got her into too much trouble
already) but the reasoned virtues of self-command: *just* consideration of others, *knowledge* of her own heart.

A very different example will show the same belief. In the walk
which most of the principal characters of *Persuasion* take to Winthrop, Mary has an opportunity to show more than her usual snobbery: when her husband and her sister-in-law go off to pay a call on
their cousin Charles Hayter, a pleasant young clergyman with no
genteel blood, Mary remarks scornfully to Captain Wentworth:

> 'It is very unpleasant having such connexions! But, I assure
> you, I have never been in the house above twice in my life.'
> She received no other answer than an artificial, assenting
> smile, followed by a contemptuous glance, as he turned away,
> which Anne perfectly knew the meaning of.[1]

We are surely meant to assume the rightness of Wentworth's
conduct here. We can be sure of that, since Jane Austen's attention
(and ours) is fixed on Anne, and her embarrassment over Mary;
Wentworth's reaction is merely a passing assurance of how badly
Mary is behaving. And that assurance is not given by any outburst,
any expression of the contempt he feels; though Wentworth (like us)
is disgusted at this snobbery, he is well-bred enough to give the
necessary 'artificial, assenting smile'.

These are not passing instances: Jane Austen really believed that
every impulse must be submitted to the inspection of the judgement, and, if necessary, restrained; just as she really believed that
happiness depended on virtue. She is sure that Wickham and
Lydia will not be happy, since 'they were only brought together
because their passions were stronger than their virtue'. We may
think of all the novelists who have pitied the unhappy couples
brought together only because their virtue was stronger than their
passions.

From restraint it is a short step to discipline: from a view that
children must be treated strictly, to a view that life is stern and
must be met sternly. Jane Austen's steady admiration for the
navy must not be set down merely to her affection for her sailor
brothers: she really admires what the navy represents, and sees

---

[1] *Persuasion*, ch. 10

that it has stiffened William Price's character in a way his family could never have done. It is not wholly fantastic, even, to draw a momentary parallel with the navy's great novelist, Joseph Conrad: Jane Austen at her sternest touches something like his stoicism. She can even speak, on the last page of *Mansfield Park*, of 'the consciousness of being born to struggle and endure'. To Conrad, this would be a phrase about the human condition; in its context, it has a narrower meaning—Sir Thomas is admitting the advantages of 'early hardship and discipline' as a form of education, and the consciousness is not that of mankind but of the Prices— but the phrase seems to lift itself out of this immediate context, and to remain in the mind as a token of the stoical streak occasionally showing itself in Jane Austen, and most of all in *Mansfield Park*.

In *Persuasion* the admiration for the navy is even steadier and more prominent. The attractive but shallow Louisa Musgrove, seen at her best when she has taken a fancy to Captain Wentworth, is kindled to 'raptures of admiration and delight on the character of the navy', and though her enthusiasm is a sign of her youth and shallowness, the fact that she chooses to use it on the navy is a sign of a better influence on her. The novel actually ends with a tribute to the navy, in the last sentence; and earlier Jane Austen even pays to it the most effective compliment in her power, the indirect compliment of having it slighted by one of her silly characters. Anne's praise ('sailors work hard enough for their comforts, we must all allow') is less eloquent than Sir Walter's solemn reply: 'The profession has its utility, but I should be sorry to see any friend of mine belonging to it.'

High principles, then, and knowledge of the heart: Jane Austen believes that the principles are powerful and the knowledge obtainable. The human heart is not a mystery to her: she knows the reason for everything. Why are the Crawfords depraved? 'Henry Crawford, ruined by early independence and bad domestic example, indulged in the freaks of a cold-blooded vanity a little too long.' The admiral, his mistress and his dissipations, do not really form part of the book: but they have to be mentioned so that there will be a cause for the depravity. Why is Darcy proud? 'As a child I was taught what was *right*, but I was not taught to correct my temper. I was given good principles, but was left to follow them in pride and conceit.' Why is Willoughby wicked? 'Elinor made no answer. Her thoughts were silently fixed on the irreparable injury which too early independence and its consequent habits of idleness, dissipation and luxury had made in the mind, the character, the happiness of a man who, to every advantage of person and talents, united a disposition naturally open and honest, and a feeling, affectionate temper.' How easy it all is: no one in Jane Austen, except the fools, would ever talk like Deronda's mother:

> 'Oh—the reasons of our actions!' said the Princess, with a ring of something like sarcastic scorn. 'When you are as old as I am, it will not seem so simple a question—"Why did you do this?" People talk of their motives in a cut and dried way. Every woman is supposed to have the same set of motives, or else be a monster.'[1]

It does not matter, for the moment, that George Eliot is withholding her full sympathy from the Princess at this point: the application may be the Princess's, and may be erroneous, but the imaginative grasp that speaks here is the author's own.

Jane Austen believes that she understands not only the causes of character growth but also the observable details of how people behave. If anyone's conduct provides a puzzle, there is always an explanation—a single, clear explanation. When Darcy at last visits the Bennets with Bingley, he does not behave as Elizabeth expected:

> When occasionally . . . she raised her eyes to his face, she as often found him looking at Jane as at herself, and frequently on no object but the ground. More thoughtfulness and less anxiety to please than when they last met were plainly expressed.[2]

The reason, as she later discovers, is a quite definite one: he has not come to court her, but to observe her sister.

'I occasionally caught her,' says Mrs Vernon in *Lady Susan*, 'observing his countenance with exultation'; and Susan herself is even more observant:

> Oh! how delightful it was, to watch the variations of his countenance while I spoke, to see the struggle between returning tenderness and the remains of displeasure.[3]

---

[1] *Daniel Deronda*, ch. 51
[2] *Pride and Prejudice*, ch. 53
[3] *Lady Susan*, letter 25

There is no difficulty in reading off emotions from the face: they are 'plainly expressed'. Human personality is no mystery to Jane Austen. She does not believe that the springs of action are beyond the discovery of common sense, or that the feelings of others are concealed from us by their complexity and our limitations. For this reason she values plot not only for its aesthetic delights but also for its usefulness in explaining. If a character in one of her novels has imposed on others and has to be shown up, she is sure to provide the evidence: there always turns out to have been some particular bad action, something that would satisfy a jury. The most obvious example is the exposure of Mr Elliott in *Persuasion*. We may have an uneasy feeling about Mr Elliott, we may distrust his charm as much as Anne does, but that isn't proof. Hence the clumsy mechanism of Mrs Smith and her revelations: 'Hear the truth, therefore, now, while you are unprejudiced. Mr Elliott is a man without heart or conscience. . . .' and Mrs Smith knows the rules: stuff like this isn't proof either.

> My expressions startle you. You must allow for an injured, angry woman. But I will try to command myself. I will not abuse him. I will only tell you what I have found him. Facts shall speak. . . .'[1]

This is, as everyone recognises, the main blemish in *Persuasion*: it is too melodramatic to dig up this convenient villainy from the past, and we may guess that if Jane Austen had lived the ending of the book would have been revised. Neither Henry Crawford nor Wickham was exposed in this way: each of them showed his villainy by running off with a woman, and in each case against his own interests. I have never been able to find a convincing reason why Henry Crawford eloped with Maria. He had nothing to gain (except sex: and was he so hard up for that?), and a great deal to lose. In the case of Wickham we are offered a cursory explanation:

> She would have wondered why, without violently caring for her, he chose to elope with her at all, had she not felt certain that his flight was rendered necessary by distress of circumstances; and if that were the case, he was not the young man to resist an opportunity of having a companion.[2]

---

[1] *Persuasion*, ch. 21
[2] *Pride and Prejudice*, ch. 51

Who can find this convincing? It is altogether too convenient that Wickham should be thinking of running away just when the plot requires that Lydia should be run away with; and perhaps Jane Austen's own uneasiness at the explanation is betrayed by her giving it as a speculation of Elizabeth's rather than (for she has no objection to being the omniscient author) a statement of her own. No: both Crawford and Wickham elope for the same reason, that they have to prove their villainy. The flavour of distaste that Jane Austen had so brilliantly stirred into their portrayal was not proof.

Is it an accident that both these actions concern sex? We might speculate (we can never do more) that Jane Austen's avoidance of mystery and her preference for evidence is, ultimately, an avoidance of sex. Realising that—in the world of the love story—villainy must show itself in sexual offences, she perhaps did not dare handle these in a way that showed the quality of behaviour involved, and was therefore glad to treat them merely as facts, to tell us that Henry Crawford ran off with Maria and leave it at that. Such (if I understand it right) is the argument of Marvin Mudrick with respect to Wickham; and it is a natural enough speculation for us nowadays. I doubt if it is true: first, because there is a good deal of implied sex in Jane Austen as it is—Mr Knightley is redeemed from priggishness by his sexual attractiveness, and Henry Crawford's flirtations are treated with quite as much outspokenness as would have been needed for the elopement; and second because this insistence on the factual runs through Jane Austen's whole treatment of character. We can maintain if we like that its psychological basis is avoidance of sex, but we are then talking not about her books but about her personality.

There is another villain in Jane Austen who is finally trapped by the evidence of her guilt. 'I am in agonies,' writes Mrs Johnson to Lady Susan when all the wrong people have met each other, and all the cats are out of the bag, 'and know not what to do, nor what *you* can do.' Then comes a chronicle of what has been found out. 'What could I do? Facts are such horrid things!' Lady Susan's 'intellect and manner' may charm and deceive; but the facts do not let us down. In this age of motivations, there is a simple integrity about such respect for evidence which gives it an almost nostalgic charm. It is not surprising that Jane Austen makes fun of the man of feelings; and she does so entertainingly enough, in her portrait of Sir Edward Denham, in *Sanditon*:

He began, in a tone of great taste and feeling, to talk of the sea and the sea shore—and ran with energy through all the usual phrases employed in praise of their sublimity, and descriptive of the *undescribable* emotions they excite in the mind of sensibility.[1]

But this is funniest to the reader who is not a man of sensibility himself: Jane Austen can ridicule the excesses of feeling because she is not greatly attracted by the real thing. Her best people have their feelings under control, and measure them out appropriately to the occasion.

'It seems very odd,' said Maria, 'that you should be staying at home instead of Fanny.'

'I am sure she ought to be very much obliged to you,' added Julia, hastily leaving the room as she spoke, from a consciousness that she ought to offer to stay at home herself.

'Fanny will feel quite as grateful as the occasion requires,' was Edmund's only reply, and the subject dropped.[2]

The reply was made to Julia's sarcasm, but it could have been made to the enthusiasm of Sir Edward—or of Marianne Dashwood (of whom I shall speak in a moment). The heroes and heroines of Jane Austen will always feel as much gratitude—as much pity, as much indignation, as much love—as the occasion requires. To them all we apply Aziz' complaint to Fielding: 'Is emotion a sack of potatoes, to be measured out by the pound?'

3 First Objection; Jane Austen and Love

Now there are, of course, objections to the view of Jane Austen I have just outlined: if there weren't, would we bother to read her? Briefly, there are two, of which the second is more important, and more valid. First, are these really Jane Austen's views: does she come out so unequivocally for control and against feeling? And second, whatever her official views, are they her real views: do her novels really sustain the doctrine they are meant to exemplify, or do they work to undermine it?

First, then, for her explicit view. The objection here claims that Jane Austen values love more than anything—she is after all writing love stories; and that it is not by applying principles but by

---

[1] *Sanditon*, ch. 7   [2] *Mansfield Park*, ch. 8

loving that her characters really learn. Fanny's true education comes through her love for Edmund, as Frederica Vernon's through her love for Reginald. This is most certainly the case with George Eliot:

> In fact it is probable that but for Mary's existence and Fred's love for her, his conscience would have been much less active both in previously urging the debt on his thought and in impelling him not to spare himself after his usual fashion by deferring an unpleasant task, but to act as directly and simply as he could. Even much stronger mortals than Fred Vincy hold half their rectitude in the mind of the being they love best.[1]

Would not Jane Austen have endorsed this?

There are those in Jane Austen who love and are not redeemed by it: is Frank Churchill much better as a result of his love for Jane Fairfax? Perhaps he will be the better for it when they are married, as Henry Crawford (we are told) would have been better for marrying Fanny. It is difficult to press arguments like this too far. To measure Edmund's overwhelming influence on Fanny against Elizabeth's milder influence on Darcy and Jane Fairfax's lack of influence on Frank Churchill, and then to estimate how far Jane Austen believed in the redeeming power of love, is too legalistic for criticism, even for criticism that is seeking the underlying values of the novels. Jane Austen may write to exemplify a moral scheme, but not to illustrate a formula.

We can surely say, however, that Jane Austen does not believe in putting all her money on love, for she has given us one case of a woman who did just that—Mrs Price. Mrs Price marries for love on the first page of *Mansfield Park*, and then disappears: when she returns to view, we—and Fanny—see the disastrous result:

> Mrs Price was not unkind; but instead of gaining on her affection and confidence, and becoming more and more dear, her daughter never met with greater kindness from her than on the first day of her arrival. The instinct of nature was soon satisfied, and Mrs Price's attachment had no other source.[2]

Even mother love needs to be encouraged by circumstances.

If love redeems and teaches as nothing else can, it is surely because it transfigures the imagination, giving to every experience

---

[1] *Middlemarch*, ch. 23   [2] *Mansfield Park*, ch. 39

a quality it did not have before, investing others with an importance that now gives them a claim on our affections.

> *This light, this glory, this fair luminous mist,*
> *This beautiful and beauty-making power*[1]

—Coleridge's joy—issued, like the love that transfigures, from the soul itself:

> *And thence flows all that charms or ear or sight,*
> *All melodies the echo of that voice*
> *All colours a suffusion from that light.*[2]

This is what love signally does not do to Mr Knightley, the man who loves most wisely in Jane Austen. He loves and censures Emma: he does not hear the echo of her voice in all melodies, but he sees her with a cool judgement that (it seems) has taken no imprint, suffered no transfiguration, through his passion. 'I cannot see you acting wrong,' he says to Emma, 'without a remonstrance.' We admire his judgement; we admit (if we know the story) that he is probably suffering; but—*transfigured?* Anything but that. When he makes his declaration he speaks 'in a tone of . . . sincere, decided, intelligible tenderness'. Mr Knightley is always intelligible, always himself.

What is the opposite to this? Lydia Bennet, perhaps. Lydia loves Wickham without judgement or restraint: she is blinded by love:

> Lydia was exceedingly fond of him. He was her dear Wickham on every occasion; no one was to be put in competition with him. He did everything best in the world; and she was sure he would kill more birds on the first of September than anybody else in the country.[3]

What a fool Lydia is. Besotted with Wickham, she wearies everyone with her garrulous infatuation. Facts are not horrid things for her, she simply adjusts them to her desires. When Elizabeth marries Darcy, she gets a letter of congratulation from Lydia.

> My Dear Lizzy,—I wish you joy. If you love Mr Darcy half so well as I do my dear Wickham, you must be very happy. It is a great comfort to have you so rich; and when you have

---

[1] Coleridge, *Dejection: an Ode*, ll. 62-3
[2] Ibid., ll. 73-5
[3] *Pride and Prejudice*, ch. 51

nothing else to do, I hope you will think of us. I am sure Wickham would like a place at court very much; and I do not think we shall have quite money enough to live upon without some help. Any place would do of about three or four hundred a year; but, however, do not speak to Mr Darcy about it, if you had rather not.[1]

Could anything be more delightfully, selfishly *stupid* than this? Lydia has learnt nothing about the world, or about other people. This is Jane Austen's satire at its most sparkling. And yet, whether she intended to or not (she surely did not), Jane Austen has given to Lydia, in however distorted a form, the one overwhelming virtue that love teaches. She has forgotten herself in someone else. She does not say to Lizzy that *she* would like to be the wife of someone at court, she says that Wickham would like it. Since Jane Austen is making fun of Lydia's wish to use her sister, this distinction must have seemed unimportant to her. But it is not unimportant: it is in one way the most important of all. Lydia is exploiting her sister with gay unscrupulousness, but she is not exploiting her simply for herself. The letter is stupid, and grasping, but is it selfish? Lydia is still shallow, but she has learnt to put her shallowness at the service of someone else. Her emotions are now invested in her husband. She is as foolish as ever, but in that sort of folly lies a kind of happiness.

Impulsive, scatter-brained, highly sexed, self-deceiving, Lydia loves according to her nature. Jane Austen values such love less than Mr Knightley's love for Emma, and no doubt she is right. But the element which Mr Knightley hasn't (the forgetfulness of self and even of principle in the intensity of otherness), and which Lydia has in distorted form, is the element that can lead us to the finest love of all. It can (for instance) lead us to

'Oh you are a wise man, are you not? You know all about life and death. Advise me. Think what I can do. He has been labouring all his life and looking forward. He minds about nothing else. And I mind about nothing else—'

For years after Lydgate remembered the impression produced in him by this involuntary appeal—this cry from soul to soul, without other consciousness than their moving with kindred natures in the same embroiled medium, the same troublous fitfully-illuminated life.[2]

[1] *Pride and Prejudice*, ch. 51   [2] *Middlemarch*, ch. 30

The love that Jane Austen values is neither openly sexual, nor like that of Anne Brangwen, in *The Rainbow*, 'a great steadiness, a core of living eternity', but is born of gratitude and esteem. Nor is it love at first sight:

> If gratitude and esteem are good foundations of affection, Elizabeth's change of sentiment will be neither improbable nor faulty. But if otherwise—if the regard springing from such sources is unreasonable or unnatural, in comparison of what is often described as arising on a first interview with its object, and even before two words have been exchanged—nothing can be said in her defence, except that she had given somewhat of a trial to the latter method, in her partiality for Wickham, and that its ill success might, perhaps, authorize her to seek the other less interesting mode of attachment.[1]

The whole plot of *Pride and Prejudice* is a defence of the less interesting mode of attachment. And while we are reading, this paragraph is surely an unexceptionable and consistent reflection: it is only if we look at it in isolation, freed from the spell of the context, that we pause to doubt. (And as I say this I realise that I have nakedly exposed my critical method to the rejection of those for whom the aim of reading is simply to submit oneself, as completely as possible, to a book's spell.) Is there not, as we weigh up the tone of that paragraph, something defensive to it, a careful disdain for the 'infatuation' that is being rejected? 'Arising on a first interview with its object'—why did Jane Austen feel it necessary to call the beloved an *object*? It's a mild joke to be sure—but why did she feel it necessary to joke? The irony of the final phrase ('the other less interesting mode of attachment') is too effective: it is as if she is daring us to disagree, and we realise that we wish to. There is a resistance to emotion underlying this paragraph that it is very tempting to call old-maidish.

The love that Jane Austen admires is reasonable. When Elizabeth is able to say to herself that she regards Darcy 'with an interest, if not quite so tender, at least as reasonable as what Jane felt for Bingley', then we know all will be well: tenderness will wait on reason, though the reverse could never be assumed. To debate on the reasonableness of one's emotions would be, in a Lawrence character, a sign of emotional sterility, of timidity and fear of

[1] *Pride and Prejudice*, ch. 46

surrender; if we could translate it into Lawrence's so utterly
different style, could we not picture the following as the author's
comment on, say Clifford Chatterley, on Dr Mitchell of *The Lost
Girl*, on other characters in whom the springs of feeling have died.

> (I) look with a degree of contempt on the inquisitive and
> doubting fancies of that heart which seems always debating
> on the reasonableness of its emotions.[1]

But the speaker is Lady Susan; the 'inquisitive and doubting fancies'
are those of the sympathetic Reginald, and the sentence is a summary of all that Jane Austen invites us to fear and dislike in her
villainess.

4 Second Objection; the anti-Jane

The second objection is perhaps more interesting: it concerns
what I will call the anti-Jane. Even if Jane Austen held to these
beliefs, runs this objection, even if she placed principle before love,
and love based on principle before love based on passion or impulse,
did she *really* hold them? Did the novelist always support the moralist: or do the principles impose a check on, even contend against,
the very emotions that her creative power engenders? If this is so,
the ambivalence will be most evident in those characters who charm
but are to be rejected: those too attractive for the stern check which
the moral scheme of the book imposes on them: those who embody
too much of the kind of energy Jane Austen rejects, but cannot
make us reject. I have already mentioned Lydia Bennet, and before
moving on to two more complex figures I will say another word
about her. Has anyone remarked the resemblance between Lydia
and her sister Jane: that Lydia's blindness to the faults of Wickham
is not unlike Jane's blindness? Not that Bingley has many faults,
but his sisters have, and Jane cannot see them. Elizabeth once
takes her to task for this:

> 'Oh, you are a great deal too apt, you know, to like people in
> general. You never see a fault in anybody. All the world are
> good and agreeable in your eyes. I never heard you speak ill
> of a human being in my life.'
> 'I would wish not to be hasty in censuring any one; but I
> always speak what I think.'

[1] *Lady Susan*, letter 16

'I know you do; and it is *that* which makes the wonder. With your good sense, to be so honestly blind to the follies and nonsense of others!'[1]

What is Jane Austen's attitude to such honest blindness? In Lydia she questions its honesty, and disapproves; in Miss Bates she makes it gloriously comic, a comedy whose underlying attitude is surely little better than a kindly contempt; and even in Jane she can't really think well of it. What we are to admire is Elizabeth's attitude: her sharp perception of Jane's folly, and her indulgence of it because she is fond of Jane—or perhaps we should continue to prefer principle to affection, and say 'because Jane is good, not bad'. Jane Austen has a low opinion of indulgence or generosity if they are based on imperceptiveness: she respects those who forgive faults they have perceived, not those who fail to perceive them.

But the anti-Jane lives most vigorously not in *Pride and Prejudice* but in *Sense and Sensibility* and *Mansfield Park*; the characters who threaten to escape from their creator's rein, far more than Lydia Bennet, are the Crawfords and Marianne Dashwood. I begin with Mary Crawford.

Almost everyone who reads *Mansfield Park* is drawn to Mary. How like Elizabeth Bennet she is—how like Jane Austen too, for that matter.

> (Marriage) is, of all transactions, the one in which people expect most from others, and are least honest themselves.[2]

This is not one of the scintillating comments of the author herself, but is made by Mary Crawford to Mrs Grant. Mary not only has her creator's wit, she has her discernment too: she sees Dr Grant for what he clearly is:

> an indolent, selfish, *bon vivant*, who must have his palate consulted in everything; who will not stir a finger for the convenience of any one; and who, moreover, if the cook makes a blunder, is out of humour with his excellent wife.[3]

She can behave with a graciousness that far exceeds mere politeness: when Maria Bertram is indulging her own silly vanity in describing the extent of Mr Rushworth's estate:

[1] *Pride and Prejudice*, ch. 4   [2] *Mansfield Park*, ch. 5   [3] Ibid., ch. 11

Miss Crawford was not slow to admire; she pretty well guessed Miss Bertram's feelings, and made it a point of honour to promote her enjoyment to the utmost.[1]

The feelings she guesses are Maria's chagrin that Henry has invited Julia and not herself to sit next to him; and Miss Crawford's behaviour shows both delicacy in realising this and kindness in reacting accordingly. As for Mary Crawford's treatment of Fanny, it could hardly be bettered: when Mrs Norris had just insulted Fanny with even more than her usual viciousness, Mary said, 'with some keenness "I do not like my situation; this *place* is too hot for me",' sat next to Fanny, and 'with pointed attention continued to talk to her, and endeavour to raise her spirits, in spite of being out of spirits herself'. That last detail is high praise indeed, in Jane Austen: and it was hardly necessary for her to add the comment that Mary had been 'almost purely governed' by really good feelings—a comment which wholly agrees, for once, with the impact made by the scene itself.

Is this the Mary Crawford who tempts Edmund from the true love he feels—or ought to feel—for Fanny; who is wicked because selfish, and dangerous because charming; and who is finally exposed, to Edmund and to us, when her comments on the elopement of Henry and Maria reveal her lack of true moral standards ('no harsher name than folly given!')? It is all too much for us to accept. Jane Austen set herself what we can see to be a version of the problem of how to depict Satan: we can see this, and sympathise; but to sympathise is not to grant success. Mary Crawford has to be made attractive, or there will be nothing to reject at the end; but the more attractive she is, the harder it is to make the rejection convincing. And Mary Crawford is never more alive than when most sympathetic: never less convincingly drawn than during the rejection. It must have been a temptation to the author to make Mary commit some obviously wicked action, so as to expose her thoroughly in our eyes; and we must admire her integrity in renouncing so cheap, so grossly inconsistent an effect, and in exposing her simply through what she says to Edmund. Indeed, what she says to Edmund ('What can equal the folly of our two relations?') is almost plausible: she spoke of the clergy in a very similar tone, before she knew that Edmund was to be a clergyman. Yet though scruple might not

---

[1] *Mansfield Park*, ch. 8

have prevented her speaking thus, good sense surely would have. She still wishes to marry Edmund, and if she has even a fraction of the sensitivity we saw in her earlier scene with Fanny, she must know what effect such speaking is likely to have on him.

And even if we grant the plausibility of Mary Crawford saying it all, must we not find the whole episode a rather feeble exposure, in a book where actions count for so much ('facts are such horrid things'). Jane Austen had to choose between the more thorough exposure of Henry Crawford, that does not convince, and the more convincing one of his sister, that does not thoroughly expose.

I have no doubt that, consciously or not, Jane Austen was not wholly satisfied with this scene. For one thing, she reports it instead of describing it direct: a common way for her to avoid some crisis or major revelation that she does not feel up to handling (such as Mr Knightley's love-talk to Emma). For another, there is the hollowness of Edmund's rhetoric ('No reluctance, no horror, no feminine—shall I say no modest loathings?': this is rather much, even from Edmund). Above all, there is the final, melodramatic moment when Mary, all pretence of resemblance to her earlier self now gone, makes her last, symbolic appeal:

> I had gone a few steps, Fanny, when I heard the door open be-hind me. 'Mr Bertram,' said she. I looked back. 'Mr Bertram,' said she, with a smile; but it was a smile ill suited to the conver-sation that had passed—a saucy, playful smile, seeming to invite, in order to subdue me; at least it appeared so to me. I resisted —it was the impulse of the moment to resist—and still walked on. I have since, sometimes, for a moment, regretted that I did not go back; but I know I was right.[1]

I do not believe that Jane Austen, if asked, would have been able to give a plausible account of what Mary Crawford was after at at that instant. The calling back suggests a change of heart from her recent mocking speech; but a change of heart would interfere with our final impression of her wickedness (for we are not to see her again), and she is therefore given her ill-suiting smile. Jane Austen has, for once, completely lost interest in the motivation of a character, transforming her into nothing less than Temptation itself. It is the most symbolic moment in all her novels—and one of the least convincing. This scene fails for the very reason that,

[1] Ibid., ch. 47

for so much of the book, Mary Crawford succeeds: she embodies the qualities that *Mansfield Park* was written to assail, but she also embodies more of the book's creative energy than anyone else— more than Fanny, and far, far more than the worthy and dreary Edmund, who comes to life only when he is material for comedy (as in Chapter XIV). *Mansfield Park* is a book divided against itself.

So is *Sense and Sensibility*: and it is worth mentioning that (after *Emma*, the undoubted masterpiece) these are the two most powerful and disturbing of the novels. *Pride and Prejudice* may be a more perfect work of art, but it does not touch us to the quick as can these two mixed-up books. *Sense and Sensibility* is mixed-up in the most radical way imaginable. It is meant to be a comedy in which we come to realise the superiority of Sense: we are to be fond of Marianne, but we are to smile at her, and we are to see that Elinor's restraint and wisdom are more valuable than her emotionalism. And so Marianne makes her appearance as someone we are not to take wholly seriously: we are told that Colonel Brandon appears to her 'an absolute old bachelor, for he was on the wrong side of five and thirty' and if we know that she is eventually to marry him we smile. When she sings at the Middletons, he is the only one who listens to her:

> His pleasure in music, though it amounted not to that ecstatic delight which alone could sympathise with her own, was estimable when contrasted against the horrible insensibility of the others; and she was reasonable enough to allow that a man of five and thirty might well have outlived all acuteness of feeling and every exquisite power of enjoyment. She was perfectly disposed to make every allowance for the colonel's advanced state of life which humanity required.[1]

This is how Marianne is treated before the appearance of Willoughby and right at the end of the book she is married off in the same tone:

> Marianne Dashwood was born to an extraordinary fate. She was born to discover the falsehood of her own opinions, and to counteract, by her conduct, her most favourite maxims. She was born to overcome an affection formed so late in life as at seventeen, and with no sentiment superior to strong esteem and lively friendship, voluntarily to give her hand to another!— and *that* other, a man who had suffered no less than herself

[1] *Sense and Sensibility*, ch. 7

under the event of a former attachment, whom two years before, she had considered too old to be married,—and who still sought the constitutional safeguard of a flannel waistcoat.[1]

The tone of this, surely, is not quite right: the tone, or its content. 'No sentiment superior to strong esteem and lively friendship': does Jane Austen then not believe in love? Does the love which is based on gratitude and esteem turn out simply to *be* gratitude and esteem? And that last old-maidish joke about the flannel waist-coat: can we not hear too audibly the relief that marriage is not going to contain anything excessive, anything violent, anything common?

Yet on its own the paragraph is not likely to jar; and it would not jar if we turned straight to it after reading the first eight chapters. For *Sense and Sensibility* begins as pure comedy, and continues so for eight chapters, chapters of unmixed delight. If we are disturbed at finding this note at the end, it is because we have in the meantime read the tragedy of Marianne.

> 'Oh! Elinor,' she cried, 'you have made me hate myself for ever. How barbarous have I been to you!—you, who have been my only comfort, who have borne with me in all my misery, who have seemed to be only suffering for me!—is this my gratitude? Is this the only return I can make you? Because your merit cries out upon myself, I have been trying to do it away.'[2]

Such an outburst shatters the shell of comedy, and puts Marianne in front of us as a suffering woman, not affecting sensibility, but feeling passion; and it is not an isolated moment, but a carefully prepared climax. For the thirty-nine central chapters of the book she has been learning her lessons too painfully for banter.

And by not remaining a comedy *Sense and Sensibility* fails in its professed aim: it does not succeed in winning us to the side of Sense. The two faults are one. Jane Austen set herself the task of making fun of Marianne, and engaging sympathy for Elinor: if sympathy for Marianne becomes too violent, if Marianne more than Elinor seems to embody the book's positives, then we shall not be led to the intended conclusion. And this is what happens: Marianne, in the intense seriousness with which she is presented, engages our sympathy at a level that makes us want to locate the positives in *her*:

---

[1] Ibid., ch. 50   [2] Ibid., ch. 36

This was the season of happiness to Marianne. Her heart was devoted to Willoughby, and the fond attachment to Norland which she brought with her from Sussex, was more likely to be softened than she had thought it possible before, by the charms which his society bestowed on her present home.[1]

The gentle, leisurely second sentence could have been written of Elinor: but not the blunt brief opening sentence. Its immediacy, its impulsive directness—this is the way Marianne is spoken of, and Marianne only.

To illustrate what I mean by saying that Marianne embodies the strongest positives in the book, I must quote at length. The Dashwood sisters—like all Jane Austen heroines—have to spend a good deal of their time in the company of malicious and importunate women. Elinor finds it hard to put up with the Misses Steele: for Lucy Steele confides in her in order to gratify her envy, and Ann is a nuisance through sheer stupidity. The Misses Steele call in the middle of Marianne's grief, and the elder says 'I am sorry we cannot see your sister, Miss Dashwood. I am sorry she is not well.' Elinor does her best to put her off, but the silly woman insists that Marianne will see 'such old friends as Lucy and me'.

> Elinor, with great civility, declined the proposal. 'Her sister was perhaps laid down upon the bed, or in her dressing-gown, and therefore not able to come to them.'
>
> 'Oh, if that's all,' cried Miss Steele, 'we can just as well go and see *her*.'
>
> Elinor began to find this impertinence too much for her temper; but she was saved the trouble of checking it, by Lucy's sharp reprimand.[2]

The effect of such episodes is to feed our irritation. We too find the impertinence (of the Steele sisters, of Mrs Ferrars, of Fanny Dashwood) too much for our tempers, and as we move through the book our impatience mounts, our need to put a check to this constant and insensitive insolence. And then comes an episode in which the irritation is released. At the dinner party which the Dashwoods give in Chapter XXXV, almost all the ill-will and cattiness in the book is gathered together. As the gentlemen enter the drawing-room, they notice, and admire, a pair of screens that Elinor

[1] *Sense and Sensibility*, ch. 11   [2] Ibid., ch. 32

has painted for her sister-in-law; the screens are passed round, and justify their presence in the novel by the rich variety of comments they excite.

Mrs Ferrars, not aware of their being Elinor's work, particularly requested to look at them; and after they had received the gratifying testimony of Lady Middleton's approbation, Fanny presented them to her mother, considerately informing her at the same time that they were done by Miss Dashwood.

'Hum'—said Mrs Ferrars—'very pretty,'—and without regarding them at all, returned them to her daughter.

Perhaps Fanny thought for a moment that her mother had been quite rude enough,—for, colouring a little, she immediately said,

'They are very pretty, ma'am—an't they?' But then again, the dread of having been too civil came over her, for she presently added,

'Do you not think they are something in Miss Morton's style of painting, ma'am? She *does* paint most delightfully. How beautifully her last landscape is done!'

'Beautifully indeed. But *she* does everything well.'

Marianne could not bear this. She was already greatly displeased with Mrs Ferrars; and such ill-timed praise of another, at Elinor's expense, though she had not any notion of what was principally meant by it, provoked her immediately to say with warmth,

'This is admiration of a very particular kind! What is Miss Morton to us? Who knows or cares for her? It is Elinor of whom *we* think and speak.'

And so saying, she took the screens out of her sister-in-law's hand to admire them herself as they ought to be admired.

Mrs Ferrars looked exceedingly angry, and drawing herself up more stiffly than ever, pronounced in retort this bitter phillipic: 'Miss Morton is Lord Morton's daughter.'

Fanny looked very angry too, and her husband was all in fright at his sister's audacity. Elinor was much more hurt by Marianne's warmth, than she had been by what produced it; but Colonel Brandon's eyes, as they were fixed on Marianne, declared that he noticed only what was amiable in it; the affectionate heart which could not bear to see a sister slighted in the smallest point.[1]

---

[1] Ibid., ch. 34

I have quoted at length; but no quotation could be long enough to convey the effect of this moment when we come upon it: for the tension that Marianne releases has been building up not only all through dinner, but all through the visit to London—indeed, all through the book. When Elinor feels such an impulse, she bottles it up, or is saved by circumstances from uttering it; but now at last Marianne has spoken to one of these vicious old women as they deserve. No one else would have done it, for those two patterns of masculine behaviour, Edward Farrars and Colonel Brandon, are impeccable in observing propriety; and where propriety demands restraint (as it usually does), restraint there will be. Colonel Brandon may be endangering Marianne's happiness if he doesn't reveal the horrid truth about Willoughby, but he has no right to speak, so he resists the improper impulse. The tension in this scene has built up so strongly because of Jane Austen's unique combination of truthtelling and acceptance. Jane Austen is a conservative in manners, and doesn't want impropriety from her sympathetic characters; but such propriety assumes a certain evasiveness (Elinor is the one on whom 'the whole task of telling lies when politeness required it always fell'), and is undermined by the ruthless analysis that the novels offer. So when at last Marianne allows her impulses to follow where the satiric analysis has pointed— when she yields to rudeness and snaps at Mrs Ferrars—the whole novel has been straining towards the assent we give her.

But if *Sense and Sensibility* is inviting us to feel as Marianne does about Mrs Ferrars, it is also urging us to condemn the expression of such feeling. Convention and truthtelling—the conservatism of propriety and the radicalism of satire—jostle unreconciled in the last paragraph of this quotation. Jane Austen's own comment is probably Elinor's, who 'was much more hurt by Marianne's warmth, than she had been by what produced it'; but if we want to cry shame on Elinor, we can do so with Colonel Brandon, blinded by love into transcending his author's preferences.

Marianne, says Marvin Mudrick, is 'the life and centre of the book'; and the most brilliant chapter of his book on Jane Austen defends her against her creator. I will not repeat his arguments, but I will consider the reply we might have expected Jane Austen to make. This is that we are wrong to contrast a passionate Marianne with a prudent Elinor, for Elinor too has her passions: only she has the wisdom to control them. 'She had an excellent heart; her disposition was affectionate, and her feelings were strong: but she knew how to govern them.' That at the beginning of the book; and at the end the mother comes to acknowledge 'that in Elinor she might have a daughter suffering almost as much, certainly with less self-provocation, and greater fortitude'. So when Marianne, having discovered that Elinor's love affair has been going as badly as hers, suggests that her self-command has been made easier because she does not feel much, she is corrected in a long eloquent speech ('the composure of mind with which I have brought myself at present to consider the matter, the consolation that I have been willing to admit, have been the effect of constant and painful exertion') that wrings from Marianne the self-reproach quoted above. Nothing could make the book's intention plainer than that: and perhaps nothing could at the same time defeat the intention so clearly. Elinor is eloquent, but Marianne is moved; and in the very moment of admitting that she has wronged her sister by under-estimating her suffering, she speaks with the accent of suffering herself; an accent we never hear from Elinor.

For it is not enough that Jane Austen should tell us that Elinor feels deeply: she must convince us as an artist, not merely announce an intention. Her failure seems due to one cause above all others: that when Elinor's strong feelings are mentioned, this is almost invariably accompanied by an assurance that she was able to govern them:

> 'I did,' said Elinor, with a composure of voice under which was concealed an emotion and distress beyond anything she had ever felt before. She was mortified, shocked, confounded.[1]

The composure of voice is almost always there. This is unwise rhetoric on Jane Austen's part; and the result is that it is hard for us to believe in these strong feelings: as we hear them so continually linked to the successful effort to control them, to smile, to conceal what it would be improper to betray, we can hardly credit them with a separate existence.

I know of only one moment when Elinor's emotion rings as true as Marianne's, and it occurs in Marianne's great tragic scene, of the reception of Willoughby's letter.

> Again they were both silent. Elinor was employed in walking thoughtfully from the fire to the window, from the window

---

[1] *Sense and Sensibility*, ch. 22

to the fire, without knowing that she received warmth from one, or discerning objects through the other; and Marianne, seated at the foot of the bed, with her head leaning against one of its posts, again took up Willoughby's letter, and after shuddering over every sentence, exclaimed—[1]

Here for once Elinor's grief seems the more genuine of the two: it is Marianne who uses rhetoric, Elinor who is presented in the physical immediacy of her sorrow. And even this paragraph probably does her less good than it should in our eyes: for it is not her own grief that is in question, but her sharing of Marianne's, and coming in the midst of Marianne's tragedy, it probably rests in the mind as a reflex from that, rather than as Elinor's very own emotion.

The true heroine of *Sense and Sensibility* is Marianne; and her true conquest is not over Colonel Brandon but over the propriety in whose name the author puts her down. The result is that a perfect comedy of manners was spoilt, and a great flawed novel written.

5 'Persuasion'; a novel by the anti-Jane

In Lydia Bennet briefly, in Mary Crawford more thoroughly, and in Marianne with full and passionate intensity, we can see the anti-Jane who lived unquelled in the moralist, and tore her books apart: until, in the end, she won her mistress over. For in Jane Austen's last novel, *Persuasion*, left unperfected and published posthumously, intensity of feeling moves nearer to the centre of the book's professed values. It is Jane Austen's one romantic novel: the one book in which love is not the product of gratitude and esteem. It sets out with a pattern which might have been dictated by the anti-Jane:

> She had been forced into prudence in her youth, she learned romance as she grew older: the natural sequel of an unnatural beginning.[2]

This is the very opposite to Marianne's development, or Edmund Bertram's, or Elizabeth Bennet's. It is true that Elizabeth's love is contrasted with the caricature of prudence represented by Charlotte: but it is equally contrasted with Lydia's (or her own) infatuation with Wickham. There is no simple contrast between prudence and romance in *Pride and Prejudice*, but a threefold

---

[1] *Sense and Sensibility*, ch. 29   [2] *Persuasion*, ch. 4

scheme with Elizabeth in the middle. And since Elizabeth moves from infatuation—or a narrow escape from it—to learning to love Darcy as she discovers his merits, it would not be wholly wrong to say that her change is the reverse of Anne's.

Persuasion is shot through not with the praise of prudence, but with that of impulse. Consider, for example, the character of Admiral Croft. He is a man of 'hearty good humour' and 'open trusting liberality': impulsive, tactless, recklessly good-natured. When he takes his wife for a drive in the gig, Captain Wentworth remarks:

> I wonder whereabouts they will upset today. Oh! it does happen very often, I assure you; but my sister makes nothing of it; she would as lieve be tossed out as not.[1]

When he hears the story of Louisa's fall, this is Admiral Croft's comment:

> 'Ay, a very bad business, indeed. A new sort of way this, for a young fellow to be making love, by breaking his mistress' head, is not it, Miss Elliott? This is breaking a head and giving a plaster, truly!'
>
> Admiral Croft's manners were not quite of the tone to suit Lady Russell, but they delighted Anne. His goodness of heart and simplicity of character were irresistible.[2]

Now both these episodes show Admiral Croft behaving in a way you would normally expect to draw rebuke. If he had driven Fanny Price as he drives Anne, his author would not have let him indulge his carelessness unblamed; but she puts into Anne's mind an amused indulgence that she clearly shares. In his remark on Louisa he is causing pain to Anne by the casual reference to Wentworth's courting of Louisa—unintentionally, it is true, but that is not always an excuse in Jane Austen. In this case, however, he is not merely forgiven by the author: he delights both us and the author and Anne, and Anne's distress is (improbably) forgotten. If Admiral Croft has an equivalent in other books, it is surely Mrs Jennings (it takes us a long time before we are sure we like her) or Mr Weston, the 'unmanageable goodwill of (whose) temper' causes so much harm in *Emma*. Admiral Croft is not only more attractive than either of them, he has an equally impulsive and delightful wife.

[1] *Persuasion*, ch. 10   [2] Ibid., ch. 13

He even makes himself agreeable to children. In his case it is a 'good-humoured notice' he takes of them, quite different from the sycophancy of the Misses Steele; and it leads to this scene at parting:

> He was cut short by the eager attacks of the little boys, clinging to him like an old friend, and declaring he should not go; and being too much engrossed by proposals of carrying them away in his coat pocket, etc., to have another moment for finishing or recollecting what he had begun.[1]

This is the nearest thing in Jane Austen to George Eliot's treatment of children: the boys have sniffed out the goodness in Admiral Croft, and almost become a moral norm.

Admiral Croft is not exceptional in the scheme of *Persuasion*, but a pointer to the set of values in the book as a whole. Frederick Wentworth is the most headstrong of all Jane Austen's heroes— and the most attractive: utterly different from her one other successful portrait of a hero, the dignified, high-minded, thoughtful Mr Knightley. Wentworth's thoughtlessness almost gets him engaged to a girl he does not love; but though Jane Austen is clear that it would have been his own fault, she does not really like him the less for this, and nor do we. The action that first brings him close to Anne again is his securing her a ride in the Crofts' gig when she is tired:

> It was a reminder of former sentiment; it was an impulse of pure, though unacknowledged, friendship; it was a proof of his own warm and amiable heart, which she could not contemplate without emotions so compounded of pleasure and pain, that she knew not which prevailed.[2]

It is indeed an impulse: the gig was already driving off 'when Captain Wentworth cleared the hedge in a moment, to say something to his sister'. What more can one ask of a headstrong hero than that he should leap hedges in this way?

And Anne: she loves as no other Jane Austen heroine loves. Passion overcomes her as it never overcame Emma, or Fanny, or Elizabeth. Her scrupulous care in avoiding awkwardness when Captain Wentworth returns after eight years, her anxiety to meet him as little as possible, is standard Jane Austen: what is new is our

---

[1] *Persuasion*, ch. 6   [2] Ibid., ch. 10

involvement with her feelings, the fact that she *needs* to control her emotions. The scene in which the former lovers meet has a power we have hardly met with before, the power of rendering agitation, the confusion of sight and sound when a dreaded and exciting moment at last comes:

> . . . a thousand feelings rushed on Anne, of which this was the most consoling, that it would soon be over. And it was soon over. In two minutes after Charles's preparation, the others appeared; they were in the drawing-room. Her eye half met Captain Wentworth's, a bow, a courtesy passed; she heard his voice; he talked to Mary, said all that was right, said something to the Miss Musgroves, enough to mark an easy footing; the room seemed full, full of persons and voices, but a few minutes ended it. Charles showed himself at the window, all was ready, their visitor had bowed and was gone, the Miss Musgroves were gone too, suddenly resolving to walk to the end of the village with the sportsmen; the room was cleared, and Anne might finish her breakfast as she could.[1]

This is truly mimetic of emotion—the only occasion in all Jane Austen. The prose scampers as breathlessly as Anne's confused but intense impressions. Anne's love is as strong as Portia's: all the other passions turn to air. 'For a few minutes' (when she sees Captain Wentworth at Bath) 'she saw nothing before her: it was all confusion.' I have said that no other Jane Austen heroine loves like this, but of course that is not quite true. Marianne Dashwood does: only she is not quite a heroine. Marianne is as violent in her passion, and more intemperate in her grief. She differs from Anne not in feeling but in conduct: Anne never behaves foolishly, as Marianne does. Excessive feeling blinds Marianne and causes her not to notice the distress of her sister: such at any rate is the intention, though we may feel that we too cannot always see Elinor's distress. Anne is never blinded: strong feeling never leads her into egoism. She is sense and sensibility combined: she behaves as well as Elinor, and has the passionate sensibility of Marianne.

Persuasion is the one book in which Jane Austen ceased to see any contrast between sense and passion, and in which what distinguishes the heroine from the other characters—what makes her the heroine ,almost—is the intensity of her emotions. Anne and Marianne are the two Jane Austen heroines who come closest to

---

[1] *Ibid.*, ch. 7

tragedy. Once or twice, Anne's thoughts disturb us on a level deeper than the gay comedy of Jane Austen can altogether control. One such moment occurs when she is speaking to Captain Harville, knowing now that she loves Wentworth, but not yet sure if he returns it.

> 'All the privilege I claim for my own sex (it is not a very enviable one: you need not covet it), is that of loving longest, when existence or when hope is gone!'[1]

She speaks to Captain Harville but she thinks of Wentworth: and the words emerge from the ironic situation to strike us direct with their meaning. It is another of those rare glimpses of a Conrad in Jane Austen.

Another such moment comes when Wentworth's first impression of her is reported to Anne: that he had found her 'so altered that he should not have known her again'. Having once or twice seen Jane Austen as Conrad, I will here take an even wilder flight of fancy and see her as Proust: discovering the effect of time on identity, and the fact that it is a blend of subjective and objective change:

> No: the years which had destroyed her youth and bloom had only given him a more glowing, manly, open look, in no respect lessening his personal advantages. She had seen the same Frederick Wentworth.[2]

Has Anne changed more than Wentworth? Or is he looking with eyes that perceive change, and she with eyes that do not. Of course Jane Austen is not like Proust, who would have discussed with sad eloquence how difficult it is to know. But at least she has recorded the starting-point of such a discussion.

Such then are the resemblances between Jane Austen's two most passionate women. The difference between them is part of a difference in technique between the two novels. In *Sense and Sensibility* the point of view is regularly that of Elinor, and we see Marianne only from the outside; but in *Persuasion* the point of view is Anne's, so that we see the passionate love from within. This ought—ought it not?—to lead to a more immediate sympathy.

But does it? Do we feel involved with Anne in the same way that, despite the book's official self, we feel involved with Marianne? We ought not to underrate the importance of point of view: every

---

[1] *Persuasion*, ch. 23   [2] Ibid., ch. 7

time Anne suffers, the author now has an opportunity to show her feelings with a directness that will mobilise all the natural habits of the novel-reader in sympathy. With some novelists—with George Eliot, with Lawrence, with Tolstoi—this would almost guarantee a sympathy with Anne beyond the reach of anything felt for Marianne. But there are also those novelists with whom it wouldn't: Conrad, James, Flaubert, perhaps Stendahl—and Jane Austen. These are the ironists, the masters of point of view and its shifting effects; these are the writers who involve us most deeply with those characters they have brooded about most carefully, deciding, perhaps, just what to tell us and what not to tell us about them, and through whose eyes we shall see each detail. These are the novelists who can arouse sudden, surprising sympathies by a shift in viewpoint, by an understanding which feeds on the mingling of inside and outside views. We feel all the more deeply for Lord Jim as a result of the difficulty of being quite sure about him. And Jane Austen, working with so fine a brush on her 'little bit (two inches wide) of ivory' perhaps belongs with these. Her genius was not for the direct rendering of intense states of consciousness; and the passion of Marianne, struggling against that genius, has in the end, perhaps, a force greater than that of Anne Elliott.

Persuasion is a much loved novel: more loved than praised. Almost everyone agrees that it might have opened a new vein in Jane Austen: Mr Mudrick entitles his essay on it 'The Liberation of Feeling'. But few critics are willing to say that it really achieves the kind of power that Jane Austen had not previously had. Perhaps there is a beginning: at least she has shed the evasiveness of her earlier love scenes (or non-scenes). There is no more of:

> What did she say? Just what she ought, of course. A lady always does.[1]

We now have an attempt to treat the declaration-scene without coyness:

> There they exchanged again those feelings and those promises which had once before seemed to secure everything, but which had been followed by so many, many years of division and estrangements. There they returned again into the past, more exquisitely happy, perhaps, in their reunion, than when it had

[1] *Emma*, ch. 49

171

been first projected; more tender, more tried, more fixed in a knowledge of each other's character, truth, and attachment; more equal to act, more justified in acting. And there, as they slowly paced the gradual ascent, heedless of every group around them, seeing neither sauntering politicians, bustling housekeepers, flirting girls, nor nursery-maids and children, they could indulge in those retrospections and acknowledgements, and especially in those explanations of what had directly preceded the present moment, which were so poignant and so ceaseless in interest.[1]

This has a directness that is new in Jane Austen: it is the one love-scene with no touch of the old maid. But to shed coyness is only a negative virtue; to have cleared obstacles from one's path need not mean one has walked along it. And though there is an honest eloquence in this passage, and perhaps a flavour of the vivid half-seeing of the lovers absorbed in each other, it is only eloquence; just as the intensity of Anne's feelings, though well stated, is (except for the agitation of the first meeting) only stated. We cannot be certain that *Persuasion* would have led to new powers in Jane Austen. We cannot be certain that it marked a permanent change of direction: there is, after all, *Sanditon*, which followed, and there are parts of *Persuasion* itself—Sir Walter and Mary, for instance—which are plain Jane. Even if the change had come, and Jane Austen had lived to write more novels like it, her new vein might have been more pleasant, more attractively open, and paid for this with the loss of her genius.

II D. H. LAWRENCE

1 'The Plumed Serpent': the Pernicious and the Bad

Though I have had to modify my assertion that Jane Austen thought impulses should be restrained, the modifications are not such as to blunt the edge of the contrast I shall now draw with Lawrence. Lawrence will need more space than Jane Austen, not only because he wrote more, and is a more complex figure, but also because he lacks her splendid epigrammatic clarity.

Every reader of Lawrence, except the blindly prejudiced or the

---

[1] *Persuasion*, ch. 23

besotted disciple, feels the need to make discriminations in his work. No modern writer cries out for it more urgently. So much greatness and so much hot air; so much insight and so much pernicious nonsense, and the insight and the nonsense so intimately and perilously related. How are we to sort one from the other?

There is of course only one way to do this: book by book, response by response. The way to sort the good from the bad in Lawrence is to read his works with critical sensitivity—the sensitivity which accepts *The Rainbow* and rejects *The Plumed Serpent*. The Aristotelian critic will do this, perhaps arranging his discussion chronologically, moving from one book to the next, and offering a balanced view of the success and limitations of each. Every critic must be able to do this, but the Platonic critic will try something riskier: he will want to know if there is a principle, a formula, that describes in more general terms how Lawrence's success differs from this failure. And for a deeply committed writer like Lawrence, he will want to state this principle, not in purely aesthetic terms, but in relation to his view of life. Has artistic success and failure in Lawrence some correspondence with what is quick or diseased in his conception of man? I believe it has: and I have constructed my discussion of Lawrence accordingly, beginning with a critique of a single novel to show that its artistic faults are connected with what is pernicious in the message.

I am sad to begin with *The Plumed Serpent*: the worst of all Lawrence's novels. I begin with it for a methodological reason, and hope that it will not introduce a sour note into the discussion. It is, alas, often easier to establish one's critical position negatively, just as hostile criticism often finds more occasion to be eloquent than laudatory criticism. I hope no one will count the pages of praise and blame that follow, and take them to represent the fractions of like and dislike in my view of Lawrence.

The three novels of Lawrence's middle period, *Aaron's Rod*, *Kangaroo* and *The Plumed Serpent*, are sometimes called the 'fascist' novels. They are Lawrence's worst, and *The Plumed Serpent* is the worst of all: yet because it is the most ambitious (and the most fascist) it is bad in a more unified, more coherent way than the others. I cannot feel it necessary to discuss all three at dutiful length, and will confine myself to this one. My aim is to describe the badness not in purely aesthetic terms (a failure of

Lawrence's creative power) but as a consequence of the book's design. Can we say that it is bad *because* it is fascist?

The story is perfunctory. Kate Leslie, a widow nearing forty, comes to Mexico worn out and uncertain after two marriages; there she meets the two leaders of a neo-Aztec religious revival, Don Cipriano, whom she eventually marries, and Don Ramon, who is to be the dictator of the new regime. The new religion is described at length, and Lawrence quotes abundantly from its hymns; it is established in blood, as a number of disloyal followers are murdered. After long hesitation, Kate decides to stay in Mexico, and submit to the demands of the new cult.

There is no question that this is a book with positives, a book deeply committed to its message. The message is the religion of Quetzalcoatl, the eagle and serpent. Its ideal is embodied, in the intense male dignity, the authority and strength of Don Ramon—as seen at moments like this:

> 'But give me the pose before you go,' said the artist.
> Ramon slowly took off his blouse-skirt, and stood with naked torso, the sash with its blue and black bars tight round his naked waist. For some moments he stood gathering himself together. Then suddenly, in a concentration of intense, proud prayer, he flung his right arm up above his head, and stood transfixed, his left arm hanging softly by his side, the fingers touching his thigh. And on his face that fixed, intense look of pride which was at once a prayer.[1]

The artist is very impressed by this: frightened, but inspired. When Ramon goes, 'with a proud, white look of joy in his face, he turned again to his work'. It is true that Kate has fits of violent hostility towards the new religion—one particularly convincing one at the end of Chapter XXII, when she refuses to be 'swallowed up', tells Cipriano to go back to Ramon because 'you only care about him and your living Quetzalcoatl and your living Huitzilopochtli', and finds herself longing for her old self, for London and Paris and New York, and loathing the sound of the 'high-flown bunk' Ramon and Cipriano want to put over her.

> . . . they want to put it over me, with their high-flown bunk, and their Malintzi. Malintzi! I am Kate Forrester, really. I am neither Kate Leslie nor Kate Tylor. I am sick of these men

[1] *The Plumed Serpent*, ch. 11

putting names over me. I was born Kate Forrester, and I shall die Kate Forrester. I want to go home. Loathsome, really, to be called Malintzi.—I've had it put over me.[1]

But Kate does not stay in this frame of mind. It is a negative phase that she passes through, and two chapters later she is invested as Malintzi; just as her next revulsion gives place to the decision, on which the book ends, to stay in Mexico. Lawrence has been careful to throw the full weight of his book behind the religion of Quetzalcoatl.

Nor is there any question, surely, about what is wrong with this positive: if it is not fascism, it is too like it for the difference to matter.

> The races of the earth are like trees; in the end they neither mix nor mingle. They stand out of each other's way, like trees. Or else they crowd on one another, and their roots grapple, and it is the fight to the death. . . . Only the Natural Aristocrats can rise above their nation; and even then they do not rise above their race.[2]

When Don Ramon interviews the Bishop he insists that he wants peace between him and the church—the usual dictator's peace: if you don't resist, we shan't have to fight.

> 'Nay! You would invade the Churches of Christ and the Blessed Virgin, I heard you say.'
> 'You know my intentions. But I do not want to quarrel with the Church of Rome, nor have bloodshed and enmity, Father. Can you not understand me? Should there not be peace between the men who strive down their different ways to the God-Mystery?'
> 'Once more desecrate the altars! Bring in strange idols. Burn the images of Our Lord and Our Lady, and ask for peace?' said the poor Bishop, who helplessly longed to be left alone.
> 'All that, Father,' said Ramon.[3]

The religion of Quetzalcoatl has a programme on the family and personal level too. Its view of sex is, quite simply, that women must not have orgasms. There is no ambiguity about the passage in which this is explained: Kate's final lesson is 'how all her old love had been frictional, charged with the fire of irritation and the spasms of frictional voluptuousness'. Cipriano teaches her to do without

[1] Ibid., ch. 22   [2] Ibid., ch. 17   [3] Ibid., ch. 17

this. 'When, in their love, it came back on her, the seething electric female ecstasy, which knows such spasms of delirium, he recoiled from her.' The 'white ecstasy of frictional satisfaction' is repulsive to him, and so she comes to feel its worthlessness, it becomes 'external to her'.

It gives one pause to realise that the author of *Lady Chatterley's Lover* rejected orgasm. It hardly needs saying that Lawrence is inconsistent on this, that *The Plumed Serpent* represents an aberration in his thought. Perhaps one might have guessed this from internal evidence—from such a sentence as

> Her strange seething feminine will and desire subsided in her
> and swept away, leaving her soft and powerfully potent, like
> the hot springs of water that gushed up, so noiseless, so soft,
> yet so powerful, with a sort of secret potency.'[1]

I do not recall any other occasion when Lawrence coupled together 'will and desire'—usually opposites in his vocabulary, the former forced and mental, the latter coming from 'the candle-flame, forever upright and yet flowing'. And it is hard to imagine any adjective less appropriate to the quenching of sexual desire than 'potent'.

It is perhaps not necessary to demonstrate at length how pernicious the message of this book is; so I will only briefly mention the murder of the traitors, the long ritualistic slaying that would be frightening if it were not ludicrous. What *is* frightening is Kate's subsequent reaction:

> So, when she thought of him and his soldiers, tales of swift
> cruelty she had heard of him: when she remembered his stabbing
> the three helpless peons, she thought: Why should I judge him?
> He is of the gods. . . . What do I care if he kills people? His
> flame is young and clean. He is Huitzilopochtli, and I am Mal-
> intzi. What do I care, what Cipriano Viedma does or doesn't
> do? Or even what Kate Leslie does or doesn't do![2]

There is no such thing, we see, as rising above morality. The ecstasy which drives Kate to feel 'what do I care', drives her to condone very specific acts that exist on a down-to-earth level. It is never safe to say of any man 'he is of the gods'.

All this, then, to show that *The Plumed Serpent* is a wicked book.

[1] *The Plumed Serpent*, ch. 26   [2] Ibid., ch. 24

It is now my argument that what makes it wicked is very close to what makes it bad. What makes it bad is, of course, the haziness of what is offered. The ritual and the ecstasy are perceived through a mumble of words: the religion has no artistic life in the book.

I opened the novel at random and paged through it till I came to one of the hymns: it happened to be the Fourth Hymn ('What Quetzalcoatl saw in Mexico') and it is as good, and as bad, as any of the others. It is a denunciation of economic colonialism that moves into an apocalyptic vision of the destruction caused by the dragons of the world. Perhaps this is an exhortation to revolution, perhaps it is a gloating prophecy of the doom of the peons: no one can be sure. The language of the hymn is as vague as its message: when it ceases to be vague it becomes absurd.

> I see dark things rushing across the country.
> *Yea, Lord! Even trains and* camiones *and automobiles.*

The imagery is either commonplace

> —*There are dead that cluster in the frozen north, shuddering
>   and chattering among the ice—*

or a rash mixing of metaphors

> —*Being dead, you shall rove like dogs with broken haunches
>   Seeking the offal and garbage of life, in the invisible lanes of the
>   air.*[1]

There is clearly a link between the vagueness of the language and the vagueness of the programme: these long monotonous lines, with no genuine rhythm, with no imagery that arrests, surely lull the reader who is prepared to be sympathetic into a state in which he will accept any suggestion as long as it is indefinite enough. He will not know at the end if he has been committed to a programme or not. Of course he has.

There are many analogous vaguenesses in the book. It does not need a Marxist to see that Don Ramon is exploiting his peasants; and there is a surprising (for Lawrence) lack of shrewdness in Kate's protestations of social innocence:

> A people without the energy of *getting on*, how could they fail
> to be hopelessly exploited. They had been hopelessly and cruelly
> exploited, for centuries. And their backbones were locked in
> malevolent resistance.

[1] Ibid., ch. 17

'But,' as Kate said to herself, 'I don't want to exploit them. Not a bit. On the contrary, I am willing to give more than I get. But that nasty insinuating insultingness is not fair in the game. I never insult them. I am so careful not to hurt them. And then they *deliberately* make these centipede attacks on me, and are pleased when I am hurt.'[1]

One word makes me certain that Lawrence accepts what Kate is here saying: that is the word 'as'. What she said to herself is offered as an illustration of the just comment. Now on a strict basis of *meum et tuum*, Kate perhaps gives more than she gets. But Lawrence is not often so naïve: Kate is rich, and she can give because she has already got. We might expect the passage to show some awareness of this. Kate need not think it, but Lawrence ought to.

Even the opening of the novel, which is usually praised for a vigour and realism that recall Lawrence at his best, is not free from the faults of the rest.

'Look at that!' said Owen. 'Isn't that fun!'
'No,' said Kate, her little *alter ego* speaking out for once, in spite of her will-to-happiness. 'No, I don't like it. I really hate common people.'[2]

This is a surrender to jargon—to fake jargon—as abandoned as the later surrender to violence. The embarrassed crudity of 'her little *alter ego* speaking out for once' is kin to the crudity of 'seeking the offal and garbage of life'. And in the conversation between Kate and Owen that opens Chapter II there is a detail as revealing as any in the book:

'I think,' interrupted Kate, 'if I knew that some of those tore-adors were going to be tossed by the bull, I'd go to see another bull-fight. Ugh, how I detest them! The longer I live the more loathsome the human species becomes to me. *How* much nicer the bulls are!'
'Oh, quite!' said Owen vaguely. 'Exactly. But still there was some very skilful work, very pretty. Really very plucky.'[3]

This illustrates very neatly the relation I have suggested between the pernicious and the slovenly. There are touches of slovenliness: Kate is allowed to sprawl among the cliché of 'The longer I live the more loathsome the human species becomes to me'. And there is a viciousness that consists not simply in letting Kate express

[1] *The Plumed Serpent*, ch. 9   [2] Ibid., ch. 1   [3] Ibid., ch. 2

this stereotyped misanthropy, but in the way it is bolstered. Owen's reply is made evasive, spineless, *stupid*, to the point of implausibility. It is a way of surreptitiously agreeing with Kate.

I will not prolong these illustrations: the anatomising of a tedious book must not expect to escape tedium. I will conclude by saying that the book is false to its own intermittent best self. The most vivid of all the passages here quoted was surely the second—that in which Kate objects to being swallowed up. It comes at the end of an argument with Don Cipriano:

> 'You treat me as if I had no life of my own,' she said. 'But I have.'
>
> 'A life of your own? Who gave it you? Where did you get it?'
>
> 'I don't know. But I have got it. And I must live it. I can't be just swallowed up.'
>
> '...How often you say *Not*, today!—I must go back to Ramon.'
>
> 'Yes. Go back to him. You only care about him, and your living Quetzalcoatl and your living Huitzilopochtli.—I am only a woman.'
>
> 'No, Malintzi, you are more. You are more than Kate, you are Malintzi.'
>
> 'I am not! I am only Kate, and I am only a woman. I mistrust all that other stuff.'
>
> 'I am more than just a man, Malintzi.—Don't you see that?'
>
> 'No!' said Kate. 'I don't see it. Why *should* you be more than just a man?'
>
> 'Because I am the living Huitzilopochtli. Didn't I tell you? You've got dust in your mouth today, Malintzi.'[1]

But what good clean dust! Kate listens to the everlasting sing-song periods of Cipriano, the pretentious questioning ('Who gave it you? Where did you get it?'), the smothering of fact in names ('You are more than Kate, you are Malintzi')—listens to it all and, for once, she answers back. It is a relief as great as when Marianne Dashwood answers back, and it is as firmly (though not as hurriedly) rejected by the book. And it brings the dialogue to life as nothing else has done for hundreds of pages: 'I am only Kate, and I am only a woman. I mistrust all that other stuff.' This is the exact note of the irritation that has been building up in the reader. Even the transition from her annoyance with Quetzalcoatl to her annoyance with men is plausible, and must quicken sympathy in male as well as

[1] Ibid., ch. 22

female readers. 'I was born Kate Forrester, and I shall die Kate Forrester.' What a fuss men make, with names and words and putting it over. This is the Lawrence who wrote *In Love* or the eleventh chapter of *The Rainbow*, or the conclusion of *St Mawr*, those masterpieces of feminine sensibility. And in *The Plumed Serpent* this Lawrence is beaten down.

If *The Plumed Serpent* were a great novel, and grew to be studied like *Paradise Lost* in future generations, there would arise among its critics a dissident sect who claimed that Lawrence, being a true poet, was really of the woman's party, that he wrote in fetters when writing of Quetzalcoatl and at fitful liberty when writing of Kate Leslie, who was the true hero of the book, and was tragically beaten down. And these dissidents would be severely rebuked by scholars who pointed out that Lawrence's intention was to justify the ways of Ramon and Cipriano, who quoted from his letters his own praise of the book, and who reminded us that a work of literature can only be appreciated in the light of the author's intention.

2 The Dialectic: Blood and Mind

This by way of preliminary: of showing that Lawrence's view of man matters, that it bit deep into his imagination, and that we must begin by understanding it. And to understand it, it is best to begin with his contrast between blood and mind.

> We must discriminate between an ideal and a desire. A desire proceeds from within, from the unknown, spontaneous soul or self. But an ideal is superimposed from above, from the mind: it is a fixed, arbitrary thing, like a machine control. The great lesson is to learn to break all the fixed ideals, to allow the soul's own deep desires to come direct, spontaneous into consciousness. . . .
> The living self has one purpose only: to come into its own fullness of being, as a tree comes into full blossom, or a bird into spring beauty, or a tiger into lustre.[1]

Though the terminology changes, this contrast runs through all Lawrence's writing: the contrast between the living self, the true creative act, the flame of genuine individuality, the whole man alive; and the dead, mental self, the thoughts that are not fed by the blood, the withered abstractions of the merely ideal. He states it

[1] 'Democracy', § 4; *Phoenix*, p. 713

in his essays, he embodies (and, often enough, states) it in his novels.
We must begin with this, for it is the very centre of Lawrence.

> My great religion is a belief in the blood, the flesh, as being wiser
> than the intellect. We can go wrong in our minds. But what our
> blood feels and believes and says, is always true. The intellect
> is only a bit and a bridle. What do I care about knowledge. All
> I want is to answer to my blood, direct, without fribbling
> intervention of mind, or moral, or what-not. I conceive a man's
> body as a kind of flame, like a candle flame, forever upright
> and yet flowing: and the intellect is just the light that is
> shed on to the things around. . . . The real way of living is to
> answer to one's wants. Not 'I want to light up with my intelli-
> gence as many things as possible' but 'For the living of my full
> flame—I want that liberty, I want that woman, I want that
> pound of peaches, I want to go to sleep, I want to go to the pub
> and have a good time, I want to look a beastly swell today, I
> want to kiss that girl, I want to insult that man.' Instead of that,
> all these wants, which are there whether-or-not, are utterly
> ignored, and we talk about some sort of ideas. I'm like Carlyle,
> who, they say, wrote 50 volumes on the value of silence.[1]

> *We've made a great mess of love since we made an ideal of it . . .*

> *Love is like a flower, it must flower and fade;*
> *if it doesn't fade, it is not a flower,*
> *it's either an artificial rag blossom, or an immortelle, for the*
>   *cemetery.*

> *The moment the mind interferes with love, or the will fixes on it,*
> *or the personality assumes it as an attribute, or the ego takes*
>   *possession of it,*
> *it is not love any more, it's just a mess.*
> *And we've made a great mess of love, mind-perverted, will-*
>   *perverted, ego-perverted love.*[2]

Here are a positive and a negative statement of Lawrence's
doctrine (though few of his statements, of course, are simply one
or the other—even in these he makes his point by contrasting the
two); it may be significant that the positive one is from an early
letter, the negative is from his later, embittered years. That letter
to Ernest Collings is the most important Lawrence ever wrote,
and he never ceased to believe what he there says—nor (perhaps)

---

[1] Letter to Ernest Collings, 17 January, 1913
[2] 'The Mess of Love', from *Pansies*

did he ever find a better image for it than the 'candle flame forever upright and yet flowing'. We see in this passage, what will engage us a great deal in a moment, his belief that to obey the flame is to be emotionally honest and admit to all one's wants, untrammelled by superficial rules about those that are and aren't approved.

Since I shall have occasion to quote so many of Lawrence's explicit statements of his views, and since so many of them are cloudy, contradictory, even perverse, I will state straight away what criterion I think they should be judged by. Lawrence is a creative writer, and he interests us because he did not merely state; yet to dismiss all his own attempts to formulate his position would be as presumptuous in his case as in George Eliot's. These attempts will have one kind of value if they fulfil the criteria to which we submit any statement: clarity, consistency and truth. They have another kind of value if we can feel that they have taken on something of the authority of creative writing: if their language seems to hold in itself a pressure of experience as well as an ability to generalise. It is because the language of statement can take on such a literary dimension that George Eliot and Lawrence have so much to say to us.

Lawrence's list of wants, tossed out almost casually in the course of his letter, seems to me to have a touch of this authority. It is not merely an illustration of the assertion that has gone before: it exists, in itself, as the expression of an upsurge of feeling, moving from the pallid theoretical beginning ('I want that liberty') through 'I want that woman' to the splendid alliterative thump of a purely physical desire 'I want that pound of peaches'—and so on through the casual and the colloquial. And its conclusion ('I want to kiss that girl, I want to insult that man') tells us without fuss that though these two wants may be quite different according to morals, they can be the same according to the test of genuineness. We see too in this passage, with its disarming last sentence, the charm of the early Lawrence, a self-deprecating charm that with the growth of age and bitterness begins to disappear from the letters. And we see that *what* the intelligence lights up does not matter:

> All the best part of knowledge is inconceivable. We know the sun. But we cannot conceive the sun, unless we are willing to accept some theory of burning gases, some cause-and-effect nonsense. And even if we do have a mental conception of the

sun as a sphere of blazing *gas*—which it certainly isn't—we are just as far from knowing what *blaze* is. Knowledge is always a matter of whole experience, what St Paul calls knowing in full, and never a matter of mental conception merely.[1]

Such passages are not, alas, rare in Lawrence; and towards the end of his career they grew more obscure without growing any less false. When he wants to say that knowing with the whole man is more important than mental knowledge, Lawrence (for whom it was always more important to know where the emphasis lay than to be fair) is quite happy to say that the mental knowledge isn't true. And since scientific knowledge is mental knowledge, his writings are scattered with casual denials of evolution, of astronomy and—of course—of a good deal of psychology.

The brusqueness towards science is not the only nonsense from which we have to extract his doctrine. Sometimes he tells us not merely what the nature of the blood-mind contrast is, but what caused it: usually the cause involves some pretentious cultural history, but in *Introduction to these Paintings* there is a more bizarre suggestion:

I know nothing about medicine and very little about diseases, and my facts are such as I have picked up in casual reading. Nevertheless I am convinced that the secret awareness of syphilis, and the utter secret terror and horror of it, has had an enormous and incalculable effect on the English consciousness and on the American. . . . I am convinced that *some* of Shakespeare's horror and despair, in his tragedies, arose from the shock of his consciousness of syphilis.[2]

Then, too, Lawrence mixes up his point with some extraordinary anatomy. He is not always content to talk of 'the deep affective centres': he will often tell us *where* true consciousness is situated.

That is, at the great solar plexus an infant *knows*, in primary, mindless knowledge; and from this centre he acts and reacts directly, individually, and self-responsibly. The same from the cardiac plexus, and the two corresponding ganglia, lumbar and thoracic.[3]

Indeed, if we pause to think of what is perhaps Lawrence's favourite

[1] *Psycho-analysis and the Unconscious*, ch. 2
[2] 'Introduction to these Paintings' (1929); *Phoenix*, p. 554
[3] 'Education of the People' § 5; *Phoenix*, p. 620

word for the true, the genuine way of experiencing—the word 'blood'—we can wonder if Lawrence always remembered that it is a metaphor only. That the blood thinks would be no more far-fetched than that the solar plexus knows.

But for all the nonsense, this contrast underlies and shapes all Lawrence has to say about man's nature, and some of his most memorable theorising is based on it. Let us take a passage from what is perhaps the finest of all his essays, *Apropos of Lady Chatterley's Lover*.

The body feels real hunger, real thirst, real joy in the sun or the snow, real pleasure in the smell of roses or the look of a lilac bush; real anger, real sorrow, real love, real tenderness, real warmth, real passion, real hate, real grief. All the emotions belong to the body, and are only recognised by the mind. We may hear the most sorrowful piece of news, and only feel a mental excitement. Then, hours after, perhaps in sleep, the awareness may reach the bodily centres, and true grief wrings the heart.

How different they are, mental feelings and real feelings. Today, many people live and die without having had any real feelings—though they have had a 'rich emotional life' apparently, having showed strong mental feeling. But it is all counterfeit. In magic, one of the so-called 'occult' pictures represents a man standing, apparently, before a flat table mirror, which reflects him from the waist to the head, so that you have the man from head to waist, then his reflection downwards from waist to head again. And whatever it means in magic, it means what we are today, creatures whose active emotional self has no real existence, but is all reflected downwards from the mind. Our education from the start has *taught* us a certain range of emotions, what to feel and what not to feel, and how to feel the feelings we allow ourselves to feel. All the rest is just non-existent. The vulgar criticism of any new good book is: Of course nobody ever felt like that!—People allow themselves to feel a certain number of finished feelings. So it was in the last century. This feeling only what you allow yourselves to feel at last kills all capacity for feeling, and in the higher emotional range you feel nothing at all. This has come to pass in our present century. The higher emotions are strictly dead. They have to be faked.[1]

[1] 'Apropos of Lady Chatterley's Lover'

How hard it always is to separate the quick from the dross in Lawrence. Even when he is writing at his intense and spontaneous best—as here—he treads the edge of the Slough of Nonsense.

What may at first seem the greatest weakness of the passage—the mind/body dualism it assumes—is a weakness more apparent than real. Certainly, a great deal of what I have said in praise of these three novelists would be undermined if we went back to believing that man is a ghost in a machine; but it is surely not *that* dualism which Lawrence is using.

In the *Study of Thomas Hardy*, in fact, Lawrence was at pains to reject a dualism of body and spirit:

> How can a man say, 'I am this body', when he will desire beyond the body tomorrow? And how can a man say, 'I am this spirit', when his own mouth gives the lie to the words it forms?[1]

We have to convict Lawrence of a shift in terminology from one essay to the other. It is not possible to maintain both that those who 'circumscribe (their) consummation within the body' are melancholy, hollow and miserable (as he does in the *Study*) and also that the body's feelings are the real ones. The reason for this inconsistency is that Lawrence constantly hesitated between a two-term and a three-term dialectic. At times he will contrast bodily and mental feelings, to the advantage of the first; at other times he will reject both in favour of an integration of the two by the whole man alive. The *Study of Thomas Hardy* (in so far as it does anything consistently) uses the three-term dialectic; and so does *St Mawr*. Yet even within *St Mawr* it is hard to be sure if Lawrence is consistent—about this, or about anything else. Both because it concerns the present point, and also because of the significant unevenness of its quality, a word on *St Mawr* will be appropriate here.

3 The Dialectic Exemplified: 'St Mawr'

The three-term dialectic is sketched in a conversation between Lou and her mother, just after Mrs Witt has humiliated the groom, Lewis, by cutting his hair. She wonders if Lewis' hair seems so important because he is 'just an animal', and she goes on to con-

---

[1] 'Study of Thomas Hardy', ch. 8; *Phoenix*, p. 469

trast those men who are mere animal with those who have a mind.

> 'Why, mother!' said Lou impatiently. 'I think one gets so tired of your men with mind, as you call it. There are so many of that sort of clever men.'[1]

The discussion continues for several pages, and though they are apparently disagreeing, there seems little doubt that an area of agreement emerges from what they say, and is implicitly endorsed by the book.

> '. . . don't misunderstand me, mother! I don't want to be an animal like a horse or a cat or a lioness, though they all fascinate me, the way they get their life *straight*. . . . If we could get our lives straight from the source, as the animals do, and still be ourselves.'[2]

This clearly suggests a threefold contrast. At the one extreme is the mere animal; at the other are the clever intellectuals that both women despise: 'old women knitting the same pattern over and over again'. Between is what Mrs Witt calls real mind, and Lou the pure animal man: 'lovely as a deer or a leopard, burning like a flame fed straight from underneath'. *St Mawr* is the story of two women's quest for this. Mrs Witt thinks she is looking for it, but she is not: her attitude is too merely negative. Lou is more genuinely looking, and has perhaps begun to find something when the book ends.

Such seems to be the book's intention, and if it were achieved it would be a little masterpiece, and a vindication of the integrated man against both mere body and mere cleverness. It is fitfully achieved, for some parts of this disorganised book are brilliant; but other parts are unachieved, and especially the parts most germane to this discussion.

St Mawr is a passionately committeed book: bitter, sardonic, ambitious, idealistic. This kind of commitment needs a coherent attitude towards the people and actions of the story, but that, alas, is what Lawrence does not give us. Towards Mrs Witt in particular our attitude is extremely uncertain. She is the most vivid character in the book, and more observation and impassioned satire has gone into her than into any of the others. The same absorbing interest that caused the vividness may also have caused the uncertainty.

[1] *St Mawr* (Phoenix edition, p. 44)   [2] Ibid., p. 46

At least once we are invited explicitly to dissociate ourselves from Mrs Witt:

> Perhaps she despised the younger generation too easily. Because she did not see its sources of power, she concluded it was powerless.[1]

But there is a limit to what an assurance like this can undo: it is precisely at the moment when she is most violently attacking the younger generation that Mrs Witt drags out the author's intensest identification. Her rudeness to the young man who is sure he exists, or to Dean Vyner and his wife, discredits and exposes them in our eyes as well as hers. With meticulous care Lawrence shows us her satire at their expense ('You meant, didn't you, if you poured tea in her hat, to put cream and sugar in first'), while he confirms every detail of it by discrediting the couple themselves.

> Here Mrs Vyner rose as if a chair-spring had suddenly propelled her to her feet. She was streaky pink in the face.
>
> 'Mrs Witt,' she panted, 'you misdirect your sympathies. That poor young man—in the beauty of youth.'
>
> 'Isn't he *beautiful*—' murmured Mrs Witt, extravagantly in sympathy. 'He's my daughter's husband!'[2]

When Lawrence works as hard as this to make a fool of Mrs Vyner, he may undo some of his own effect: he may fill us with a dislike of Mrs Witt that will overspill into a dislike of the author who is so coolly using her as a weapon of satire.

This suspicion is confirmed when we see how often the writing goes flabby when Mrs Witt is presented: flabby because the author's critical sense is suspended, and he allows her to get away with often flagrant cliché. When talking to two foolish men, Mrs Witt 'looked from one man to the other, as if she were dropping them down the bottomless pit'; later she says to one of them 'Really! Is that so!' and Lawrence adds:

> If irony could have been condensed to prussic acid, the fair young man would have ended his life's history with his reminiscences.[3]

It is at the moments when she is behaving most cheaply that the writing gets cheap.

[1] Ibid., p. 89   [2] Ibid., p. 77   [3] Ibid., p. 59

187

There is a good deal of flabby writing in *St Mawr*. The most prominent weakness is Lou's vision of evil, the feeling that there are 'dark-grey waves of evil rearing in a great tide' that comes over her shortly after the horse has thrown Rico. It has some very tired writing

—She felt that from the core of Asia the evil welled up, as from some strange pole, and slowly was drowning earth—

and (worse still) some adolescent mouthing:

But ideal mankind would abolish death, multiply itself million upon million, rear up city upon city, save every parasite alive, until the accumulation of mere existence is swollen to a horror.[1]

Lou's vision of evil is so close to the evil that is released from the Marabar Caves and spreads over the surrounding plain and the city, that a parallel is tempting and a direct influence is very possible (Lawrence was reading *A Passage to India* in July 1924, and wrote *St Mawr* that same summer). In both cases, a day's outing to a famous attraction in the hills leads to a disastrous accident, and to the terrifying sense of a very old evil beginning to spread and destroy. The tact with which Forster stops just short of the supernatural, the completeness with which the newly released evil is embodied in the book's action and yet retains a further, numinous quality, have made this one of the most brilliant and disturbing episodes in modern fiction. And if we look at Lawrence's comment on *A Passage to India* we can perhaps see more clearly why he comes so badly out of this comparison:

Life is more interesting in its under-currents than in its obvious; and E. M. does see people, people and nothing but people: *ad nauseam*.[2]

Lawrence has too glibly shouldered aside the people for the undercurrents. He has accepted too easily Lou's own crude formulation of her 'vision'; and he has simply not been able to embody the new evil in action because *St Mawr* is so riddled with moral uncertainty: a strong contrast to the never didactic but morally very clear and firm Forster.

It is not surprising then that the three-term dialectic that Law-

---

[1] *St Mawr* (Phoenix edition, p. 65)
[2] Letter to Martin Secker, 23 July, 1924

rence set up as the book's framework is one that he does not succeed in maintaining consistently: it is invaded by the same uncertainty as other parts of the book. For we have naturally to ask what embodies 'good intuitive mind', thinking that is 'quick like fire', getting one's life 'straight from the source'. We need not, of course, expect too clear-cut an answer: in particular, we need not insist that any single man in the story represents it. Indeed, to do so would be to reject one of the book's essential and most moving features: the fact that there *are* no such men, that Lou's stubborn quest is an impossible one, and that it must therefore culminate in a withdrawal from the civilised world, and a rejection of sex.

> 'What I *know* is, that the time has come for me to keep to myself. No more messing about.'[1]

Despite the over-insistent italics, this is a fitting climax to Lou's long frustrated search: Lou is less vividly created than Mrs Witt, but more steadily seen. How compelling we find her search, how tragic her failure, must depend on how powerfully we are shown what she is searching for. We are shown it in several ways. Once in the magnificent image (given, significantly, to Mrs Witt) of the man in whom Pan hasn't fallen. The unimportant Cartwright develops this:

> In those days you saw the thing, you never saw the god in it: I mean in the tree or the fountain or the animal. If you ever saw the God instead of the thing, you died. If you saw it with the naked eye, that is. But in the night you might see the God. And you knew it was there.[2]

This calm animism has the restraint and genuineness of someone who does not need to goad himself to make his point: it is far more convincing than most of Lawrence's more excited appeals to the Dark Gods.

A more extended symbol for the book's positives is Lou's ranch. *St Mawr* like *The Lost Girl* ends with a strange and moving journey into the hills, an invitation to take part in man's frustrated struggle to colonise hostile nature—frustrated, bitter, savagely portrayed, and yet ultimately exhilarating. In both cases, it is hard to convince ourselves that the end really belongs to the rest of the book:

---

[1] *St Mawr* (Phoenix edition, p. 146)   [2] Ibid., p. 51

as we conclude our reading we feel moved but cheated. And in both cases (I wonder if this is more than a coincidence?) the very last page concludes on a trivial and discordant detail: *The Lost Girl* on Ciccio saying he will go to America, *St Mawr* on a cheap sarcasm from Mrs Witt.

The account of the building of the ranch before Lou bought it is one of Lawrence's finest pieces of writing: utterly unsentimental, even bitter, yet awed before the grandeur of the task and the fitful exultation of the doing. And it has its place at the end of this book, for its suggestion of an unfinished and perhaps impossible task surely fits Lou's sadly futile quest for a real man. It is hard, however, not to accept Graham Hough's criticism that we are hardly entitled to give Lou any of the credit for this task: she did not colonise the ranch but has merely bought it—and will probably grow dissatisfied and sell it in a few months. And from that we can move to a larger criticism: if this final symbol is to be attached to the book as a whole, we must be able to say what it corresponds to, what it repeats or varies or makes explicit. We have to ask what symbolises the real man whose life is 'straight from the source' during the rest of the book. And here there is one sadly obvious answer: it is the horse himself, St Mawr.

The greatest failure of this book surely lies in the horse: and for several reasons. First, the moments when we are asked to thrill most intensely to his pure energy are those when he behaves in an ecstasy of pure destruction: above all when he kicks young Edwards in the face. This is a criticism of the book's norms as well as its execution, and I will put it aside here since it anticipates the climax of this discussion. Second the symbolism is crude and obvious: indeed, it is not always clear whether St Mawr is a symbol at all— whether he does not quite simply possess rather than symbolise what Lou is seeking. And finally—arising out of this—he destroys all attempt to make a three-term dialectic. St Mawr is an animal, and he does not behave like a man in whom Pan is unfallen: what human behaviour he evokes is either spiteful or commonplace. (Hough makes another good point when he observes that 'the English countryside is full of young women who like horses better than men'.)

I must therefore conclude that as an attempt to describe and embody how men could get their lives 'straight from the source as animals do and still be (them)selves', *St Mawr* is a failure. The man

190

in whom Pan is unfallen remains a shadowy image, and the only alternative to the old women knitting their intellectual patterns is after all the mere animal.

4 The Articulateness of 'Women in Love'

I have no doubt that Lawrence was happier with a twofold contrast: that between animal and knitting, between blood and mind, or, to come back to *Apropos*, between real feelings and mental feelings. But his flirtings with the threefold contrast have shown us how to read this one. 'Mental feelings' are those felt by the divided self: they are the result of dualism. Bodily feelings are those of the whole man. To write 'body' instead of 'whole man alive' is a rhetorical strategy on Lawrence's part, a way of stressing the physical element in total experience, of directing his attack at the knitting.

All this is indefensible, certainly, and annoying. But perhaps it is only annoying: it reveals Lawrence's cavalier treatment of his readers rather than a fundamental confusion. And granting the terms of the passage, we may say surely that it rings very true to something in the experience of all of us. The example that ends the first paragraph has a blunt and familiar eloquence that once again touches statement with the authority of imaginative language.

Turning now to Lawrence's next paragraph, I cannot write of it with the same enthusiasm. That occult picture, of the man reflected from head to waist, happens to be an exact reversal of another and more famous image: to set these two opposites against each other may be revealing:

I pardon that man's life. What was thy cause? Adultery? Thou shalt not die: die for adultery! No, the wren goes to't, and the small gilded fly goes lecher in my sight. Let copulation thrive; for Gloucester's bastard son was kinder to his father, than my daughters got 'tween the lawful sheets. To't, Luxury pell-mell! for I lack soldiers. Behold yond simpering dame, whose face between her forks presages snow; that minces virtue, and does shake the head to hear of pleasure's name. The fitchew, nor the soiled horse goes to't with a more riotous appetite. Down from the waist they are Centaurs, though women all above; but to the girdle do the gods inherit, beneath is all the fiend's. There's hell, there's darkness, there is the sulphurous pit; burning, scalding, stench, consumption; fie, fie, fie! pah, pah! give me an ounce of civet, good apothecary, to sweeten my imagination:[1]

We must notice, but not set too much store by, the fact that Shakespeare is writing a play and Lawrence an essay: that Lear is expressing a particular mood, caused by the circumstances of the plot, and Lawrence a philosophy of man. For much of the power of *King Lear* lies in its ability to transcend the plot and speak to the human condition: we are so involved with Lear because at moments like this he expresses a neurosis so widespread, a disgust so human, that we cannot rest on the comfort of attributing it merely to his circumstances. And Lawrence's 'philosophy' is not just philosophy—it is an attempt to classify and evaluate experiences, it is based on (and implies) a view of life expressed in the novels. It therefore seems to me valid to compare the two.

And they compare very neatly: they show us that, whereas Shakespeare fears a surrender to impulse, Lawrence fears the withering of impulse. We could not ask the contrast with Jane Austen to be more vividly indicated. Lawrence's fearful vision is of man from waist to head, then from waist to head again: Lear's (Shakespeare's?) is

Down from the waist they are Centaurs, though women all above.

For Lawrence, 'marriage is no marriage that is not basically and permanently phallic'; for Lear

but to the girdle do the gods inherit, beneath is all the fiend's.

We are back with the three-term dialectic: with the help of Shakespeare, Lawrence's statement can define itself more carefully than it could on its own. Lawrence's real feelings have to contrast with the magic picture, and they have to contrast with Lear's magic picture as well: if they do that, we will believe they express the whole man. Ultimately, the only way to decide if they do will be to trace them into the novels; but in the meantime we can notice in this second paragraph an element that was not present in the first, and that robs it of some of the ring of truth. I mean the references to 'now'. It is in our present century that mental feelings have

[1] *King Lear*, IV, vi, 112ff

killed real feelings, it is nowadays that the higher emotions are dead.

This is something very common in Lawrence. He is very fond of harking back to a happy past, contrasting the empty present with a time when the abstractions of the mind had not usurped the place of true blood awareness. It comes in essays, poems, stories and novels, and it includes some of his sloppiest and most superficial writing.

The Golden Age is a lady of easy virtue: she will lie down with any author who enjoys denouncing the present, and her price in truthfulness is never high. Like any easy lay, she corrupts those who use her, for at least two reasons. First, such contrasts of the present with the better past easily contradict themselves: *when* was that better time? As you go back further or less far, what counts as the present at one moment may be moved to the other side of the fence at another, and count as past. Thus in *Apropos* Lawrence has to go right back to the eighteenth century to find real feelings, but in the opening chapters of *The Rainbow* he found them in the mid-nineteenth century. Second, and more important, an idealised past that has been created as a projection of one's indignation with the present will be imaginatively thin, with no life of its own. So when Wordsworth denounces the present he falls, as he idealises, into his most verbose:

> *Oh where now is the character of peace,*
> *Sobriety and order and chaste love,*
> *And honest dealing and untainted speech,*
> *And pure goodwill, and hospitable cheer;*
> *That made the very thought of country life*
> *A thought of refuge for a mind detained*
> *Reluctantly amid the bustling crowd.*[1]

Idealisation which is a mere by-product of one's indignation will never be achieved bodily in the writing. Wordsworth can give no reality to this ideal country life, he drops so drearily into the tamest of adjectives ('honest dealing', 'pure goodwill'), into mere lists of abstractions unquickened by the rhythm, because his interest in it at this moment is derived, not genuine. The point is particularly clear in this case, since this is the very subject on which Wordsworth could write so magnificently when his interest was immediate.

---

[1] *The Excursion,* VIII, 239ff

Lawrence suffers from the same fault: 'the old England of hamlets and yeomen' does not often engage his living self, his fullness of being—it is there for a purpose, a thin, indignant, hysterical purpose. And the point grows clear for Lawrence in the same way it did for Wordsworth, if we turn to the closing chapters of *The Lost Girl* and see with what sharp reality, what poetic genuineness, he can render 'the lovely, pristine morning of the world, before our epoch began' when he is writing without this polemical purpose.

But apart from the damage which Lawrence's Golden Age attitude does to his writing, one wants to say that by his own theories one would not expect it to be true. If the emotions belong to the body, we can accept that the mind only recognises them, cannot create them: the mind is rudder, not motor. But how then can it destroy them? On this point I find Lawrence evasive: he asserts it frequently, but never with that immediate ring of truth we saw in the first paragraph above. In *The Novel and the Feelings*, for example, he describes something very like the Freudian concepts of libido ('we ourselves only exist because of the life that bounds and leaps into our limbs and our consciousness, from out of the original dark forest within us') and repression:

> Man is the only creature who has deliberately tried to tame himself. He has succeeded. But alas! it is a process you cannot set a limit to. Tameness, like alcohol, destroys its own creator.[1]

But whereas Freud would now go on to tell us that what is repressed is not destroyed, that it continues its clandestine existence in the unconscious, shooting occasionally to the surface in the progressively more distorted forms of errors, jokes, dreams and neurotic symptoms, that it may in fact have a more powerful influence on our lives than any conscious factors—Lawrence we find believes none of this. For him the effect of repression is, quite simply, that it succeeds.

I have already, in discussing *Apropos*, begun the interrogation to which, later in this chapter, I shall submit Lawrence: for the moment, however, it is the positive side of this view I am concerned with, and his consequent treatment of human relationships. Lawrence's view of human relationships, it is still widely believed, was that nothing mattered except sex. This is true, but in such a

[1] 'The Novel and the Feelings'; *Phoenix*, p. 757

misleading sense that it would be better to call it untrue. It is so important to relate Lawrence's emphasis on sex to the 'candle flame, forever upright and yet flowing' of the body, that I have begun by stressing that, and saying as little as possible about sex. It is not that the popular view has exaggerated Lawrence's emphasis on sex—it hasn't: but it has narrowed the meaning he gave to it:

> And what is sex, after all, but the symbol of the relation of man to woman, woman to man? And the relation of man to woman is wide as all life. It consists in infinite different flows between the two beings, different, even apparently contrary. Chastity is part of the flow between man and woman, as to physical passion. And beyond these, an infinite range of subtle communication we know nothing about. . . . The long course of marriage is a long event of perpetual change, in which a man and a woman mutually build up their souls and make themselves whole. It is like rivers flowing on through new country, always unknown.[1]

This essay and *Apropos* (they belong closely together) offer us a splendidly dignified view of the relations between man and woman: reverent, and concerned for the integrity of another's personality. It is as far as could be from some popular views of what Lawrence stands for.

> This is sex, if you like. But it is no more sex than sunshine on the grass is sex. It is a living contact, give and take: the great and subtle relationship of men and women, man and woman.[2]

This then is Lawrence's theory. Many of his statements of it are more complex than I have been able to indicate, and many are far more cluttered up with confusions, anti-science and verbiage than I have let show. But I hope this account does justice to his view of man: as far as clarity and consistency are concerned, it perhaps does more than justice. The next task is clearly to turn to the relationships between men and women that he actually creates.

It is not, however, a clear transition. We have seen that the language of Lawrence's theorising can take on an imaginative glow; and it hardly needs repeating that his imaginative writing is shot through with theory. This is especially true of *Women in Love*, his most ambitious novel, and in the opinion of many admirers his

[1] 'We need one another' (1930); *Phoenix*, p. 193   [2] Ibid., p. 191

finest. The status of theory in that novel is crucial and, in a sense subversive: it leads to a confrontation which lies at the heart of Lawrence's conception of love, and which I am surprised his critics have paid so little attention to.

The high ambitious attempt of *Women in Love* consists in the fact that it unites the qualities of (say) *The Rainbow* and *We Need One Another*: an imaginative and a discursive treatment of the subject. The principal characters of *Women in Love* are all intelligent, self-conscious people, used to analysing their own emotions, interested in understanding why they do or don't get on with one another, or with themselves. Lawrence puts into their heads and mouths a complex and sustained commentary on their own feelings —not as an alternative to expressing these feeling through image, dialogue and action, but as well as that—indeed, as part of such expression. Here is the difficulty, of course: to take a piece of subtle analysis by Birkin or Gerald on its own terms is not to regard it as expression of that person's feelings, so that Lawrence is constantly drawn into losing distance from his characters, failing to see them objectively when he is interested in what they are saying. This is particularly so with Birkin.

There are moments, in *Women in Love*, when Lawrence splendidly achieves his aim of rendering the shape of a human relationship. When lovers quarrel, the impulses they follow are only poorly represented by what they actually say to one another. We all know that the most violent quarrels, the tenderest reconciliations, can be about apparent trivialities: for the quarrel is an enacting of a deeper rhythm than the complaints and apologies that may mark its apparent course. Resentment and need direct the ebb and flow of love, episodes of everyday living provide the content of what is said. Lawrence's genius consists in knowing this, and in showing us the true course of quarrels or of coming together. Any one of a number of scenes in *Women in Love* would illustrate this: I shall choose the outing of Birkin and Ursula in Chapter 23 ('Excurse'). It is an account of a quarrel and reconciliation. Birkin fetches Ursula after school, to take her for a ride. 'She consented. But her face was closed and unresponding, and his heart sank.' He gives her some rings he has bought for her: she is enchanted by them, and as she puts them on they are drawn together. But when he announces that he must return to have dinner with Hermione (Ursula's predecessor) the quarrel breaks into the open. She rages against Hermione and his 'spiritual brides', denounces the dirt and foulness that lie beneath their true and 'spiritual' union, and in the end she storms away. Birkin is left thinking of what she is saying—'tired and weak' but also relieved. He recognises that Ursula is partly right, but there is a darkness over his mind. Then when Ursula comes walking back, they are reconciled. She receives back from him the rings she had flung into the mud; they drive together into Southwell, to see the Minster and take a meal together, affectionately, intimately. Then they spend the night together, in Sherwood Forest, sleeping in the car. Out of the quarrel has come their deeper intimacy.

Does not the greatness of the scene lie in its sheer truthfulness—in Lawrence's rendering of what quarrels are like, in that eye for details which shows his responsiveness to the deepest levels of their emotional life? In—for example—a detail like this:

'No, you want *yourself*, and dirt and death—that's what you want. You are so *perverse*, so death-eating. And then—'
'There's a bicycle coming,' he said, writhing under her loud denunciation.
She glanced down the road.
'I don't care,' she cried.
Nevertheless she was silent. The cyclist, having heard the voices raised in altercation, glanced curiously at the man and the woman, and at the standing motor-car as he passed.
'—Afternoon,' he said cheerfully.
'Good-afternoon,' replied Birkin coldly.
They were silent as the man passed into the distance.[1]

How perfectly Lawrence has caught the poise and tug between keeping up appearances and the impatient impetus of the quarrel itself; how much is contained in that silence of the last sentence. And when the quarrel is healed, it is not by words at all—they stay apart from each other, and we stay with Birkin as his rage simmers down into indifference. Then comes this:

She was coming back. He saw her drifting desultorily under the high hedge, advancing towards him slowly. He did not move, he did not look again. He was as if asleep, at peace, slumbering and utterly relaxed.
She came up and stood before him, hanging her head.

[1] *Women in Love*, ch. 23

'See what a flower I found you,' she said, wistfully holding a piece of purple-red bell-heather under his face. He saw the clump of coloured bells, and the tree-like, tiny branch: also her hands, with their over-fine, over-sensitive skin.

'Pretty!' he said, looking up at her with a smile, taking the flower. Everything had become simple again, quite simple, the complexity gone into nowhere. But he badly wanted to cry: except that he was weary and bored by emotion.[1]

Lawrence's eye is true because he knows what is going on. Such a detail as 'desultorily' captures, surely, the whole nature of Ursula's timid return, hesitating on the edge of reconciliation. Lawrence focuses our attention on the flower because their attention was on it: at this moment he must deal with their feelings but not talk about them. And how justly Lawrence renders the tired healing of the breach, the mixture of positive and negative in the emotion of reconciliation, by saying that Birkin was bored by emotion. What does it matter what they quarrelled about, we say: this is how quarrels end.

And yet. This will not do, for it does matter. The content of their quarrel is the theme of the book. Lawrence means us to pay attention to their analyses of one another, he has put these in for themselves, not merely as symptoms. And what they are saying concerns Birkin's attempt to bully her. Has he not been bullying her all along, wanting her to marry him before she is ready in herself? Ursula and her sister have said of Birkin that 'his own voice is too loud—he cries you down'. He has wanted to shape Ursula, to detach her from her family, her own outlook—and in this scene she hits back. But Birkin wins, in the end: he and Ursula find a satisfying love, on his terms. This must mean that she submits, that they yield their obstinacy, that they find unity in renouncing the bitter mutual hostility of their contending individualities. So when they make love:

She had her desire of him, she touched, she received the maximum of unspeakable communication in touch, dark, subtle, positively silent, a magnificent gift and give again, a perfect acceptance and yielding, a mystery, the reality of that which can never be known, vital, sensual reality that can never be transmitted into mind content, but remains outside, living body of darkness and silence and subtlety, the mystic body of reality.[2]

[1] *Women in Love*, ch. 23   [2] Ibid., ch. 23

Is this the pattern of Birkin's relationship with Ursula? It is a fair account, is it not, of the course of their emotions, and corresponds to the feeling we take from the book. And yet, in another respect, it is the very opposite of what happens. For if we look at what they say to each other, we find that Birkin does not preach domination, but separateness; that Ursula does not say she wants to keep her individuality, she wants to merge with him. 'At the very last,' Birkin maintains, 'one is alone, beyond the influence of love.' He insists that they should cling to the 'real impersonal me', he believes in 'mutual unison in separateness'.

> She knew he would never abandon himself *finally* to her. He did not believe in final self-abandonment. He said it openly. It was his challenge. She was prepared to fight him for it. For she believed in an absolute surrender to love. She believed that love far surpassed the individual. He said the individual was *more* than love, or than any relationship.[1]

And in that case, the love that Birkin and Ursula finally achieve is not a merging but an acceptance of separateness. I cut short the last quotation but one. After speaking of 'the mystic body of reality', Lawrence goes on:

> She had her desire fulfilled. He had his desire fulfilled. For she was to him what he was to her, the immemorial magnificence of mystic, palpable, real otherness.[2]

Did Lawrence believe love was a merging or a separateness, a yielding or a holding apart? We are faced here with the same inconsistencies, the same shifts in terminology, that bedevilled our discussion of the body/mind dichotomy. It is hard to know how much contradiction there is between, say, his reverence for 'the strange reality of Otherness' in *Democracy* and his attack on the war because it will make:

> each one of us so completely a separate entity, that the whole will be an amorphous heap, like sand, sterile, hopeless, useless, like a dead tree.[3]

It is easier, certainly, to fit the reverence for otherness into the belief in yielding than the reverse: to say, for instance, that by

[1] Ibid., ch. 19   [2] Ibid., ch. 23
[3] Letter to Lady Cynthia Asquith, 2 November, 1915

surrendering our own individuality we learn to respect that of others. But like all such ingenious reconciliations, this ends by robbing the sharp, aggressive terms of a good deal of their meaning. It is wiser to point to the overwhelming, often unambiguous belief in merging that we can find at almost any point in Lawrence's career—abundantly in the early phase, of course; or in a letter of 1924, in which Lawrence pleads for 'a return to the older vision of life':

> It needs some welling up of religious sources that have been shut down in us: a great *yielding*, rather than an act of will: a yielding to the darker elder unknown, and a reconciliation.[1]

or in the passage from *Apropos* which I have used as an epigraph:

> This old maid typifies 'personality' instead of character, the sharp knowing in apartness, instead of knowing in together-ness, and she is, to my feeling, thoroughly unpleasant, English in the bad, mean snobbish sense of the word.[2]

Indeed, if we think of Jane Austen, and then of Jack Fergusson letting 'his heart yield' to Mabel, we cannot doubt that in any acceptable sense of the term, love for Lawrence is a yielding. He rises to his greatest eloquence in saying this:

> As a rule, when he started love-making, the emotion was strong enough to carry with it everything—reason, soul, blood—in a great sweep, like the Trent carries bodily its back-swirls and intertwinings, noiselessly. Gradually, the little criticisms, the little sensations, were lost, thought also went, everything borne along in one flood. He became, not a man with a mind, but a great instinct.[3]

I have quoted that because it is explicit and short: but we ought to see it as a pendant to the magnificent scene in which Paul makes love to Clara in the open field: 'they had met and included in their meeting the thrust of the manifold grass-stems, the cry of the pee-wit, the wheel of the stars'.

And then, when Lawrence came to write his most sustained and ambitious love story he took most of this back. *Women in Love*

[1] Letter to Rolf Gardiner, 4 July 1924
[2] 'Apropos of Lady Chatterley's Lover'
[3] *Sons and Lovers*, ch. 13

contrasts the failure in love of Gerald and Gudrun with the success of Birkin and Ursula. It is a hard-won success, for Birkin has to be healed from the frenetic, willed influence of Hermione, and Ursula has to learn to accept a new and harder conception of love. Though they win through to this only slowly, it is offered to us, in statement, from the very beginning: Birkin is quite clear on what he is striving towards. Lawrence is admirably objective in his treatment of Birkin as a man, but much less objective with his view of love. This is not presented as a personal trait or weakness, but as the book's own description of the relationship he and Ursula are striving to attain.

> There is a real impersonal me, that is beyond love, beyond any emotional relationship. So it is with you. But we want to delude ourselves that love is the root. It isn't. It is only the branches. The root is beyond love, a naked kind of isolation, an isolated me, that does *not* meet and mingle, and never can.[1]

This is Birkin's account of the 'mutual unison in separateness' that he is urging on Ursula. No doubt it is nothing like the sharp knowing in apartness that Lawrence so loathed in Jane Austen, but if we read the words it is hard to see much difference between separateness and apartness.

If this were simply a difference between *Women in Love* and Lawrence's previous work, we could explain it as a shift in Lawrence's views; though even that would not entitle us to shrug it off as unimportant. The more committed a writer, the more we must be disturbed when he changes sides. Changing sides is the gift of the debater, not the committed moralist, and it must lead us to wonder if what we took for literary power is not mere rhetorical competence. But we cannot, in any case, treat this contradiction in that way. In the first place, the passages I have quoted in favour of yielding come from both sides of *Women in Love*—as early as 1915, as late as 1930. Second, and more important, the contradiction exists within the novel: it is Birkin who preaches the need for each one remaining a separate entity, yet he is the one who tries to impose his will on Ursula. The action of the novel seems to contradict what the characters say.

There is one way out of the difficulty that will be suggested by many readers, and might have been suggested by Lawrence him-

---

[1] *Women in Love*, ch. 13

self: that is to use the magic words polarity or duality. For there are occasions in his discursive prose when Lawrence recognises that there are contrasting, even contradictory kinds of love. Perhaps the most relevant to our present purpose comes in his essay on *Love*, published in January 1918 (after *Women in Love* was written, but before it was published).

> There must be brotherly love, a wholeness of humanity. But there must also be pure, separate individuality, separate and proud, as a lion or a hawk. There must be both. In the duality lies fulfilment.[1]

Once again, Lawrence's own terminology gets in the way of understanding: to call these two principles sacred and profane love ('sacred' the desire for union, 'profane' the desire for separateness) adds nothing but confusion. Whatever the terms, the two principles are clearly those of love as yielding and love as otherness; and after the drive towards the merging of sacred love you will, Lawrence claims, feel a reaction of detestation. That is why both are necessary.

Love is not an essay of much intrinsic value. It blinds with metaphors ('what is the infinity of love but a cul-de-sac or a bottomless pit?'), and its language seems to me to have none of the authority of creation. But it is of interest when placed next to *Women in Love*, since it appears to contrast the same two attitudes to love. The difference, however, is that what I have called inconsistency, even contradition, Lawrence calls duality.

But that is merely an evasion. Lawrence's love stories are not about the possibility of a fruitful union between 'sacred' and 'profane' love, or the need for both in our emotional life. There is no duality in *The Rainbow* or *Women in Love* or *Lady Chatterley's Lover*: there is conflict. Two views of love meet and struggle, and one (with the aid of the novel) ousts the other. Ursula's love for Skrebensky must be outgrown and rejected, Skrebensky must be shown to be dead within; there must be a gradually clarifying contrast between the love of Ursula and that of Gudrun, we must realise that when one spells life the other spells death. This is clearer in *Lady Chatterley's Lover*, since the plan of that book is so much cruder: it is a simple, violently emphasised contrast between Connie's bond with Clifford and her bond with Mellors, and these we can only call—and are meant to call—the false and the true.

---

[1] 'Love' (1918); *Phoenix*, p. 155

When therefore, in an otherwise unmemorable essay, we find Lawrence telling us that there must be both, that in duality lies fulfilment, we have to say that the essay is not a key to the book, that it cannot take us out of the impasse which the book has led us into. Duality is not an easy way of contradicting oneself with impunity.

But although we may reject the essay as a solution, we cannot despise Lawrence for getting into the difficulty. For when he tells us that love is a yielding, and then has to tell us that it is a holding apart, the paradox he has landed himself in is—I don't want to mince this—true. And when the partner who bullies does so in the name of keeping one's individuality, and the partner who resists does so in the name of love that includes everything, any criticism is artificial which does not begin from the central fact of the plausibility of this. It is hard to develop this point without exceeding the proper bounds of literary criticism: the way to appeal to the experience of the reader is to write not a commentary but a poem or novel. This is not the place for that; and I have therefore simply to say that Lawrence's inconsistency results from his insight, not from an artistic perversity.

On at least one occasion Lawrence found a perfect symbol for this dual, even contradictory nature of love. In the scene in *The Rainbow* when Anna and Will bring in the sheaves, the rhythm of their work is played against their attraction to each other in the way separateness is played against merging in their emotions. 'They worked together, coming and going, in a rhythm, which carried their feet and their bodies in tune.' This rhythm keeps them separate from each other.

> And always, she was gone before he came. As he came, she drew away, as he drew away, she came. Were they never to meet? Gradually a low, deep-sounding will in him vibrated to her, tried to set her in accord, tried to bring her gradually to him, to a meeting, till they should be together, till they should meet as the sheaves that swished together.[1]

As they stay apart, each dominated by the movement of the work, a deeper unison arises between them. This low, deep-sounding will is born only of the growing tension of their work: the meeting they now long for will be the release of what they have built up as they carry the sheaves.

[1] *The Rainbow*, ch. 4

Till at last, they met at the shock, facing each other, sheaves in hand. And he was silvery with moonlight, with a moonlit, shadowy face that frightened her. She waited for him.

'Put yours down,' she said.

'No, it's your turn.' His voice was twanging and insistent.[1]

For a moment Anna yields to a short cut: and though he is longing only to take her in his arms and melt into her, he resists—his voice is twanging and resistent. Love is now a ritual of work that must not be skimped: their merging is the result of their ceremonial preservation of their individualities.

This scene is the most splendid in Lawrence: I believe, indeed, that it is the greatest love-scene in English fiction. The marvel lies in the underlying ritual wooing (this is any pair of lovers, in any century) as they cross and recross in their silent work; in the delicacy of perception that hovers on its surface (the 'faint, keen clash' as Anna sets down the sheaves, the 'twanging, insistent' voice in which Will tells her it's her turn); and in the power with which Lawrence goes to the quick of love in his account of what is stirred in Anna by Will's kisses:

Trembling with keen triumph, his heart was white as a star as he drove his kisses nearer.

'My love!' she called, in a low voice, from afar. The low sound seemed to call to him from far off, under the moon, to him who was unaware. He stopped, quivered, and listened.

'My love,' came again the low, plaintive call, like a bird unseen in the night.

He was afraid. His heart quivered and broke. He was stopped.

'Anna,' he said, as if he answered her from a distance, unsure. 'My love.'

And he drew near, and she drew near.

'Anna,' he said, in wonder and the birthpain of love.

'My love,' she said, her voice growing rapturous. And they kissed on the mouth, in rapture and surprise, long, real kisses.[2]

There is nothing to say about this scene. It illustrates the ideas of *Democracy*, *Apropos of Lady Chatterley's Lover*, and *We Need One Another*, but it does not need these essays. It does not need anything, except a reader who has been in love.

---

[1] *The Rainbow*, ch. 4   [2] Ibid., ch. 4

There is nothing as perfect as this in *Women in Love*, no symbol which so completely contains the duality in itself. In reading it we are witnesses, not of a clash between what characters say and what they are, but of a true representation of a complex relationship, a mimesis of attraction and distance. We can lament this lack in the later book; but we must add that it was not Lawrence's aim to write such scenes in *Women in Love*. Since its characters are themselves so highly articulate, the rise and fall of emotions takes place through a discussion of them.

Then we find that such discussion is beyond the powers of a Birkin. So subtle, so penetrating is Lawrence's understanding of how feelings move, that the only way Birkin (or even Lawrence in his own person) can keep up with them is by contradicting himself. To illustrate, not the inconsistencies of the formulation, but the truth of the underlying understanding, we have had to turn to a scene that foregoes the double ambition of *Women in Love*, and exempts Will and Anna from being able to say anything coherent about their feelings. The expression of an emotion cannot absorb a coherent analysis of it.

I salute and respect the attempt of *Women in Love* to write about articulate people; and if there is a way in which the book fails, it lies in Lawrence's uncertainty how reliable their version of their own relationships are. It would have been easy to let Birkin and Gerald talk about love, and make it clear that nothing they said was of intrinsic value, everything was there so that we could see why they said it. It would have been equally easy to put into their mouths as much understanding of their motivation as the author himself has. It is a sign of Lawrence's integrity and ambition that he rejected both these extremes even though the result is the inconsistency I have been pointing out.

5 *Two Tales*

Perhaps the most perfect expression of love in Lawrence is found in his tales. They cannot, of course, do what a full-length novel can do: they cannot show the 'long event of perpetual change, in which a man and a woman build up their souls and make themselves whole'. A tale like those of Lawrence is a cross section through such a complex relationship, often taken at a single moment in its development, showing us the actual state of feeling, the traces of what was, and the seeds of what is to come. A few of the best of the tales concentrate on the moment, with little attention to the before and after, dealing perhaps with a relation between several people: *Tickets Please* is a superb example of this. But most of them contain, however carefully hidden, a sense of process, a before and an after, absorbed into the action of the moment with that skill which is the mark of the natural short-story writer. The two stories I want now to discuss have the great merit that they do not achieve their goal easily. In both of them we see a relationship so casual, so eccentric or so brutal that we must think three times before consenting to call it love.

You Touched Me is the story of the Rockleys: Ted Rockley, midlands industrialist, rich, retired, widowed, dying of a kind of dropsy in the Pottery House, next door to his now disused pottery; his two daughters, Matilda and Emmie, already old maids (Matilda, the elder, is thirty-two), because they will have ten thousand each on his death, and 'in a thorough industrial district, it is not easy for the girls who have expectations above the common to find husbands'; and Hadrian, the charity schoolboy, about ten years younger than the girls, whom Ted Rockley had adopted because he had no son, who had grown up in the family with 'a subtle, jeering look on his face', and who went off to Canada at the age of sixteen 'without a word of thanks'. Hadrian joins the army during the war, and when the war is over writes to say he is coming to the Pottery House on a visit. During this visit he persuades the old man that Matilda ought to marry him: and Ted Rockley threatens that if she doesn't he will leave everything to Hadrian. The girls threaten Hadrian and protest to their father ('it's so *indecent,*' Matilda says) but the dying man insists 'with malevolent satisfaction'. 'He seemed to have a strange desire, quite unreasonable, for revenge upon the women who had surrounded him for so long, and served him so carefully.' Matilda suddenly agrees, she marries 'the indomitable dangerous charity boy', and the story ends with the dying man murmuring 'That's right! That's right!'

Now certainly this looks like the story of a nasty plot—a conspiracy by a scheming young man to get his stepsisters' money by exploiting a dying man's perversity. But that is the story Lawrence could have written, and did not write. Although reason and common sense must urge us to share the sisters' indignation, Lawrence wishes to show us that Hadrian, for all his pettiness, is on the side of life: that Matilda is not being victimised, but helped. It is not only that Hadrian's motives are not quite as mean as Emmie makes out:

> He knew, in his subtle, calculating way, that it was not for money he wanted Matilda. He wanted both the money and Matilda. But he told himself the two desires were separate, not one. He could not do with Matilda, *without* the money, But he did not want her *for* the money.[1]

It is that there is a link between Hadrian and Matilda of a different and deeper kind from the consciousness that seeks for money or cries 'unfair'. This is what the title refers to. Matilda, coming into her father's room in the middle of the night to comfort him, forgetting that he is sleeping downstairs, touches Hadrian by mistake. He is strangely moved by her touch: 'the soft, straying tenderness of her hand on his face startled something out of his soul'. It is this incident that gives him the idea of marrying her, and that justifies the outrageous suggestion in his own eyes. 'If you were anything decent,' Matilda says to him, 'you'd know that was a mistake, and forget it.' But she had established contact with him on a level where words like 'mistake' are meaningless. And Matilda, for all her protests, is partly aware of this: Lawrence never makes her as indignant or as bitter as her sister (though she is the one who has, reasonably, more cause to be), and when she finally comes round we are meant neither to feel too surprised nor to believe that something in her has been violated. Her father's spite and Hadrian's charity-boy cunning have outwitted the grey, dreary empty house, the old-maid respectability that had awaited the sisters.

Now has Matilda's unknown spontaneous self, her fullness of being, been destroyed or fulfilled? It is hard to say—it usually is, when Lawrence is at his best. It is not those who *talk* of reverence for the individual who help in this fulfilment—it may be the spiteful, the cunning, the greedy. When Lawrence appears, in his stories, to be flouting his own belief in individuality, he may simply, in his honesty, be making things hard for himself. As a matter of fact, we can see this very conveniently in the case of *You Touched Me*, for this story was once adapted for the stage by Tennessee Williams: adapted with such insensitivity that a simple comparison of the two will point direct to the merits of the original. Williams

[1] 'You Touched Me' (Phoenix edition of the complete Short Stories, p. 406)

turns Matilda into a young and beautiful girl, gives Emmie a ludicrous clergyman as a suitor, full of uplift and announcing tactfully (if improbably) that he doesn't intend actually to sleep with his wife, cuts out the father's spite and malevolent gleam, and turns Hadrian's charity-boy cunning into a wordy idealism, full of long speeches about the fine future that awaits the post-war world when it has thrown off stuffy conventions. Perhaps the comparison makes things too easy, since Williams has systematically vulgarised every detail of the story; but it is still worth saying that Williams has not increased but diminished the respect for the true living self. It is the very reluctance with which Matilda's accidental touch awakes Hadrian's feelings, and Hadrian's scheming awakes hers, that speaks for the genuineness of what is born in each of them.

The same reluctance appears in *The Horse Dealer's Daughter*, another of Lawrence's most moving stories, one which offers a more positive assurance of the awakening of love, but still a powerful tug against it from what might appear to be, but isn't, the individual self of the central figure. Jack Fergusson saves from drowning a young girl whose life has collapsed with the family fortunes, who has been told by her brothers that unless she goes to live with the sister she evidently dislikes she will have to find herself lodgings on the kerbstone. Mabel replies, in dumb obstinacy, that she won't go to her sister, and walks out into the cold black clayey pond to throw herself under just as Fergusson (who is a doctor, and a friend of her brothers') is passing. Fergusson saves her impersonally, as a doctor, takes off her wet clothes and wraps her in a blanket. When she comes round, and realises what has happened, she tells him—unreasonably, absurdly—that he must love her:

> 'You love me,' she murmured, in strange transport, yearning and triumphant and confident. 'You love me. I know you love me, I know.'
> And she was passionately kissing his knees, through the wet clothing, passionately and indiscriminately kissing his knees, his legs, as if unaware of everything.[1]

The girl is crazy. Fergusson hardly knows her, has no personal feelings towards her; feels, in fact, that his professional honour is being violated: yet she too has made contact with him at a level below common sense, reasonableness and professional honour.

[1] 'The Horse-dealer's Daughter' (Ibid., p. 453)

With an inward groan he gave way, and let his heart yield towards her. A sudden gentle smile came on his face. And her eyes, which never left his face, slowly, slowly filled with tears. He watched the strange water rise in her eyes, like some slow fountain coming up. And his heart seemed to burn and melt away in his breast.[1]

The element of otherness, of withdrawal, which in *Women in Love* had to be treated so prominently and explicitly, need not be mentioned in these tales: it is provided by the situation. They show us the slow, reluctant awakening of love from dislike, despair, common sense or simple inexperience; and a love that is forcing itself into awareness against such resistance can only take the form of a movement towards. When passion and sensual abandonment are struggling to master the personality, they will appear single and total, not ambivalent: pride, fear, money and honour provide all the separateness that is needed. And so in the tales, more completely than in many of the novels, we can see a yielding, a merging, that dramatises totally for us the contrast with Jane Austen.

6 Never trust the Artist

Delightful as it would be to linger on simple praise, I must now turn to the necessary, difficult task of setting praise against blame. If there were only good Lawrence—*Sons and Lovers, The Rainbow*, most of *Women in Love*, the ending of *The Lost Girl, The Virgin and the Gipsy*, most of the tales, and on a less intense level some of the letters and travel sketches—how grateful we would be. And yet, perhaps, how misled too. For what makes the badness in Lawrence so important, and so hard to identify and separate, is the intimate, the incestuous relationship it seems to have with his greatness.

To separate the genuine from the fake is, according to Lawrence's own view, to save the books from their author. A generation before Wimsatt and Beardsley wrote their famous essay on *The Intentional Fallacy*, Lawrence formulated the doctrine in a sentence: 'Never trust the artist, trust the tale.' It is a doctrine that grows very naturally from Lawrence's views: we can see this if we turn to his essay *The Novel and the Feelings*. It is a lament that man has been 'tamed', and will not easily be able to 'sow wild seed' again—

[1] Ibid., p. 454

not one of Lawrence's best, but culminating in a paragraph of sudden, fierce beauty:

> How shall we even begin to educate ourselves in the feelings? Not by laying down laws, or commandments, or axioms and postulates. Not even by making assertions that such and such is blessed. Not by words at all.
>
> If we can't hear the cries far down in our own forests of dark veins, we can look in the real novels, and there listen-in. Not listen to the didactic statements of the author, but to the low, calling cries of the characters, as they wander in the dark woods of their destiny.[1]

The artist, when he speaks in his own person, speaks from 'the theory of knowledge, the metaphysic of the man' which is 'much smaller than the man himself' (*Study of Thomas Hardy*): therefore Lawrence urges us not to believe 'old-fashioned Nathaniel, with his little boy charm', or the Tolstoi who 'denied all that was great in him, with vehement cowardice', but to trust their books instead, the creative quick of the books and not the commentary imposed by the authors, for there we will hear 'the low, calling cries of the characters as they wander in the dark woods of their destiny'.

The most memorable statement of the doctrine comes in the essay on *The Novel*:

> It is such a bore that nearly all great novelists have a didactic purpose, otherwise a philosophy, directly opposite to their passional inspiration. In their passional inspiration, they are all phallic worshippers. . . .
>
> Oh give me the novel. Let me hear what the novel says. As for the novelist, he is usually a dribbling liar.[2]

To save the tales of Lawrence from the artist who created them is more difficult than in the cases of Jane Austen and George Eliot. For Lawrence is as much of a dribbling liar as any other great novelist; and his lies were mostly about phallic worship. To save *his* tales from their creator is to shoulder out of the way the very doctrine in whose name, according to Lawrence, we are supposed to be acting.

Through the whole of Lawrence runs a contrast between two kinds of men. It is something like Hardy's contrast between the

---

[1] 'The Novel and the Feelings'; *Phoenix*, p. 759
[2] 'The Novel'; in *Reflections on the Death of a Porcupine*

gentleman and the peasant, but more defiant, more violent, more deep-searching. On the one hand, there are men like the younger Tom Brangwen (Ursula's uncle) and Skrebensky in *The Rainbow*, Dr Mitchell in *The Lost Girl*, Rico in *St Mawr*, the vicar in *The Virgin and the Gipsy*, Mr Massey in *The Daughters of the Vicar*, Owen in *The Plumed Serpent*, and Clifford Chatterley. These men are sophisticated, spiteful, often intellectuals, often rich, and always against life. On the other hand are Morel in *Sons and Lovers*, Cicio in *The Lost Girl*, the two grooms in *St Mawr* (Lewis more than Phoenix, and neither of them fully, for the character who really belongs here is the horse itself), the gipsy in *The Virgin and the Gipsy*, Arthur in *The Daughters of the Vicar*, both Ramon and Cipriano in *The Plumed Serpent*, and Mellors. These men are often working class, sometimes foreign, full of a smouldering, sullen energy, impulsive, unintellectual, contemptuous of reasonings, and highly sexed.

Looking at these lists (both of which could be much longer, especially if we included the tales) we must be struck with one thought: that with a single exception, they do not show Lawrence at his best. For this contrast, that Lawrence draws over and over again, is a contrast to do with phallic worship: he draws it in order to assert his doctrine, and in it he does not, or not often, speak the speech of art, the 'only true speech'.

> 'Yes, I will come,' he said, still watching the bicycle tube, which sprawled nakedly on the floor. The forward drop of his head was curiously beautiful to her, the straight, powerful nape of the neck, the delicate shape of the back of the head, the black hair. The way the neck sprang from the strong loose shoulders was beautiful. There was something mindless but *intent* about the forward reach of his head. His face seemed colourless, neutral-tinted and expressionless.[1]

That is not the speech of art, it is a mechanical doling out of Lawrentian phrases (above all, 'mindless but *intent*'). Cicio has not been seen, we have nothing but an assertion of his power, of the fact that he stands for a force of life in the book. And how the doughy, dull presentation of Cicio contrasts with the vivid reality of the Houghtons and the world of Woodhouse.

I said there was one exception to this: and that of course is

---

[1] *The Lost Girl*, ch. 8

Morel. Lawrence hardly ever created a character more convincing, more coherent (without being merely predictable) and more alive than this version of the father he resented and regarded as having dragged his mother down. To illustrate the power with which Morel is created one would need to quote the whole book, but I will mention two episodes in particular. One is the birth of Paul. Mrs Morel (who has a hard time) is helped by a neighbour, Mrs Bower; the baby is born while Morel is at work and he returns, tired, hungry and dirty, to find a strange woman in possession:

> Morel, thinking nothing, dragged his way up the garden path, wearily and angrily. He closed his umbrella, and stood it in the sink; then he sluthered his heavy boots into the kitchen. Mrs Bower appeared in the inner doorway.
> 'Well,' she said, 'she's about as bad as she can be. It's a boy childt.'
> The miner grunted, put his empty snap-bag and his tin bottle on the dresser, went back into the scullery and hung up his coat, then came and dropped into his chair.
> 'Han yer got a drink?' he asked.
> The woman went into the pantry. There was heard the pop of a cork. She set the mug, with a little, disgusted rap, on the table before Morel. He drank, gasped, wiped his big moustache on the end of his scarf, drank, gasped, and lay back in his chair. The woman would not speak to him again. She set his dinner before him, and went upstairs.[1]

If sympathy lies anywhere in this scene, it is surely with the man. Lawrence is showing us the sex war, and it is the woman (as so often on occasions of childbirth) who is the aggressor. Morel is completely self-centred, but he has the excuse of exhaustion; Mrs Bower is concerned about Mrs Morel but, we see here, in a way that uses sympathy as fuel for indignation: instead of her anger with Morel being the consequence of her concern for his wife, the concern almost exists to feed the anger. And all of this is conveyed in that one completely apt physical detail, the 'little, disgusted rap' of the mug on the table—too actual for a symbol, but enclosing in itself the whole meaning of the incident.

In the very next incident, we see another side of Morel. He returns home to find the Congregational clergyman having tea in the house:

[1] *Sons and Lovers*, ch. 2

Morel took off his coat, dragged his armchair to the table, and sat down heavily,

'Are you tired?' asked the clergyman.

'Tired? I ham that,' replied Morel. '*You* don't know what it is to be tired, as *I'm* tired.'

'No,' replied the clergyman.

'Why, look yer 'ere,' said the miner, showing the shoulders of his singlet. 'It's a bit dry now, but it's wet as a clout with sweat even yet. Feel it.'

'Goodness!' cried Mrs Morel. 'Mr Heaton doesn't want to feel your nasty singlet.'

The clergyman put out his hand gingerly.[1]

Once again, what we must notice is the perfect truth of the scene, the sharpness with which Lawrence has seen everyone's behaviour —so sharply that in its last detail the passage is almost comic. The sympathy we were offered for Morel is hovering again as the scene begins: Mrs Morel's exclamation is a token of her alienation from his habits, so automatic that she cannot be blamed, but none the less cruel. But when Morel comes in he forfeits it all by dramatising his position, enjoying his moral advantage over the clergyman in exactly the same way Mrs Bower had enjoyed hers over him.

It is a sign of Lawrence's mastery that in so short a space he can show us Morel in two such different lights, and convince us that they are not merely compatible but complementary, that the man who behaved in one way is likely to behave in the other. Both these scenes come early in the book, but the character of Morel continues to develop and to be explored, even until he is an old man, no longer in the foreground, tamed by age and still under Lawrence's scrutiny.

In later life Lawrence confessed that he thought he had been unjust to his father, and said that if he were to write the book again he would be more sympathetic to the father, and less to the mother. How thankful we can be that he never did this! For it cannot be coincidence that Morel, the most successful of Lawrence's surly sexed and vital men, is the one against whom he bears a grudge: it is that grudge which stiffened Lawrence's treatment of him, caused him to see Morel with ruthless clarity, and kept away the indulgence and hysteria that caused Lawrence to ruin so many other versions of such a character (and whose seeds no doubt

[1] Ibid., ch. 2

were already present in what gave Morel his vitality). The resentment is, of course, personal in origin: Lawrence hates Morel because it is his father. From this we can conclude that here is an author who writes better, not worse, for incompletely detaching himself from an autobiographical situation. When Lawrence made his recantation he had perhaps detached himself enough from his memories to feel calmly about his father; but that calmness would merely have laid Morel open to the forces in Lawrence that would have wanted to make him another Cicio, another Annable.

The reason why this contrast between two kinds of men recurs so regularly is that it is a sign of the very contrast with which we began: that between blood and mind. This can be used as a guide through Lawrence's fiction in other ways than as a method of sorting out the characters. If we ask ourselves what these violently committed books are asking us to accept and reject, we will find that we are indicating the full range of human experience that he covers. And we can express our disquiet by saying that there is too much in what he rejects that is admirable, even necessary, too much in what he accepts that is pernicious. What he rejects is too like reason, what he accepts is too like brutality. I will deal with these one at a time, though the distinction is rather artificial.

7 What Lawrence Rejects

What he rejects. To say that Lawrence rejects reason is to fall foul of many of his present admirers. It is common nowadays to stress Lawrence's intelligence, to say that 'he almost always made it clear in his later work that he meant that *the blood, the flesh, the instincts, should operate in balance with the intellect*, and not alone'. This remark, by Harry T. Moore, can be paralleled from Leavis, Hoggart, Spilka, Alvarez and others, and it is usually the anti-Lawrentians who deny it. I hope it is not necessary to join the anti-Lawrentians to say that Mr Moore's 'almost' covers a concession so gigantic that it would be less misleading simply to say his remark is untrue.

It would not be difficult to make a list of the occasions when Lawrence said more or less the opposite to what Mr Moore claims he said: from his remark to Aldous Huxley 'All scientists are liars', to Ramon saying in *The Plumed Serpent* 'Man is a column of blood, with a voice in it. And when the voice is still, and he is only a column of blood, he is better.'[1] (And in a letter to Secker Lawrence asserted that what Ramon means in the book is what he means.) But it would not be difficult, either, to make a list of counter-quotations, and to match them against one another is not to talk about literature. What is disturbing is not a number of casual remarks made by Lawrence in his letters: Lawrence's explicit statements, as I am wearisomely insisting, matter because Lawrence is an artist: and what I am here recording is a tendency in his art to denigrate intellect—and so to damage the art.

It is most clearly seen in *Lady Chatterley's Lover*. Not the best of Lawrence, nor even (artistically) very typical, this book is in one sense Lawrence at his most characteristic. It is constructed to show at its clearest and bluntest the contrast that more intricately informs his other work. Connie Chatterley, married to the impotent, clever and spiteful Clifford, mistress of the passionate, tender and sullen Mellors, is drawn by two contrasting worlds, and the book is the story of her movement from one to the other. What got the book into trouble was the explicitness of the love scenes, the treatment of the Mellors world: and I will not deny that by almost any feasible legal criterion it was natural to ban a book that contained such scenes. Here however, we are concerned not with law but with literature—we are not even concerned (as the law now is) with the ludicrous but no doubt necessary task of joining the two. And speaking of the book as literature, I want to say that it is the Clifford half that is bad. Connie's affair with Mellors is moving and—in places—beautiful. Mellors seen by Mrs Bolton, or in relation to the wood and the young pheasants, seems to me an imaginative success, and even the notorious four-letter words are not nearly as disastrous as often claimed. I respect Lawrence's aim in using them, and dissent only with sadness from the achievement. Where this book *is* disastrous though—where it is even vicious—is in the anti-intellectual sneer with which it portrays Clifford.

Clifford was inviting the young man of thirty at an inauspicious moment in that young man's career. Yet Clifford did not hesitate. Michaelis had the ear of a few million people, probably, and, being a hopeless outsider, he would no doubt be grateful to be asked down to Wragby at this juncture, when the rest of the smart world was cutting him. Being grateful, he would no doubt do Clifford 'good' over there in America. Kudos! A man

[1] *The Plumed Serpent*, ch. 25

gets a lot of kudos, whatever that may be, by being talked about in the right way, especially 'over there'. Clifford was a coming man; and it was remarkable what a sound publicity instinct he had. In the end Michaelis did him most noble in a play, and Clifford was a sort of popular hero. Till the reaction, when he found he had been made ridiculous.[1]

Is it possible for writing to be flatter than this? How tired the drab, unfelt, journalistic language—'inauspicious moment', 'hopeless outsider', 'did him most nobly'. Like so much of the later Lawrence, this writing is poised between the author's account of Clifford's intentions and actions, and Clifford's own account: it does not report what Clifford was thinking, but it does describe his thoughts in the sort of sloppy, careless language he might himself have used. The same is true of *St Mawr*, most of which has the faults, but not the virtues, of confining itself to Mrs Witt's point of view (and her slangy, limited vocabulary). Reading stuff like this, one can see the point of Yvor Winter's fantastic claim that the dramatic mode is the enemy of literature, because it confines the author within the insensitivity of his characters:

> Let us suppose that the dramatist is imitating the speech of a character of moderate intelligence in a situation of which the character does not in any serious sense understand the meaning. This presents an almost insoluble problem. If the poet is endeavouring to communicate his own best understanding of a human situation, that is one thing. If he is endeavouring to communicate approximately a plausible misunderstanding of a situation on the part of an imaginary character much less intelligent than himself, that is quite another.[2]

The answer to this is long and complex: partly it is that dramatic convention, in writers from Racine to Ivy Compton Burnett, allows the characters of a play to retain all their other limitations but to be granted the gift of articulateness; and partly it is that drama does imply a regard for our fellowmen, a belief that everyone's viewpoint is worth expressing. Perhaps this latter is the reason why the one character to whom the writer ought not to confine himself is a character he despises—and perhaps that is what is wrong with *St Mawr*, and with half of *Lady Chatterley's Lover*. Yet

[1] *Lady Chatterley's Lover*, ch. 3
[2] 'Problems for the Modern Critic of Literature, § 7; in *The Function of Criticism*

the worst thing in this passage is the moment at which Lawrence seems to agree with Winters, seems to realise that he is using terms in the same shoddy way as Clifford, and ought to do something about it. What does he do? He adds inverted commas: that is to say, he *admits* that words like 'good' and 'over there' are inadequate, but does nothing about it. Or he extends the inverted commas into a phrase: 'a man gets a lot of kudos, *whatever that may be. . .*'. Another admission that the whole vocabulary is tired and useless—admitted in the same shoddy, tired vocabulary.

It is not surprising, then, as we look at this cursory paragraph and ask ourselves what sort of plays Michaelis wrote, what it was Michaelis said of Clifford in his play, what caused the reaction, that we realise that Lawrence has not even begun to trouble himself towards giving us an answer.

Why is Lawrence so unfair, so glib, in his treatment of Clifford? Because he so hates what Clifford stands for that he wants only to claw it down. He does not trouble, therefore, to create what he is attacking in order that we shall be convinced of its limitations: he merely abuses what he has not troubled to create. Let us turn to a longer scene—and here I must quote at length, though not as great length as is perhaps desirable: the scene in Chapter XVI in which Clifford talks about the popular scientific book (by Julian Huxley, perhaps, or James Jeans) that he has been reading.

'What do you think of this, by the way?' he said, reaching for his book. 'You'd have no need to cool your ardent body by running out in the rain, if only we had a few more aeons of evolution behind us. Ah here it is!—"The universe shows us two aspects: on one side it is physically wasting, on the other it is spiritually ascending".'

Connie listened, expecting more. But Clifford was waiting. She looked at him in surprise.

'And if it spiritually ascends,' she said, 'what does it leave down below, in the place where its tail used to be?'

'Ah!' he said. 'Take the man for what he means. *Ascending is* the opposite of his *wasting*, I presume.'

'Spiritually blown out, so to speak!'

'No, but seriously, without joking: do you think there is anything in it?'

She looked at him again.

'Physically wasting?' she said. 'I see you getting fatter, and I'm not wasting myself. Do you think the sun is smaller than he used to be? He's not to me. And I suppose the apple Adam offered Eve wasn't really much bigger, if any, than one of our orange pippins. Do you think it was?'

'Well hear how he goes on: "It is thus slowly passing, with a slowness inconceivable in our measures of time, to new creative conditions, amid which the physical world, as we at present know it, will be represented by a ripple barely to be distinguished from nonentity".'

She listened with a glisten of amusement. All sorts of improper things suggested themselves. But she only said:

'What silly hocus-pocus! As if his little conceited consciousness could know what was happening as slowly as all that! It only means *he's* a physical failure on the earth, so he wants to make the whole universe a physical failure. Priggish little impertinence!'

'Oh, but listen! Don't interrupt the great man's solemn words!—"The present type of order in the world has risen from an unimaginable past, and will find its grave in an unimaginable future. There remains the inexhaustive realm of abstract forms, and creativity with its shifting character ever determined afresh by its own creatures, and God, upon whose wisdom all forms of order depend."—There, that's how he winds up!'

Connie sat listening contemptuously.

'He's spiritually blown out,' she said. 'What a lot of stuff! Unimaginables, and types of order in graves, and realms of abstract forms, and creativity with a shifty character, and God mixed up with forms of order! Why it's idiotic!'

'I must say, it is a little vaguely conglomerate, a mixture of gases, so to speak,' said Clifford. 'Still, I think there is something in the idea that the universe is physically wasting and spiritually ascending.'

'Do you? Then let it ascend, so long as it leaves me safely and solidly physically here below.'

'Do you like your physique?' he asked.

'I love it!' And through her mind went the words: It's the nicest, nicest woman's arse as is!

'But that is really rather extraordinary, because there's no denying it's an encumbrance. But then I suppose a woman doesn't take a supreme pleasure in the life of the mind.'[1]

This scene is lazy, cheap and ineffective. It is lazy because Lawrence has simply put down what will provide a convenient contrast

[1] *Lady Chatterley's Lover*, ch. 16

with the previous love-scene with Mellors: he has not troubled to make it plausible in itself. It is thoroughly improbable that Clifford would begin with that laboured reference to running out in the rain —quite unconnected with what he is saying, offered to us in a rhythm not even remotely like that of real speech: but it has to go in, so that Lawrence can make sure we are busy contrasting Clifford with Mellors. And as he unfolds to us the contents of the book Clifford is reading, we see how easy Lawrence has made things for himself. He does not really want to tell us what the scientific-religious attitude is, he merely wants to make fun of it: he has set up what is only too easy to knock down. And it was not enough to make the author write badly—Lawrence has to get Clifford to join in the denigration, so that there shall be no mistake.

> I must say, it is a little vaguely conglomerate, a mixture of gases, so to speak.

More remarkable still is Clifford's remark: 'Oh, but listen! Don't interrupt the great man's solemn words!' I find this completely baffling. Is Clifford serious? And if so, does Lawrence really want us to believe that he would speak with such crass pomposity? Or is he ironic—in which case, why is the Clifford who can be so relaxed and impartial at this moment given so much hot air to speak in the rest of the scene? The kindest explanation I can find is that Lawrence was here being careless.

The scene is cheap because Connie's criticisms of the book are so crude, so sneering and so stupid that they remove any sympathy we might have for her. The scene in which Mellors, fondling her buttocks, had said to her 'Tha's got such a nice tail on thee', and had gone on to describe, quietly and frankly, all her bodily functions, had a genuine if misguided dignity: I respect what Lawrence was getting at there. But in this conversation, where Connie is meant to be still under the charm of that earlier scene, she speaks with a sniggering crudity that has no trace of dignity:

> 'Physically wasting?' she said. 'I see you getting fatter, and I'm not wasting myself.'

And not only Connie—Lawrence sniggers too:

> She listened with a glisten of amusement. All sorts of improper things suggested themselves.

And the scene is ineffective because it is cheap. So completely are we alienated by the way Connie talks, that we can no longer be sure that what she speaks for is any better than what the book was saying. And beneath such doubt lies the more radical doubt whether, in a scene as dead, as unrealised as this, it is worth bothering which side we are on.

8 'How beastly the bourgeois is': Lawrence's Poetry

It is not only Lawrence's fiction that is disfigured by his sneers: so is his poetry, and especially those most typical, those most admired late poems called *Pansies*. I choose one of the most famous.

How beastly the bourgeois is
especially the male of the species—

Presentable, eminently presentable—
shall I make you a present of him?

Isn't he handsome? Isn't he healthy? Isn't he a fine specimen?
doesn't he look the fresh clean englishman, outside?
Isn't it god's own image? tramping his thirty miles a day
after partridges, or a little rubber ball?
wouldn't you like to be like that, well off, and quite the thing?

Oh, but wait!
Let him meet a new emotion, let him be faced with another
man's need,
let him come home to a bit of moral difficulty, let life face him
with a new demand on his understanding and then watch him
go soggy, like a wet meringue.
Watch him turn into a mess, either a fool or a bully.
Just watch the display of him, confronted with a new demand on
his intelligence,
a new life-demand.

How beastly the bourgeois is
especially the male of the species—

Nicely groomed, like a mushroom
standing there so sleek and erect and eyeable—
and like a fungus, living on the remains of bygone life
sucking his life out of the dead leaves of greater life than his
own.

220

And even so, he's stale, he's been there too long.
Touch him, and you'll find he's all gone inside
just like an old mushroom, all wormy inside, and hollow
under a smooth skin and an upright appearance.

Full of seething, wormy, hollow feelings
rather nasty—
How beastly the bourgeois is!

Standing in their thousands, these appearances, in damp
  England
what a pity they can't all be kicked over
like sickening toadstools, and left to melt back, swiftly
into the soil of England.[1]

This poem is quite interesting in itself; and very interesting indeed as a specimen of Lawrence. Its lively opening promises us something sharp and deadly—

> *How catty our Bertie can be*
> *—And he a lad from the mines!*

Its flippancy, its sprightliness, are of a kind that places the speaker as well as the subject. The deliberate clichés in that charming rhythm—a rhythm of gay, almost neurotic conversation; the brittle joke on 'presentable'; you can *see* the speaker, wearing a tight skirt and long hair, holding a sherry glass, nervously tapping the ash off a cigarette in a long holder. Intelligent, sharp, witty, but not really free of what she's attacking. How perfectly Lawrence has caught her:

> *Isn't it god's own image? tramping his thirty miles a day*

The pronouns ('isn't *it*', '*his* thirty miles') reveal just that touch of patronage laced with malice that shows the speaker not quite free of involvement. Why didn't Lawrence always write like this? Why, oh why, didn't he always trust to this sure instinct?

And then, as we read on, we realise it's meant to be taken straight. It's a serious denunciation of the bourgeois—it isn't satire at all, just denunciation. And so the poem goes soggy, 'like a wet meringue'. The language gets abstract, the rhythm disappears:

> *let him come home to a bit of moral difficulty, let life face him*
> *with a new demand on his understanding.*

[1] 'How Beastly the Bourgeois is', from *Pansies*

221

We can remind ourselves of Lawrence's own defences of free verse, in his letters:

> I think, don't you know, that my rhythms fit my mood pretty well, in the verse. And if the mood is out of joint, the rhythm often is. I have always tried to get an emotion out in its own course, without altering it.[1]

Break the rhyme rather than the stony directness of speech.[2]

There is no stony directness in 'let life face him with a new demand on his understanding'. It no longer thrusts its clichés at us with a bright smile, as in 'especially the male of the species'; it slips them over in the sag of the rhythm, hoping they won't be noticed. And if that 'fits his mood'—well, we can say that the mood is out of joint, instead of saying that the rhythm is a clumsy expression of it: as a criticism of the poem, they come to the same thing.

Satire needs formality more than any other kind of poetry. The iron couplets of Pope serve two important functions: the wit and the aesthetic satisfaction give the reader a shiver of delight that enables him to take the bitterness: and the discipline they are evidence of transforms the emotion from self-indulgence to something fierce. Without formality, satire too easily becomes grumbling—as does this poem. The flood of abstract nouns in the fourth verse is the sign that Lawrence has lost control; and as we ask what these nouns remind us of ('a bit of moral difficulty') we realise with a shock that the poem has turned into a sermon.

Now, for the rest of the poem, the sermon fights the sharp, cruel liveliness. The latter is still there

—watch him go soggy, like a wet meringue—

(the girl puts down her sherry glass to hold one up; it sticks to her finger; the party's drawing to a close), but so is the preaching:

—sucking his life out of the dead leaves of greater life than his own.

The girl's lip is seen to curl disdainfully once or twice

—rather nasty—

but by the end it is all Lawrence, mouthing in fury, out of control:

[1] Letter to Edward Marsh, 18 August, 1913
[2] Letter to Catherine Carswell, 11 January, 1916

what a pity they can't all be kicked over
like sickening toadstools.

This is abuse of the kind that impedes the clear expression of any emotion. And the emotion it does, however clumsily, betray is not a pleasant one, and not all that rare in Lawrence. It is the delight Lawrence takes in St Mawr ('the glossy powerful haunches of St Mawr swaying with life, always too much life, like a menace') kicking the foppish young man in the teeth.

While that unpleasant moralising gentleman who takes himself so seriously is denouncing the bourgeois in one corner of the room, the girl's shrill voice rises cattily above the party: 'rather nasty,' she says, talking—we realise with a shock—about *him*.

A single phrase betrays the weakness of this poem: the 'oh but wait!' that introduces the fourth verse. This always rang false to me, but it was only after much thought that I was able to decide why. The reason, I now see, is that it announces a transition, and one assumes it will introduce a change of attitude:

Oh but wait! female of a not so different species,
    Aren't you god's own image, tapping your little rubber ball of phrases
after the man you want to catch.

But it does nothing of the sort. There is no transition, no standing back to view the critic critically. We continue as before, abusing the bourgeois: the phrase was a false alarm.

The trouble with Lawrence as a poet is twofold. The first is his formlessness. I think the very fact that this charge is so obvious has caused critics to hesitate, and not make it; but there are times when criticism needs to state the obvious. Because his lines, and his poems, have no shape, the emotion has no shape either. I realise that I have put this the wrong way round: it is the shape of the emotion that should determine the shape of the poem ('I have always tried to get an emotion out in its own course, without altering it'). But there is, after all, such a thing as technique: by writing you discover just what you want to say. If you always try to get an emotion out in its own course—if you never *work* at it—you are making yourself helpless: a poem then is a hit or miss affair, and when the mood is not out of joint it may, by luck, come right of itself. Every poet knows that a poem's success depends largely on luck: few have gone so far as Lawrence in relying on nothing else.

I have tried to sort out the lines in this poem that do and don't fit the emotion, without asking that they fit any formal pattern: I have tried, that is, not to reproach the poem for being in free verse. But I don't want to conceal the fact that I regard free verse with misgiving. A successful poem in free verse seems to me about as rare as any other run of good luck. As readers of poetry, we are helped by formal patterns to share the poet's emotion; and he was often helped by them to shape and even (in extreme cases) to discover it. That our minds are helped in this way by patterning may depress some, though it doesn't depress me much: but it seems to me inescapably true. We don't need to overvalue formal beauty for its own sake—we don't need to become aesthetes—to say that Lawrence's formal slovenliness made things harder for his poems.

The other great fault of Lawrence's poetry is its abandonment to gusts of emotion (the two faults are, of course, connected). Over and over, Lawrence's poems go wrong because, instead of expressing an emotion, they betray it: instead of showing us the true shape and nature of an experience, they give vent to the everyday phrases that his hate, his love or his indignation have thrust at him. Especially his indignation. Some of the indignant poems in *Pansies* are almost very good: some are awful. But almost all of them lapse, sooner or later, into a kind of mouthing. *Ships in Bottles*, for example, starts from a brilliant idea:

> *O ship in a bottle*
> *with masts erect and spars all set and sails spread*
> *how you remind me of my London friends,*
> *O ships in bottles!*[1]

If one wasn't so used to being disappointed, one would expect something sharp and memorable from this opening. Even the move from singular to plural seems pointed and effective: it corresponds, we realise, to the move from literal to figurative. It is tiny things like that which we mean by 'form'. But before the poem is over, the sermon has begun:

> *Sail, little ships in your glass bottles*
> *safe from every contact,*
> *safe from all experience,*
> *safe, above all, from life!*[1]

[1] 'Ships in Bottles', from *Pansies*

You can't get much triter than that. It is the voice of 'Lift up your hearts'; it is the voice of Lawrence being carried away; most certainly, it is not the voice of poetry.

9 What Lawrence Accepts

Perhaps we are almost repeating the same point if we turn now to what Lawrence accepts, and express disquiet at that too. A good starting-point here is the list of wants in Lawrence's letter to Collings (quoted on p. 181). It concluded with wanting to be aggressive: 'I want to look a beastly swell today, I want to kiss that girl, I want to insult that man'. Lawrence often saw aggressiveness as a form of emotional honesty—as no doubt it is. Those who deny aggressiveness and assert universal benevolence are, to Lawrence, absurd and even wicked. This is the subject of one of his best essays, *Nobody Loves Me*, which begins with an account of the complaint of a fifty-year-old New England woman. When asked how she was:

> 'Well!' she replied, glancing almost viciously out of the window at the immutable slopes and peaks opposite, 'I don't know how *you* feel about it—but—these mountains! well!— I've lost *all* my *cosmic consciousness*, and *all* my *love for humanity*.'[1]

The rest of the essay sets out to prefer emotional honesty, an acceptance of 'the condition of true egoism, and emptiness' in oneself to humanitarianism, cosmic benevolence and theoretical goodwill. It is not by accident that the woman is made a New Englander, for these are the qualities Lawrence made fun of in Emerson and Whitman, and this essay, like the study of Whitman, is written with more wit and less disabling indignation than is usual in Lawrence:

> The way to kill any feeling is to insist on it, harp on it, exaggerate it. Insist on loving humanity, and sure as fate you'll come to hate everybody. Because, of course, if you insist on loving humanity, then you insist that it shall be lovable: which half the time it isn't. In the same way, insist on loving your husband, and you won't be able to help hating him secretly. Because of course nobody is *always* lovable.[1]

[1] 'Nobody Loves Me' (1930); *Phoenix*, p. 204

Assenting to this (as we surely must) we turn to see what Lawrence makes of it in his fiction; and there we realise that it was not, in itself, a sufficient guide through human conduct.

> Aaron Sisson watched the other dark face, with its utterly exposed eyes. He was in a state of semi-intoxicated anger and clairvoyance. He saw in the black void, glistening eyes of the oriental only the same danger, the same menace which he saw in the landlady. Fair, wise, even benevolent words: always the human good speaking, and always underneath, something hateful, something detestable and murderous. Wise speech, and good intentions—they were invariably maggoty with these secret lustful inclinations to destroy the man in a man. Whenever he heard anyone holding forth: the landlady, this doctor, the spokesman at the miner's meeting—or the all-benevolent newspaper—his soul curdled with revulsion as from something foul. Even the infernal good-will and love of his wife. To hell with good-will. It was more hateful than ill-will. All righteous bullying, like poison gas![1]

In summary, this passage would seem to be saying much the same as the previous one: yet we cannot give it anything like the same assent. The scrupulousness of the first piece has gone, replaced by a fierce delight in the conclusion. Now we must be fair here: partly this change is from careful truthfulness to something cruder, but partly it is a change of speaker, from Lawrence's own essay-writing person to an angry miner. I do not mean by this that the second passage is simply dramatic, an expression of Aaron's anger, for there is no doubt that Lawrence assents to what Aaron is thinking: if the context did not make this clear, we could deduce it from the language—the word 'clairvoyance', or the syntax of 'he saw ... the same ... which he saw ...', or even the use of 'invariably'. The difference here is not simply the difference between Lawrence's opinions and Lawrence's reporting of someone else's opinions; it is the subtler, perhaps more important difference between two ways of holding an opinion—in judicious calm, or in anger.

Turning from calm to anger has not brought sheer loss. Nothing in the first passage quite had the bite of

> Wise speech and good intentions—they were invariably maggoty with these secret lustful inclinations to destroy the man in man.

[1] *Aaron's Rod*, ch. 2

But nothing in it corresponds to the rant into which the second piece degenerates at the end: the cliché of 'holding forth', the tired sneer of 'all-benevolent newspaper', the final, gratuitous cliché of 'like poison gas'.

This anger of Aaron's is something between the honesty that Lawrence pleaded for in *Nobody Loves Me*, that recognises the *fact* of aggressive impulses, even their use to him who feels them; and an acceptance, a glorifying of brutality in the name of such honesty. Turning to the end of *Aaron's Rod* we find what we can only call brutality glorified and asserted. In the conversation between Aaron, Lilly, Argyle and Levinson, in Chapter **XX**, it is not easy to be sure where the book's sympathies lie. Lilly's denunciation of humanitarianism does seem to be offered for our approval:

> The ideal of love, the ideal that it is better to give than to receive, the ideal of liberty, the ideal of the brotherhood of man, the ideal of the sanctity of human life, the ideal of what we call goodness, charity, benevolence, public spiritedness, the ideal of sacrifice for a cause, the ideal of unity and unanimity—all the lot—all the whole beehive of ideals—has all got the modern bee-disease, and gone putrid, stinking.[1]

It is true that Lilly remarks, a few minutes later, that he does not mean what he is saying—'I'd say the blank opposite with just as much fervour'—but that seems to apply only to the positive part of his doctrine—the belief in slavery—that Levinson goaded him into stating. There is no doubt that we are meant to despise Levinson's socialism, his belief in fairness and goodwill; and—more important than any doctrines—the weight of the book is turned against the way Levinson actually behaves, and in favour of the brutal assertiveness of Argyle and Lilly.

> 'Ah my dear fellow, are you still so young and callow that you cherish the illusion of fair play?' said Argyle.[1]

Then, for several pages, we are shown just how callow Levinson is, so that we shall share Argyle's contempt. In order to enlist us on the side of the sneers of Argyle and Lilly, Lawrence spends a good deal of time telling us that it was Levinson who sneered.

To recognise the exhilaration of emotional honesty, and to trample on the feelings of others: are these the same? Lawrence

[1] Ibid., ch. 20

almost invariably assumes that they are—to recognise the value of an impulse, is to approve the yielding to it. But this need not follow: as we can see if we turn for a moment to George Eliot:

> 'Teaching seems to me the most delightful work in the world,' said Mrs Garth, with a touch of rebuke in her tone. 'I could understand your objection to it if you had not knowledge enough, Mary, or if you disliked children.'
> 'I suppose we never quite understand why another dislikes what we like, mother,' said Mary, rather curtly. 'I am not fond of a schoolroom; I like the outside world better. It is a very inconvient fault of mine.'[1]

This is quite unlike Lawrence in method. He would have understood Mary's reaction, but might have expressed it through her manner of saying something quite irrelevant, and so gained in naturalism by blurring the point. It is like Lawrence in the way the author is behind Mary's annoyance, and we are made to feel it. But what is finally and utterly unlike Lawrence is 'rather curtly'. Even when she gives her sympathy to a burst of anger (and they are not always as mild as this), George Eliot pauses to disapprove. And this is characteristic of George Eliot. Neither Lawrence nor Jane Austen could have written the tenth chapter of *The Mill on the Floss*, in which Maggie pushes Lucy into the mud—Jane Austen because she (like Mrs Pullet) would merely have regarded Maggie as a naughty child, Lawrence because he would not have been capable of writing this:

> There were passions at war in Maggie at that moment to have made a tragedy, if tragedies were made by passion only, but the essential $\tau\iota$ $\mu\acute{\epsilon}\gamma\epsilon\theta\sigma$ which was present in the passion was wanting to the action; the utmost Maggie could do, with a fierce thrust of her small brown arm, was to push poor little pink-and-white Lucy into the cow-trodden mud.
> Then Tom could not restrain himself, and gave Maggie two smart slaps on the arm as he ran to pick up Lucy, who lay crying helplessly. Maggie retreated to the roots of a tree a few yards off, and looked on impenitently. Usually her repentance came quickly after one rash deed, but now Tom and Lucy had made her so miserable, she was glad to spoil their happiness—glad to make everybody uncomfortable. Why should she be sorry? Tom was very slow to forgive *her*, however sorry she might have been.[2]

[1] *Middlemarch*, ch. 40   [2] *The Mill on the Floss*, ch. 10

Perhaps we can even say that George Eliot chides the sin but loves the sinner. She shares Maggie's impulse to push Lucy as much as Lawrence ever would have; she—like Lawrence—can stand with Maggie and feel fiercely uncomfortable, yet unrepentant, consumed with hatred of those she ought to love. But what George Eliot does, and Lawrence would not have done, is to describe Maggie's feelings in a way that implies another standard besides fidelity to impulse. 'Tom was very slow to forgive *her*, however sorry she might have been.' By making Maggie rationalise in this way, by making her, in fact, more or less *right*, George Eliot has given to her not more sympathy but less: for by standing back from her impulse she has implied to us that impulses, when yielded to, have conse-quences.

For a contrast to this, let us turn back to *Lady Chatterley's Lover*. This book was originally called *Tenderness*, for Mellors offers Connie a relationship such as she has never found with Clifford or Michaelis, because he understands phallic tenderness. As they speak to each other, they discuss her husband and his wife:

> 'I could wish the Cliffords and Berthas all dead,' he said.
> 'It's not being very tender to them,' she said.
> 'Tender to them? Yes, even then the tenderest thing you could do for them, perhaps, would be to give them death. They can't live! They only frustrate life. Their souls are awful inside them. Death ought to be sweet to them. And I ought to be allowed to shoot them.'
> 'But you wouldn't do it,' she said.
> 'I would though! and with less qualms than I shoot a weasel. It anyhow has a prettiness and a loneliness. But they are legion. Oh, I'd shoot them.'[1]

So that is the other side of tenderness—it is for our friends only. For those who get in our way (for Mellors is here annoyed with Clifford and Bertha not because in their nature they 'frustrate life', but because their existence frustrates his plans) quite a different treatment is indicated. What are we to say of the emotional honesty of a doctrine that turns out to be so convenient?

To sum all this up is merely to gather together what has been said already. What led Lawrence astray as an artist was a didactic

---

[1] *Lady Chatterley's Lover*, ch. 18

passion. No doubt this had roots in his personal life. Never again after the war do we find quite the charm that appears in his letters —and the letters about him—just after his elopement; and as the man grew older and tenser, stridency grew more prominent in his work. For all its fitful genius, the work of his last ten years surely does not equal that of his high creative epoch (from *Sons and Lovers* to about 1920). But I have not been concerned here to relate Lawrence's work to his life, and in terms of the work alone we must see this distorting passion as an urge to castigate the present, to denigrate intellect, to impose on the forests of his dark veins some crude version of the Clifford/Mellors contrast. When this happened, Lawrence destroyed his own genius: sometimes we can see him tearing away at it, in frenetic eagerness.

10 The Personal and the Public: is Lawrence a Fascist?

Before leaving Lawrence I have one more distinction to consider not because I find it any better than those we have already considered, but because it will lead us out from his work to another of those huge issues where the Platonist rushes in. This is the suggestion that the line between good Lawrence and bad Lawrence is the line between the personal and the public: that Lawrence's view of man is valid when he is talking about—or expressing—personal relationships; that we ought never to trust him when he talks about society; and that the intruding ideas that damage his work are social ideas.

Now it is true enough that Lawrence is no guide in politics: even his warmest admirers will usually admit this. It is hard, for instance, to imagine political naïvety carried further than in the essay *Education of the People*, which contains the simplest and crudest version of the disarmament fallacy. There are three ways of defending disarmament, of which two must command respect, the third only contempt. The first is the realistic approach, that hard bargaining and shrewd talking may bring gradual concessions from both sides. The second is the pacifist approach: that to use our weapons would be so indefensible that we must abandon them and face the consequences—with a clear-sighted view of just how terrible these consequences may be. The third is the sentimental approach: that if we throw away our weapons no one will hit us. In *Education of the People* Lawrence pleads for martial training of an unmechanised sort (another Golden Age touch). 'Put your guns in the fire and drown your explosives, and you've done your share of the League of Nations.' If this does not abolish war, it will at least ensure that it will be fought with the right weapons. How can we know this? 'Send your soldiers to Ireland, if you must send them, armed with swords and shields, but with no *engines* of war. Trust the Irish to come out with swords and shields as well: they'll do it.'

It is passages such as this which make it impossible for me to respect Lawrence's pacifism. It is not merely that Lawrence was a pacifist when the mood took him, and a militarist at other times: it is that even when he held to pacifism, it was a soft, flabby kind. True pacifism is one of the hardest, most realistic of creeds: it comes of a sanctity sprung from despair. But it is very rare, and I can find no trace of it in Lawrence's rejection of the first world war; all I can find is this:

> My dear Katherine, I've done bothering about the world and people—I've finished. There now remains to find a place where one can be happy.[1]

It is revealing too to look at Lawrence's moving, uneven essay on *Nottingham and the Mining Countryside*, written right at the end of his life. Its account of the relations between colliers and their wives, and its defence of the apparent selfishness of the men, is Lawrence at his best, infused with a genuine love for the sensitivity of the miner, and a true sense of knowing his subject (though we have seen that Lawrence wrote worse fiction from this standpoint than he had done when he sympathised with the women). All that mars this early part of the essay is its touch of unthinking conservatism, the kind of conservatism which contrasts radicalism with being 'non-political':

> The great fallacy is to pity the man. He didn't dream of pitying himself, till agitators and sentimentalists taught him to. He was happy; or more than happy, he was fulfilled.[2]

Lawrence then moves to an eloquent account of how the miners have now been beaten down, and claims that the real tragedy of modern England is its ugliness. Now this view, like pacifism, can either be something more profound or more superficial than ordin-

[1] Letter to Katherine Mansfield, 7 January, 1916
[2] 'Nottingham and the Mining Countryside' (1930); *Phoenix*, p. 136

ary politics; uneasily, as one reads this essay, one feels it to be the latter:

> If the company, instead of building those sordid and hideous squares. . . had made big, substantial houses, in apartments of five or six rooms, and with handsome entrances. If above all, they had encouraged song and dancing—for the miners still sang and danced—and provided handsome space for these. If only they had encouraged some form of beauty in dress, some form of beauty in interior life—furniture, decoration. If they had given prizes for the handsomest chair or table, the loveliest scarf, the most charming room that the men or women could make! If only they had done this, there would never have been an industrial problem.[1]

Prizes for the best male-voice choir? Handicraft displays? More charming houses? Is *this* Lawrence's answer to industrialism? For all the rousing passion of his conclusion ('Pull down my native village to the last brick'), there is no true radicalism here.

If we had no other evidence than this essay, in which the often moving genuineness of the memories and responses sits so ill with the triviality of the social analysis, we might well conclude that the line between personal and social is also the line between good and bad Lawrence. Of course it isn't: in his fiction, as we have seen, the distinction is more complicated. He accepts some very ugly things on the personal level, and the seventeenth chapter of *Women in Love* contains some magnificent social analysis. And even in those of his essays where the distinction does hold, it is not one that can grant us much comfort. It is all very well to say that Lawrence has little or nothing of value to say to us on politics: before we can lie easy, we want Lawrence to say it too. And usually he refuses to say anything of the sort. 'The working man is not fit to elect the ultimate government of the country,' he wrote to Lady Ottoline Morrell in 1915. 'And the holding of office *shall not* rest upon the choice of the mob: it shall be almost immune from them.' If Lawrence insists on talking about politics (as he does, continually) we cannot pretend not to listen: if we insist that he has nothing to tell us, must we not wonder if he is dangerous? This is why the charge that Lawrence is a fascist is not one that can be dismissed.

I have dwelt on this point for two reasons. First, because it tells us something about Lawrence—more than we are happy to admit:

---

[1] 'Nottingham and the Mining Countryside' (1930); *Phoenix*, p. 138

on the level of mere opinion, the charge of fascism parallels something in the fiction. And second, because it tells us something about fascism. What I have to say now is hard to say, and the reluctances are strong: it has taken me a long time to decide that it may be true. Can we not regard fascism as the mistranslation into social terms of a true view of man's individual nature—truer, at any rate, than the liberal view?

It is a well-known paradox that the great literary masterpieces of this age of liberal humanism have most of them rejected the liberal humanist view of the world. The most famous account of this paradox is given by Lionel Trilling, in his book *The Liberal Imagination*:

> If . . . we name those writers who, by the general consent of the most serious criticism, by consent too of the very class of educated people of whom we speak [i.e. of the liberals], are to be thought of as the monumental figures of our time, we see that to these writers the liberal ideology has been at best a matter of indifference. Proust, Joyce, Lawrence, Eliot, Yeats, Mann (in his creative work), Kafka, Rilke, Gide—all have their own love of justice and the good life, but in not one of them does it take the form of a love of the ideas and emotions which liberal democracy, as known by our educated class, has declared respectable. So that we can say that no connexion exists between our liberal educated class and the best of the literary mind of our time. And this is to say that there is no connexion between the political ideas of our educated class and the deep places of the imagination.[1]

Perhaps this is too sweeping. We could add another group of modern writers, who have defended the liberal position—in so far as 'defending' is compatible with creative writing. This group would include Conrad, Forster, Auden, Sartre, Camus, Malraux—and perhaps ought to include Mann and even Proust. If these writers have invested their emotions in any world-view, it is the liberal humanist one: being poets, they have subjected the working-out of this view to the rigour of truthtelling. George Eliot belongs with these writers too: but Lawrence, as Trilling observes, clearly doesn't.

And it is not as if Yeats, Lawrence or Kafka gave their allegiance to some worthy and viable alternative to liberalism. It is very

---

[1] 'The Function of the Little Magazine'; in *The Liberal Imagination*

questionable if Kafka's terrifying work contains *any* 'love of justice and the good life'; Yeats we know was tempted by fascism in his life, and in his work he submits steadily to the lure of eccentric and crackpot superstitions; and of Lawrence I have spoken at length. How can we fail to conclude that obscurantism, superstition and even fascism have a natural appeal to those who have visited the deep places of the imagination; and how can we fail to be disturbed by this?

The modern liberal secular state has offered to its citizens an unprecedented degree of freedom. In our hatred of authoritarian regimes we forget, nowadays, that until a very few centuries ago authoritarian theocracies were accepted by most men as the natural form of government. We are so aware of the widening of the state's power to interfere in our lives, that we forget there has been a corresponding lessening of its wish to interfere. It is the countries without treason trials, without compulsory orthodoxy, without spies and informers, without prison for one's opinions (all of these found in Elizabethan England) that are the innovators. How this great change came about is not material for a passing paragraph in a work of literary criticism; but in one—superficial—sense of 'how', we can ascribe the change to a more limited conception of the field of politics. We now separate off a much larger area of human activity than before, and regard that as the sovereign territory of the individual: his religion, his reading, his personal relationships, his freedom of assembly and a great deal of his way of life is now his to choose and alter. And it is only the remaining territory that is now the concern of politics. We had to wait until the nineteenth century for Mill on Liberty.

Is it surprising, then, that a theory of man's nature which is designed to subserve this new, limited conception of politics should be a limited theory: that it should largely ignore the sovereign territory of the individual, and describe only those activities the state now claims to control. And the areas thus excluded are precisely those in which the irrational, the mysterious and the demonic hold most sway. Hence it is that the liberal view of man is overrational and—in a sense—superficial. Pentheus now holds power, and keeps the Bacchae in their place; is it surprising that his philosophy does small justice to Dionysos?

Indeed, since liberalism is beleaguered—since the world is still full of people aiming to interfere with the liberty of others for their own good (the snap definition of the illiberal), and since these people hold power in some countries—there is constant pressure on liberalism to exaggerate its claims, to build an even more tendentious, even more superficial philosophy out of the belief that man knows his own long-term good, that he seeks to harmonise this with the good of others, that he can judge all issues calmly—in short, that man is rational.

But it is not this area of man's nature that feeds literature, or in which the imagination works most splendidly: it is rather the remaining area, that now sovereign to the individual. Is it surprising, then, that the great imaginative writers of the century have been tempted to those theories that set up, against liberalism, a philosophy based on all that is most personal, intimate and terrible in our natures? We cannot regard the illiberalism of our great writers as an accidental aberration, as an attack on some distorted shadow version of the liberal idea. It is a natural (though a mistaken) derivative from what gives them their great imaginative power. On the level of social and political decisions, the mistake has been a terrible one: one of its forms led to the most horrible crimes of the century, almost of any century. But on the level of imaginative insight into the nature of the individual man, how easy it is for us to correct the mistake, how hard it was for them to win the vision that tempted them to it.

III GEORGE ELIOT

1 Impulse in George Eliot

Nothing would round off this argument better than now to present George Eliot as combining the merits of both these contrasting positions: as appreciating the value of impulse and surrender, while subjecting them, when necessary, to the scrutiny of reason. And on the whole I believe this to be the case. It is impossible to imagine Jane Austen writing as kindly as George Eliot did of such a woman as Mrs Moss, 'a large, easy-tempered, untidy, prolific woman, with affection enough in her not only for her own husband and abundant children, but for any number of collateral relations'—showing us, by some insight, or trick of style, or mixture of the two, a link between abundance of children and abundance of kindness. And it is just as impossible to imagine George Eliot writing the scene in which Hermione, with a 'terrible voluptuous thrill', hits Birkin with a ball of lapis lazuli ('her heart was a pure flame in her breast, she was purely unconscious in ecstasy'), and then making Hermione think 'she was perfectly right. She knew that, spiritually, she was right'—while Birkin, sitting naked among the primroses, reflects 'It was quite right of Hermione to want to kill him'.

No reader of George Eliot can really doubt that she was deeply drawn to emotional surrender.

> We learn to restrain ourselves as we get older. We keep apart when we have quarrelled, express ourselves in well-bred phrases, and in this way preserve a dignified alienation, showing much firmness on one side, and swallowing much grief on the other. We no longer approximate in our behaviour to the mere impulsiveness of the lower animals, but conduct ourselves in every respect like members of a highly civilised society. Maggie and Tom were still very much like young animals, and so she could rub her cheek against his, and kiss his ear in a random, sobbing way; and there were tender fibres in the lad that had been used to answer to Maggie's fondling; so that he behaved with a weakness quite inconsistent with his resolution to punish her as much as she deserved: he actually began to kiss her in return, and say—
> 'Don't cry, then, Maggie—here, eat a bit o' cake.'
> Maggie's sobs began to subside, and she put out her mouth for the cake and bit a piece; and then Tom bit a piece, just for company, and they ate together and rubbed each other's cheeks and brows and noses together, while they ate, with a humiliating resemblance to two friendly ponies.[1]

In paraphrase, this could pass for Lawrence: certainly the preference for the impulsiveness of animals over 'highly civilised society' has the sound of Lawrence. But once we look at the actual language, all resemblance disappears. Not Lawrence nor any other modern novelist would write like this. There is no hint of violence in the warm feeling to which Tom and Maggie abandon themselves; and although *Lady Chatterley's Lover* was once called *Tenderness*, its 'phallic tenderness' is something much tougher, more disturbing and more complex than the 'tender fibres' of Tom's brotherly affection. And there is an apologetic note to the introduction of the

---

[1] *The Mill on the Floss*, ch. 5

animals ('the mere impulsiveness of the lower animals') that later ('with a humiliating resemblance to two friendly ponies') becomes simply coy. There is not much sentimentality in *The Mill on the Floss* but we are very close to it here: softened by her own tender fibres, George Eliot's clear gaze is blurring with tears. Emotional surrender is valuable because it can establish the human bond as nothing else can. The greatest happiness that George Eliot's characters ever attain—the only happiness, for some—is the result of opening their hearts, of letting their feelings, and their words, flow out to another human being. Nowhere is this presented more vividly, or more movingly, than in the character of Mrs Transome. She is one of George Eliot's great tragic figures: despising her husband, disappointed in her lover and her son, bitter, old, realistic, she sits looking at herself in the mirror, unseeing, yet seeing too much.

> She was seated before the mirror apparently looking at herself, her brow knit in one deep furrow, and her jewelled hands laid one above the other on her knee. Probably she had ceased to see the reflection in the mirror, for her eyes had the fixed wide-open look that belongs not to examination, but to reverie. Motionless in that way, her clear-cut features keeping distinct record of past beauty, she looked like an image faded, dried, and bleached by uncounted suns, rather than a breathing woman who had numbered the years as they passed, and had a consciousness within her which was the slow deposit of those ceaseless rolling years.[1]

Perhaps there is no image in George Eliot more explicitly geological than this, none that makes clearer her belief that personality is built with something of the slowness of rocks, and something of the same inevitability. This passage is from Chapter 39 of *Felix Holt*, the account of Mrs Transome's conversation with Denner: a brief, moving, and terribly lucid chapter. It is as if all George Eliot has to do to wring our hearts is to *show* us Mrs Transome. Her portrait is one of those achievements in the novel where technique seems to disappear, where the events become a window through which we see nothing but the truthfulness of the author's vision: her statement of what it is like to be old, proud and lonely. For this, Mrs Transome has herself to be articulate, but George Eliot has not made her more so than her purpose demands, nor more than realism allows. Look-

[1] *Felix Holt*, ch. 39

ing at herself in self-pity and self-contempt, she is neither blinded
by the first nor rendered unsympathetic by the second. Her pain
is that she is cut off from the two men she has loved, because neither
of them needs her. It is hard to illustrate the full power of this
chapter without quoting it all, and even Mrs Transome's final and
most moving remark draws a lot from context. When Denner
protests that she at least loves her mistress with a love that has not
turned to hatred or contempt, Mrs Transome replies:

> 'Ah, then, you are a happy woman, Denner; you have loved
> somebody for forty years who is old and weak now, and can't
> do without you.'
> The sound of the dinner-gong resounded below, and Mrs
> Transome let the faithful hand fall again.[1]

Mrs Transome sees that to fulfil the need of someone else is the one
sure way of fulfilling one's own; so that the very assurance which
Denner gave to comfort her becomes a source of envy. Denner has
something that she hasn't, the one thing that she most needs. Perception like this gives to Mrs Transome the pure dignity of tragedy:
and it depends on the perfect honesty of the author, our clear
assurance that nothing is being evaded. It might therefore seem
that the most dangerous thing the author could do would be to
'rescue' Mrs Transome—to give her that emotional release whose
lack makes her tragic.

And this is what George Eliot does, in the chapter which forms
the climax of the novel. Harold Transome has learnt his mother's
secret—that Jermyn, whom he hates, is his father—and has left
her in bitter silence; her loneliness and suffering are worse than
ever they have been, when she meets Esther, who senses that there
is a new trouble (not knowing what it is), comforts her, listens to
her complaints, and persuades Harold to sit by his mother's side
as she wakes.

It is a very ambitious chapter—it is to release into the action the
full force of the book's positives—and it is not equal to the greatness that has gone before. Such chapters, alas, so seldom are. Yet
it is not a failure, and it can still draw on the emotional power that
has already been built up. All this power is evoked again by the
first two pages of Chapter 50, in which Mrs Transome, a last spring
broken inside her but maintaining her proud reserve, tells Denner

[1] *Felix Holt* ch. 39

what has happened, and takes from Denner's love what solace she
can, through their mutual reserve.

> The patient waiting-woman came back and sat by her mistress
> in motionless silence. Mrs Transome would not let her dress be
> touched, and waved away all proffers with a slight movement of
> her hand. Denner dared not even light a candle without being
> told. At last, when the evening was far gone, Mrs Transome
> said—
> 'Go down, Denner, and find out where Harold is, and come
> back and tell me.'
> 'Shall I ask him to come to you, madam?'
> 'No; don't dare to do it, if you love me. Come back.'[1]

This is the comfort that Stoicism can bring, this and no more.
A deep but qualified admiration for the dignity of Stoic resignation
runs through George Eliot's work, as it ran through her life. Her
agnostic belief in duty without reward, her sad conviction that
happiness avoids most human lives, led to many statements like
that which she wrote to Chapman in 1852:

> ... the thought which is to mould the Future has for its root a
> belief in necessity, ... a nobler presentation of humanity has
> yet to be given in resignation to individual nothingness, than
> could ever be shown of a being who believes in the phantas-
> magoria of hope unsustained by reason. ... [2]

Such a belief leads to a dignified acceptance of the human lot.
Defending agnosticism in another letter ('the "highest calling and
election" is to do without opium') she speaks of the agnostic in a
phrase that has the ring of Conrad at his bleakest and most splendid
—'those who have strength to wait and endure'.

When George Eliot uses such phrases in her letters, she is talking
about the human lot, the difficulty of living in a world without God:
her religious attitude never ceased to be stoical. But in human intercourse (and here is a crucial difference from Conrad—as from Jane
Austen) dignified withdrawal can bring little except dignity. It can
teach to bear wounds, but cannot heal them. Those who are Stoics
in personal relations (we shall see this again when we come to
Romola) are neither happy nor at the limit of their human growth:
there is something splendid about Denner's submission, her utter
devotion, her respect ('she shrank from seeming to claim an equal's
share in her mistress's sorrow'), but Denner is too like her proud

[1] Ibid., ch. 50   [2] Letter to John Chapman, 24-25 July, 1852

mistress to bring her what she most needs. This is brought by Esther, who ignores restraint and decorum.

> . . . there was no waiting. In an instant Mrs Transome felt Esther's arm around her neck, and a voice saying softly—
> 'Oh why didn't you call me before?'[1]

And in talking to Esther Mrs Transome loses her tight dignity. She utters the self-pity she has kept bottled up ('Why should I be punished any more'), and by admitting weakness she opens the possibility of a comfort more valuable than that of dignity and self-respect. Mrs Transome's last words in the novel are not about herself at all, except in their implied self-rebuke: 'If that dear thing will marry you, Harold, it will make up to you for a great deal'. A barrier within her is now down.

How successful is all this? Mrs Transome herself is surely quite successful: I am thoroughly convinced that her reserve could have been broken in this way, for the pressure of misery within it was so great, and had just been intensified; and we must all believe that she would have been the better for it. But in the case of Esther we have the same difficulty that we saw earlier with Felix: she is the 'noble nature' this time, and will she not be taken merely on trust by the author? It is true that Esther talking to Mrs Transome is not visualised with the same lucid power as Mrs Transome talking to Denner.

> Mrs Transome would not let her dress be touched, and waved away all proffers with a slight movement of her hand. Denner dared not even light a candle without being told.
>
> .   .   .   .   .
>
> A passionate desire to soothe this suffering woman came over her. She clung round her again, and kissed her poor quivering lips and eyelids, and laid her young cheek against the pale and haggard one.[2]

The contrast between these two short passages, from the same chapter, is strongly in favour of the first: in comparison to its steady seeing eye, there is a touch of gush in the second. There are seven adjectives in the second, and at least one ('*poor* quivering lips') is a direct assault on the reader; the first has one, the austerely descriptive 'slight'.

---

[1] *Felix Holt.*, ch. 50   [2] Ibid., ch. 50

George Eliot then did not altogether pull off her climax, but she did not fail disastrously. Esther as a good angel is redeemed artistically not only by the continuing vivid presence of Mrs Transome, but also by the fact that the struggle of which she is a witness speaks to her condition and leads to the making of her own decision. The end of the chapter (Esther's resignation of the estate) is deeply moving, because the power of the Transome story has, as if by an artistic sleight of hand, been given to the Esther story.

Every George Eliot novel presents emotional release as a positive, showing us how it springs from and leads towards the human bond. Confession, consolation, tears can mark the moment at which love becomes possible. There is one scene in Jane Austen that offers a convenient contrast to this, and will show once more this crucial difference between the two.

While Catherine Morland is staying with the Tilneys, she receives a letter from her brother telling her that he has not merely been jilted by Isabella Thorpe, but that she has given him up for Captain Tilney:

> Catherine had not read three lines before her sudden change of countenance, and short exclamations of sorrowing wonder, declared her to be receiving unpleasant news; and Henry, earnestly watching her through the whole letter, saw plainly that it ended no better than it began. He was prevented, however, from even looking his surprise by his father's entrance.[1]

Catherine does, in the end, confide in Henry and even allow them to read the letter; and there is no doubt that it gives her relief to do so. Yet how differently from the way Janet Dempster or Lydgate or Mrs Transome confide. An elaborate comedy is necessary before Catherine says anything, so that we may be reassured that the Tilneys are too well bred to pry:

> Henry and Eleanor were by themselves in the breakfast room; and each, as she entered it, looked at her anxiously. Catherine took her place at the table, and after a short silence Eleanor said, 'No bad news from Fullerton, I hope? Mr and Mrs Morland—your brothers and sisters—I hope they are none of them ill ?'
> 'No, I thank you,' sighing as she spoke; 'they are all very well. My letter is from my brother at Oxford.'

[1] *Northanger Abbey*, ch. 25

241

Nothing further was said for a few minutes; and then, speaking through her tears, she added, 'I do not think I shall ever wish for a letter again.'

'I am sorry,' said Henry, closing the book he had just opened; 'if I had suspected the letter of containing anything unwelcome, I should have given it with very different feelings.'

'It contained something worse than anybody could suppose! Poor James is so unhappy! You will soon know why.'

'To have so kind-hearted, so affectionate a sister,' replied Henry warmly, 'must be a comfort to him under any distress.'

'I have one favour to beg,' said Catherine, shortly afterwards, in an agitated manner—'that, if your brother should be coming here, you will give me notice of it, that I may go away.'

'Our brother! Frederick!'

'Yes; I am sure I should be very sorry to leave you so soon, but something has happened that would make it very dreadful for me to be in the same house with Captain Tilney.'

Eleanor's work was suspended while she gazed with increasing astonishment; but Henry began to suspect the truth, and something, in which Miss Thorpe's name was included, passed his lips.

'How quick you are!' cried Catherine: 'you have guessed it, I declare!'[1]

Surely the most prominent element here is the restraint which must be circumvented before confidence can begin: Henry and Eleanor give their anxious look only to one another; Eleanor's first inquiry is impeccably restrained (it must of course come from Eleanor: it would be even less proper for Henry to pry); there is no further remark until Catherine herself continues the subject, and the two remarks that Henry then feels able to make are carefully phrased so as not to look like questions. Now there are barriers to the flow of speech and feeling in George Eliot too, such as Gwendolen's dread of giving way:

Gwendolen looked at her a moment in silence, biting her inner lip; then she went up to her, and putting her hands on her mamma's shoulders, said, with a drop of her voice to the lowest undertone, 'Mamma, don't speak to me now. It is useless to cry and waste our strength over what can't be altered. You will live at Sawyer's Cottage, and I am going to the bishop's

[1] *Northanger Abbey*, ch. 25

daughters. There is no more to be said. Things cannot be altered, and who cares? It makes no difference to any one else
what we do. We must try not to care ourselves. We must not
give way. I dread giving way. Help me to be quiet.'[1]

But George Eliot describes the barrier so that we shall feel the
strength of the flow that eventually breaks it down. Jane Austen's
barrier is built up for its own sake: she values the well-bred dis-
cretion of the Tilneys, the reluctance of Catherine to speak rashly.
Who is there in Jane Austen who offers her confidence freely? Not
any of her heroines, not even Marianne, but Lucy Steele, who
'opens her heart' for the purpose of tormenting Elinor.

It is clear, then, that George Eliot values emotional surrender:
yet there are times when she seems to condemn it. The most obvious of these comes in *The Mill on the Floss*: the key chapter of the
book, that in which Maggie allows herself to be taken off with
Stephen, is actually called 'Borne along by the Tide'; and Maggie's
moral awakening consists in resisting the 'stronger presence that
seemed to bear her along without any act of her own will', in refusing to agree with Stephen that 'the feeling which draws us towards
each other is too strong to be overcome', and (let us slip into Jane
Austen's vocabulary here) in placing principle before folly.

It need not be inconsistent to approve some impulses and condemn others: this is how most of us govern our moral lives. To do
so implies a set of principles; and to describe what these are must
surely take us very near the heart of George Eliot's values. One
simple and obvious principle comes immediately to mind: she dis-
approved of self-centred impulses. It is easy to state that; what is
more important is to use it to organise one's reaction to the novels.
I propose to do this, first of all for *Romola*—this will help to work
out the recipe; then for *Middlemarch*, in a way that will raise one
of the central critical questions about the book; and finally for
The Mill on the Floss: I conclude with this because its disturbing
conclusion leads directly to my final point.

2 The Double Contrast of 'Romola'

The moral situation of *Romola* is best seen in Romola herself: not
because she is the most successful character (Tito is surely that) but

---

[1] *Daniel Deronda*, ch. 23

because she has the richest and most complex moral life. We can see this clearly enough if we contrast her with Tessa. Tessa is the woman who remains (morally) a child: her belief that she is really married; her simple-minded submissiveness; her timid attempts to snatch simple pleasures for herself and her children—these mark her as without malice and without conscience, an extreme example of William James''once-born' temperament, Romola, in contrast, is twice-born: she has never known simple happiness, simple virtue.

> One day in Greece as he (Tito) was leaning over a wall in the sunshine, a little black-eyed peasant girl, who had rested her water-pot on the wall, crept gradually nearer and nearer to him, and at last shyly asked him to kiss her, putting up her round olive cheek very innocently. Tito was used to love that came in this unsought fashion. But Romola's love would never come in that way.[1]

Romola lives in the fallen world in which tragedy is possible—even inevitable. She knows it herself, and says so, once, in what is perhaps the most haunting image in the book:

> 'You have never known that happiness of the nymphs, my Romola.'
> 'No; but I have dreamed of it very often since you came. I am very thirsty for a deep draught of joy—for a life all bright like you. But we will not think of it now, Tito; it seems to me as if there would always be pale sad faces among the flowers, and eyes that look in vain.'[2]

George Eliot sees the attraction of Tessa next to this—as Hawthorne sees the attraction of Phoebe, in *The House of the Seven Gables*; but like Hawthorne (whom she occasionally resembles, and never as much as in this book) she believes that it is necessary to fall from our first innocence in order to become fully human. Tito, alas, simply falls; and for as long as his charm clings to him (and it never quite leaves him), Romola can see that he has a grace she has never possessed.

Tito is charming: but a charming egoist. He 'tries to slip away from anything unpleasant'; he delights in pleasing others, but not if it means depriving himself of pleasure. Like Arthur Donnithorne, he genuinely wishes to do good, but cannot force himself to do so

---

[1] *Romola*, ch. 9   [2] Ibid., ch. 17

the hard way. He is a profounder study than Arthur, however, and more fiercely analysed; and he becomes totally corrupt, as Arthur does not. The stages of his degeneration too are shown us as Arthur's are not (and hardly could have been without breaking the nine-teenth-century conventions of sexual reticence). Tito does not begin by doing anything wrong, he simply argues himself out of the unattractive (and probably unnecessary) duty of going to look for Baldassare. By yielding in this way to the easy course, Tito be-comes the deed's creature. The best parts of the novel are those which then analyse and display the slow forming of Tito's character by the way he has behaved: 'that inexorable law of human souls, that we prepare ourselves for sudden deeds by the reiterated choice of good or evil which gradually determines character'. By the end, Tito has become totally unscrupulous, yet the bloom is barely off his charm.

Romola in contrast learns to live for others. It is not an easy lesson: 'she had no innate taste for tending the sick and clothing the ragged, like some women to whom the details of such work are welcome in themselves'. But she learns it, almost in an instant: the instant when Savonarola finds her leaving Florence, and tells her to turn back by saying 'You are seeking your own will, my daughter'. Romola of course already knows what it is to live for others, since she lived more for her father than herself: she too has 'prepared herself for sudden deeds', and she responds to Savona-rola's intense and persistent inspiration, and turns back.

Romola's moral life illustrates a double contrast: that between rule, duty, principle and emotional yielding; and that between living for self and living for others. We can plot her development on these two axes. She begins as a Stoic—a believer in self-sufficiency, too proud to lose dignity in surrender. 'It is a great gift of the gods,' she tells her father when we first see her (repeat-ing back to him the lesson he has taught her), 'to be born with a hatred and contempt of all injustice and meanness.' She says it to her father, because it was from him she learned it. Bardo, bitter and lonely, is not a happy man: his dignity can barely hold his self-pity in check. Because his condition is solitary, embittered and hopeless, it is better that he should maintain a proud reserve than be petty and mean: Mrs Transome wins more of our admiration than Mr Casaubon, and no less sympathy. But Stoicism in human intercourse, as we have already seen, is never more than second best for George Eliot; and Romola is not really like her father, because she has the capacity for something finer.

> The habitual attitude of her mind towards strangers—a proud self-dependence and determination to ask for nothing even by a smile—confirmed in her by her father's complaints against the world's injustice, was like a snowy embankment, hemming in the rush of admiring surprise.[1]

It is her firm, proud bearing that attracts Tito, and makes him wish to break down her reserve; and, as this image has already suggested, when the snowy embankment is down there is a great rush of feeling released.

Romola puts aside the ethic of Stoicism for that of love.'Put aside' however, might suggest something too deliberate: Romola simply reacts to the deep need of her nature, and falls in love. That is why her loss of faith in Tito is so terrible.

> The great need of her heart compelled her to strangle, with desperate resolution, every rising impulse of suspicion, pride and resentment; she felt equal to any self-infliction that would save her from ceasing to love. That would have been like the hideous nightmare in which the world had seemed to break away all round her, and leave her feet overhanging the dark-ness.[2]

(The force of these dark images in *Romola* is remarkable, and has never received enough praise: it is a kind of power that among the other books is perhaps only found in *Daniel Deronda*.)

It is Romola's total commitment to love that leaves her nothing when Tito lets her down, and causes her to run away:

> She was going to solve the problem in a way that seemed to her very simple. Her mind had never yet bowed to any obligation apart from personal love and reverence; she had no keen sense of any other human relations, and all she had to obey now was the instinct to sever herself from the man she loved no longer.[3]

At this moment, using our two axes, we can say that Romola is at the extreme of emotional yielding, and of self-regarding. When therefore she is made to return to Florence, it is presented to her in terms of duty, rule and principle: not Stoicism, which is a

---

[1] *Romola*, ch. 6   [2] Ibid., ch. 27   [3] Ibid., ch. 36

self-regarding ethic of restraint, but the ethic of the Piagnoni—
service to others, submission to discipline in order to help our fellow-
creatures. It becomes

> thoroughly her habit to reject her impulsive choice, and to
> obey passively the guidance of outward claims.[1]

Romola has progressed from self-regard to regard for others; but
she has also reverted, from the ethic of surrender to that of self-
control.

And when, after the execution of her godfather, she finally loses
faith in Savonarola and in Florence, her reversion to emotional
surrender is presented as a defeat. She loses her 'high human trust',
and 'the dignity of life sinks too'; and George Eliot then turns to
that favourite image of hers, so highly and ambivalently charged
with emotion:

> She had done enough; she had striven after the impossible, and
> was weary of this stifling crowded life. She longed for that re-
> pose in mere sensation which she had sometimes dreamed of in
> the sultry afternoons of her early girlhood, when she had fancied
> herself floating naiad-like in the waters.[2]

And this image of drifting with the stream is immediately followed by the fact of drifting:

> The imagination of herself gliding away in that boat on the
> darkening waters was growing more and more into a longing,
> as the thought of a cool brook in sultriness becomes a painful
> thirst. To be freed from the burden of choice when all motive
> was bruised, to commit herself, sleeping, to destiny, which
> would either bring death or else new necessities that might
> rouse new life in her!—it was a thought that beckoned her the
> more because the soft evening air made her long to rest in the
> still solitude, instead of going back to the noise and heat of the
> village.[3]

The moral overtones here have become so delicate that they are
barely audible: yet we are not meant altogether to forget that the
burden of choice is also a duty of choice, and that 'the noise and heat
of the village' is the link with one's fellow men that it is—in the end
—self-centred to reject. And when Romola yields to the indulgence
of drifting, to the longing (that central Romantic longing) 'to

---

[1] Ibid., ch. 52   [2] Ibid., ch. 61   [3] Ibid., ch. 61

cease upon the midnight with no pain', to 'hear the sea Breathe o'er (her) dying brain its last monotony', the novel almost abandons its claim to be a novel as it sends her to sea on a symbolic voyage that is conceived as if for a poem (except that George Eliot is never so good a poet in verse as she is in prose):

> Romola felt orphaned in those wide spaces of sea and sky. She read no message of love for her in that far-off symbolic writing of the heavens, and with a great sob she wished that she might be gliding into death.[1]

Now it is clear what the climax of the book ought to offer us. The clash in Romola between the ethic of yielding and that of service to others should be reconciled: she should in the end live for others in a way that fulfils her nature instead of denying it. She should be given another awakening like her awakening from aloofness to love of Tito, another breaking down of snowy embankments, but this time it should be to a love of 'the noise and heat of the village', it should be wholly unselfish. And this is what George Eliot has tried to do. Romola's surrender to the tide was not entirely to easeful death. The thought that beckoned her was 'to be freed from the burden of choice when all motive was bruised, to commit herself, sleeping, to destiny which would either bring death *or else new necessities that might rouse a new life in her!*' It is perhaps a weakness that we are not sure whether these italicised words are part of Romola's consciousness or inserted by the author. As the first, they are surely implausible: her yielding is too absolute for her to have such a qualifying thought at that moment. Yet for George Eliot to slip in her own assurance that this drifting may lead to good after all is too like a wink to the reader, an assurance that the plot will behave impeccably.

For it does behave well: this drifting journey of Romola's, undertaken without purpose, brings her the opportunity to fulfil herself in service. Her boat takes her to a plague-stricken village, and she stays there for months like a good angel, nursing, helping, comforting. And this time she is not checking her impulses, but obeying them; acting not out of duty but love. The yielding of self-indulgence has led directly to the yielding of service.

[1] *Romola*, ch. 61

We must surely respect this ending. Having shown us the clash of two ethical creeds, two principles of conduct, George Eliot has set out to reconcile them in the only way she found possible: by abandoning the realism of the rest of the book in order to let the emotional state of Romola create the action instead of emerging from it. The result is the same movement from realism to fable as she used in *Silas Marner*: it is appropriate that parallels from Keats and Shelley come so readily to mind. And the result, too, is a weakening of effect, an artistic decline: even in prose, George Eliot is primarily a novelist, not a poet. Though some of the passages I have quoted have a haunting power, they do not lead to that almost impossible achievement, the transcending of realism by a novel at its climax. The change of mode leads to a thinness of presentation, and Romola in the plague-stricken village is universalised the easy way. Realism is not transcended but abandoned. And when Romola, returning to Florence, seeks out Tessa, and takes care of her, we have not even what symbolic force the drifting in the boat had managed to generate, but merely a worthy and moralised Victorian ending. We can readily see this by putting next to each other the two sustained analyses of Tito's character: that by George Eliot in her own person in Chapter 23—subtle, thoughtful, compelling—and that by Romola in the Epilogue—making the same points with a flavour of moralising, pietistic almost: the tone of an adult talking down to a child. It is true that Romola *is* talking to a child; but George Eliot has taken too ready advantage of this to sweeten her own tone.

Romola then does not in the end succeed artistically in expressing its ethical preferences. Having shown, with great power, Romola abandoning impulse for duty in order to abandon self for others, it tries to reconcile these two goods, but only at the cost of a thinness of rendering. So that we are left feeling that the book's two ideals may, after all, conflict with each other, that there may be a clear choice between the abandoning of self and the yielding to impulse. Not until *Middlemarch* did George Eliot face the same problem again, and succeed.

3 Dorothea and the Theresa-complex

Dorothea Brooke is a study of what some psychologist must surely, by now, have labelled the Theresa-complex: a yearning to do good in the world which is so intense that it must answer to some emotional need in the Theresa herself. This theme is announced immediately, in the *Prelude*, which begins with an account of the young Theresa

> walking forth one morning hand-in-hand with her still smaller brother, to go and seek martyrdom in the country of the Moors.[1]

Though this account is ironic ('Out they toddled from rugged Avila'), there is nothing ironic about the central description of Theresa's flame, soaring

> after some illimitable satisfaction, some object which would never justify weariness, which would reconcile self-despair with the rapturous consciousness of life beyond self.[2]

In the same way, when the passage moves to the 'later-born Theresas', though there is once more a touch of irony ('here and there a cygnet is reared uneasily among the ducklings in the brown pond'), it once more leaves the central sympathy untouched:

> Here and there is born a Saint Theresa, foundress of nothing, whose loving heart-beats and sobs after an unattained goodness tremble off and are dipersed among hindrances, instead of centring in some long-recognisable deed.[3]

Some readers have been worried by the changes of tone in the *Prelude*, as if George Eliot's own attitude to Saint Theresa was uncertain and even confused; and this leads naturally into the larger criticism (which I shall discuss in a moment) that her attitude to Dorothea is uncertain. It is true that in the second half of the *Prelude*, which concerns the later-born Theresa, the transition from irony to sympathy is less clear-cut than in the first; but this is surely natural, and intentional: it is so much easier to sort out our attitudes when dealing with hagiography than in the realistic novel. If we take the first transition as our clue we can surely realise that the same deliberate ambivalence is present in the later paragraphs: a clear perception of the clumsinesses, the ineffectualities, the occasional absurdity of these blundering lives, but an undimmed, unhesitating sympathy for the flame itself, and for

---

[1] *Middlemarch*, Prelude   [2] Ibid., Prelude   [3] Ibid., Prelude

what it may with luck achieve. This is the attitude towards Dorothea.

It is affirmed in the very first paragraph of the first chapter, in the opening image through which she is presented:

> Miss Brooke had that kind of beauty which seems to be thrown into relief by poor dress. Her hand and wrist were so finely formed that she could wear sleeves not less bare of style than those in which the Blessed Virgin appeared to Italian painters; and her profile as well as her stature and bearing seemed to gain the more dignity from her plain garments, which by the side of provincial fashion gave her the impressiveness of a fine quotation from the Bible,—or from one of our elder poets,—in a paragraph of today's newspaper.[1]

This chapter sets up a view of Dorothea that, through all the shifts of emphasis, is never abandoned. We here see her mainly from the outside: in dialogue with Celia, and in the level commentary of her unruffled author. It is natural therefore that we should first be struck by the critical, ironic tone ('Riding was an indulgence which she allowed herself in spite of conscientious qualms; she felt that she enjoyed it in a pagan sensuous way, and always looked forward to renouncing it'), by the open reference to her love of extremes, by the self-righteousness and 'Puritan toleration' which she shows to Celia during the sharing of the jewels; and it is equally natural that when the writing shifts (as it several times does) in favour of Dorothea, it should usually be by a counter-irony, at the expense of Celia, or of a general 'you' or passive voice which disconcertingly identifies the reader with the common run of Dorothea's acquaintances and neighbours:

> Women were expected to have weak opinions; but the great safeguard of society and of domestic life was, that opinions were not acted on.[2]

A discriminating reading of the chapter will notice these shifts, and appreciate their delicacy: will perceive that the general impression is more critical than sympathetic, yet will reflect that none of the critical details is wholly to Dorothea's discredit. Yet one's reading should not be merely discriminating, or we shall miss the

---

[1] Ibid., ch. 1   [2] Ibid., ch. 1

emotional pressure behind this chapter: to read it knowing *Middle-march* can bring tears to the eyes. We can see the secret of this in the opening sentences quoted above—in such an image as that of the 'fine quotation from the Bible,—or from one of our elder poets, —in a paragraph of today's newspaper'. It is itself an ambiguous image. Its first impression is no doubt of incongruity; it describes the impression Miss Brooke gave of being out of place, the worthy but slightly boring effect she might have on 'highly civilised society'; but its further resonance is of something deeper and wholly to Dorothea's credit. The same ambiguity emerges from such a detail as the slipping in of 'or from one of our elder poets'. To wrap them up with the Bible in this way has the effect of a perfunctory gesture, the kind of vague, respectful but only half-interested reference Mr Brooke might make to 'fine things—you know'; and so suggests the lack of enthusiasm with which Dorothea's noble appearance might be greeted; yet, again, after we have paused to reflect, we can see the joining of the Bible and the elder poets is massing the evidence that reminds us of the triviality of today's newspaper: the sophisticated comment drops away, and we realise that Doro-thea is being—quite simply—compared to all that is fine. Exactly the same doubleness fits the previous image, of the paintings of the Blessed Virgin. Now we cannot really doubt that this standard by which Dorothea with her ignorance matters, and provincial fashion with its maturity doesn't matter, is the one which George Eliot really holds. If we know about Marian Evans, we cannot doubt it; if we remember the simpler irony of *The Mill on the Floss* ('conduct ourselves in every respect like members of a highly civi-lised society') we cannot doubt it. But we do not really need exter-nal evidence, we only need to know *Middlemarch* and read the passages thoughtfully. We shall then feel the passionate sympathy for Dorothea that lies almost hidden at the heart of this clear ironic portrait.

So it should not surprise us that although Dorothea's loving heartbeats and sobs after an unattained goodness lead her to folly and distress—to her imperceptiveness over Sir James Chettam's intentions, above all to her disastrous marriage—they also lead to what we are most to admire about her, to conduct and feelings that serve as a touchstone for the whole book. I cannot illustrate this as fully as I would wish, or as the novel deserves. Let us begin from the account of how Dorothea receives Mr Casaubon's proposal:

Dorothea trembled while she read this letter; then she fell on her knees, buried her face, and sobbed. She could not pray; under the rush of solemn emotion in which thoughts became vague and images floated uncertainly, she could but cast herself, with a childlike sense of reclining, in the lap of a divine consciousness which sustained her own. She remained in that attitude until it was time to dress for dinner.

How could it occur to her to examine the letter, to look at it critically as a profession of love? Her whole soul was possessed by the fact that a fuller life was opening before her: she was a neophyte about to enter on a higher grade of initiation. She was going to have room for the energies which stirred uneasily under the dimness and pressure of her own ignorance and the petty peremptoriness of the world's habits.

Now she would be able to devote herself to large yet definite duties; now she would be allowed to live continually in the light of a mind that she could reverence. This hope was not unmixed with the glow of proud delight—the joyous maiden surprise that she was chosen by the man whom her admiration had chosen. All Dorothea's passion was transfused through a mind struggling towards an ideal life; the radiance of her transfigured girlhood fell on the first object that came within its level.[1]

The full effect of this passage is lost if we have not just read the letter itself, which is too long to quote ('I am not, I trust, mistaken in the recognition of some deeper correspondence than that of date in the fact that a consciousness of need in my own life had arisen contemporaneously with the possibility of my becoming acquainted with you'). The juxtaposition thrusts at us a violent hint at what we realise steadily as we read on (or remember sadly if we know the book already), the pathetic futility of these hopes of Dorothea's. We guess, or know, that the life opening before her is not to be fuller—or if it is, only in the sense that suffering brings fullness of experience. The higher grade of initiation is into maturity but not happiness. There is direct, even crude irony in the reference to 'the light of a mind she could reverence'. The last two sentences, reminding us that Dorothea was a young girl capable of loving intensely, and therefore all the more eager to marry Mr Casaubon, are really a reminder of the true difficulty of her situation: that because she is a woman, with a woman's feelings and a nineteenth-century woman's prospects, her ardour must—in the words of the *Prelude*—

[1] *Middlemarch*, ch. 5

'alternate between a vague ideal and the common yearning of womanhood': so that either the latter replaces the former, and disappointment is obvious, or it disguises itself as the former, and disappointment lies in wait.

All this is fairly obvious, for the passage is not complex. What I here want to point out, however, is that the extent of the irony is limited. There is no hint that we are to withdraw our sympathy from the 'rush of solemn emotion' that seizes Dorothea. Her immaturity lies in the uncertainty and dimness of the prospect that she sees before her, but not in the intensity with which she welcomes it. For it is that same intensity which seizes Dorothea when she exerts her final and liberating influence on Lydgate, when for a moment she is truly Saint Theresa:

> Lydgate turned, remembering where he was, and saw Dorothea's face looking up at him with a sweet trustful gravity. The presence of a noble nature, generous in its wishes, ardent in its charity, changes the lights for us: we begin to see things again in their larger, quieter masses, and to believe that we too can be seen and judged in the wholeness of our character.[1]

And it is this intensity that sweeps Rosamund to her one moment of true goodness:

> Rosamond, taken hold of by an emotion stronger than her own —hurried along in a new movement which gave all things some new, awful, undefined aspect—could find no words, but involuntarily she put her lips to Dorothea's forehead, which was very near her, and then for a minute the two women clasped each other as if they had been in a shipwreck.[2]

There is not only the same intensity here—communicated to her from Dorothea—but even the same dimness, the same blur ('some new, awful, undefined aspect'). We cannot doubt, in the light of these passages, that the portrait of Dorothea when 'she fell on her knees, buried her face, and sobbed' is more compassionate than ironic; that foolish as she is, such folly is no necessary consequence of a tendency to rushes of solemn emotion. And we must conclude that the finest moments in *Middlemarch*, those moments which serve as touchstones for the behaviour shown elsewhere in the book, are those in which characters yield to such rushes.

[1] *Middlemarch*, ch. 76   [2] Ibid., ch. 81

We are told of Dorothea in Chapter X that

> all her eagerness for acquirement lay within that full current of sympathetic motive in which her ideas and impulses were habitually swept along.[1]

and in the same chapter Lydgate first meets Dorothea and reacts more or less unfavourably:

> 'She is a good creature—that fine girl—but a little too earnest,' he thought. 'It is troublesome to talk to such women. They are always wanting reasons, yet they are too ignorant to understand the merits of any question, and usually fall back on their moral sense to settle things after their own taste.'[2]

Lydgate is not swept along by any 'full current of sympathetic motive', and (we see here) would not wish to be. By 'moral sense' he means such a current, something intense and highly charged with emotion: this is clear both from what we know of Dorothea, and from his own contrast with 'reasons'. Now the slow change in Lydgate's attitude to Dorothea is one of the many triumphs of *Middlemarch*. At the beginning, for all his professional idealism, he is aloof and rather patronising to women, and emotionally reserved; and here is his climax:

> Lydgate did not stay to think that she was Quixotic: he gave himself up, for the first time in his life, to the exquisite sense of leaning entirely on a generous sympathy, without any check of proud reserve.[3]

This is the one moment at which Lydgate the man behaves with the dedication and singleness of Lydgate the doctor: the 'spots of commonness' are washed away.

Now this offering of emotional release as the central positive of the book was not merely a decision on George Eliot's part: it was the transcribing into fiction of her own emotional needs. Because Marian Evans had felt 'loving heart-beats and sobs after an unattained goodness', Dorothea's feelings mattered to her more urgently than those of any other character in the book. Several critics have been perceptive enough to observe and (usually) to condemn this.

Best known of these critics is F. R. Leavis, and I shall use his criticism as starting-point for what I want next to say about

---

[1] *Middlemarch*, ch. 10   [2] Ibid., ch. 10   [3] Ibid., ch. 76

Dorothea. After enthusiastic praise of the rest of *Middlemarch*, Leavis asserts that 'the weakness of the book ... is in Dorothea'. He sees this weakness in George Eliot's too sympathetic treatment of Dorothea's 'soul-hunger', in her 'unqualified self-identification' with Dorothea:

> Dorothea ... is a product of George Eliot's own 'soul-hunger' —another day-dream ideal self. This persistence, in the midst of so much that is so other, of an unreduced enclave of the old immaturity is disconcerting in the extreme. We have an alternation between the poised impersonal insight of a finely tempered wisdom and something like the emotional confusions and self-importance of adolescence.[1]

Leavis finds 'unacceptable valuations and day-dream self-indulgences' in the love-affair with Will, and in Dorothea's relations with Lydgate, where we are given a Dorothea 'all-comprehending and irresistibly good'; and he concludes:

> Such a failure in touch, in so intelligent a novelist, is more than a surface matter; it betrays a radical disorder. ... The emotional 'fullness' represented by Dorothea depends for its exalting potency on an abeyance of intelligence and self-knowledge, and the situations offered by way of 'objective correlative' have the day-dream relation to experience; they are generated by a need to soar above the indocile facts and conditions of the real world.[2]

Although Leavis' case against this aspect of *Middlemarch* is well known, I have quoted it here because it has received so much discussion and assent. Mr I. R. Browning actually claims to know what episode in Marian Evans' life most fed this need of hers: the brief affair with John Chapman. Quoting Dorothea's temporary disillusion with Ladislaw, and Romola's permanent disillusion with Tito, he says:

> Both these scenes (and there are others like them throughout the novels and stories) betray a deflecting personal identification with the heroine: it is George Eliot who is before us. Anyone well acquainted with her biography will have no difficulty in recognising the *gentle tones* and the *soft eyes* as those of John Chapman.[3]

[1] *The Great Tradition*, ch. 2, § 2   [2] Ibid., ch. 2, § 2
[3] 'The Recriminating Female'; *Essays in Criticism*, July, 1955

And it is clear that Leavis is simply articulating a widefelt response when we find similar comments occurring in very different critics: thus Lord David Cecil remarks that George Eliot was not 'wholly immune from the frailties of her sex; like every woman novelist she tends to draw heroes less from life than in the image of her desire'.

Leavis' view has not been accepted by all critics; and it will be convenient to set against it that of David Daiches, who maintains that the *Prelude* is misleading; that the moral centre of the book is not Dorothea but Mary Garth; that 'doubt remains as to the social usefulness of sainthood'; and that Dorothea is regarded with a steady, critical detachment all through the book.[1] Both critics, for instance, mention the detail of the organ. Mr Casaubon is discussing music, and indicating a certain lofty scorn for pretty playing. He goes on to exempt 'the grander forms of music', which being Mr Casaubon, he describes in a leisurely period:

> 'As to the grander forms of music, worthy to accompany solemn celebrations, and even to serve as an educating influence according to the ancient conception, I say nothing, for with these we are not immediately concerned.'
>
> 'No; but music of that sort I should enjoy,' said Dorothea. 'When we were coming home from Lausanne my uncle took us to hear the great organ at Freiberg, and it made me sob.'
>
> 'That kind of thing is not healthy, my dear,' said Mr Brook. 'Casaubon, she will be in your hands now; you must teach my niece to take things more quietly, eh, Dorothea.'[2]

This is a perfect exposition, in miniature, of the contrasting attitudes of the three people. We can see why Dorothea accepted Casaubon: for the content of his speech expresses exactly what she thinks about music: she too regards pretty playing as trivial compared with the grander forms. The leisurely period in which he puts it all she will put down to his age and learning, rather than to the fact that his view is even more theoretic than hers—though the betraying detail is there, could she but notice it (as we, on rereading, surely do) in the fact that he feels compelled to add 'according to the ancient conception': for he prefers to speak, not of his reactions, but of what the fit reaction has been held to be.

Everyone can agree on Casaubon here; but what of Dorothea

---

[1] *George Eliot: Middlemarch* ('Studies in English Literature', No. 11)
[2] *Middlemarch*, ch. 7

and Mr Brooke? 'We can't help noting,' Leavis says, 'that it is the fatuous Mr Brooke, a figure consistently presented for our ironic contemplation, who comments, "That kind of thing is not healthy, my dear".' Daiches, however, denying the 'unqualified self-identification' with Dorothea, says of Mr Brooke—quoting this passage—that 'foolish man as he is, (he) often lays his finger precisely on what is wrong with some conduct that goes beyond comfortable normal experience'.

It is necessary to oversimplify. There is no paragraph in *Middlemarch* whose effect is not carefully integrated into the whole, and which is not fed by its context. When we disagree with a good critic, we continually want to say that his quotations are too short: they may seem to mean what he claims, but if we read on we shall see that they don't quite—and reading on really means reading the whole of the rest of the novel. I therefore cannot adequately back up the conclusion which I take from confronting these two views, but must in the end appeal (as criticism always must) to the impression made by the whole book.

But in the simplified terms in which one must work, I can now state the conclusion clearly. I think that Leavis is right and Daiches wrong about the balance of the book: Dorothea is its moral centre. But I think Leavis is wrong, and George Eliot right, about her soul-hunger.

The other half of Daiches' claim (that Mary Garth is what Dorothea isn't, the book's moral centre) is even harder to refute, for in an important sense it is true. Mary is seldom if ever wrong in her judgements, and there are moments—such as her refusal to burn the will when Featherstone is dying—when the author is totally and intensely with her. But on the whole, the Mary Garth-Fred Vincy story is the least intense, the most leisurely, the most conventional part of *Middlemarch*: it is the part Trollope could almost have written. The situation is one of Trollope's favourites: the young scapegrace, the good girl who sees all his faults but loves him all the same, and the unheroic, rather worldly clergyman, whom George Eliot prefers to the evangelical Tyke, just as Trollope's well-fed worldlies, we are to feel, do more good in the world than Mr Crawley, the poor and proud fanatic. It is the one part of *Middlemarch* that we are sure will end happily.

Of course Trollope could never have written it: in almost every scene there are punches that he would have pulled, and that George

Eliot does not pull. When Fred calls at Stone Court to tell Mary about the bill, we see his egoism with the clarity of George Eliot at her merciless best—and it is a clarity that Mary shares. Fred is genuinely sorry for what he has done, but his self-reproach is laced with self-pity: he cares that Mary should forgive him, but has not realised that she will not even think about him in her grief for her family. It is not only George Eliot who realises this, it is Mary too:

> 'What does it matter whether I forgive you?' said Mary, passionately. 'Would that make it any better for my mother to lose the money she has been earning by lessons for four years, that she might send Alfred to Mr Hanmer's? Should you think all that pleasant enough if I forgave?'[1]

That is outside the range of Trollope: it must cause any male reader to wince (Trollope never attacks his own readers). But to say this is to find Mary's limitation, which I can best describe in terms of my own argument, by saying that she represents the Jane Austen in George Eliot.

> She had already come to take life very much as a comedy in which she had a proud, nay a generous resolution not to act the mean or treacherous part. Mary might have become cynical if she had not had parents whom she honoured, and a well of affectionate gratitude within her, which was all the fuller because she had learned to make no unreasonable claims.[2]

I doubt if this is intended as a deliberate contrast to Dorothea: the unreasonable claims Mary does not make are selfish ones, whereas those which Dorothea does are claims to be able to do some vast good. All the same it is a contrast: Dorothea could not possibly view the world as a comedy, nor is she in danger of becoming cynical. Now if this account of Mary sounds like any novelist, surely it sounds like Jane Austen, in whom, too, honour and gratitude are the checks of cynicism. What keeps Mary from becoming unattractive—from being 'always right'—is her love for Fred. She does forgive Fred for robbing her parents, and though he does not deserve it, Mary is the better for doing so: she too has her sublimated egoism to conquer, the egoism of seeing through others.

I think the obvious moral shape of *Middlemarch* is also its true

---

[1] *Middlemarch*, ch. 25   [2] Ibid., ch. 12

I*   259

shape. Dorothea occupies the *Prelude* and the final pages; it is she who is the good angel of the climax, the noble nature for which others are the better; it is she with whom George Eliot is accused of 'unqualified self-identification'.

The terms of this accusation are, we may notice, dangerous, for they seem to deal not with the book but with the author. It is true that George Eliot had a Theresa-complex, and that there is a Dorothea in every book; that if Marian Evans (who was ugly) had been beautiful, it would have been with the beauty of Maggie Tulliver; and that (why should we not make the suggestion?) her art is therefore a substitute gratification, granting her vicariously what she could not have in life. But to say this is to say nothing about the merit of the books: as readers, we care not about the similarities between Janet, Maggie and Dorothea, but about the differences. If George Eliot wrote out her own tangles into her stories, we have yet to learn—from the stories themselves—whether she used this emotional pressure to deflect from or add power to the needs of the book.

Leavis does not commit (what Mr Browning, for instance, does) this error of substituting biography for criticism. He is interested in the book's origins only as explanation for a flaw he claims to find in it. If the identification with Dorothea is 'deflecting', this must mean that the author's clear vision has been blinded, that under pressure from her own feelings, she has not told the truth.

What truth? It is easiest to look at the treatment of others, if we are to find the deflecting interest most clearly manifested. If there is such deflection, then those with whom Dorothea comes into contact will be shown more harshly or more softly than the evidence warrants. If the author's sympathy with Dorothea in her marriage flares up too uncritically, we shall protest at the unfair handling of Mr Casaubon; if the need to give her a happy ending is too pressing, then Ladislaw will be passed off as more than the author has managed to make him.

Let us begin with Casaubon, and say at once that in his case the charge is absurd. He is almost the most wonderful thing in *Middlemarch*. Consider the delicate balance that must be struck when he first appears. We must be convinced that Dorothea would wish to marry him, yet we must be aware what he is really like. We are shown Casaubon direct, and also through the eyes of both sisters and (some subtle humour here, that cuts both ways) of Mr Brooke.

The most hostile view is Celia's ('Really, Dodo, can't you hear how he scrapes his spoon?'), and we must feel that she is hasty and super-ficial, yet just: Celia is not malicious or unobservant, and the Casaubon that she sees is a less important part of the man, but a more accurate version of that part, than Dorothea gives of her part. For some time we might feel that Celia's Casaubon is far nearer to George Eliot's than is Dorothea's—until George Eliot makes her startling shift from irony to compassion, in mid-sentence:

> One morning, some weeks after her arrival at Lowick, Dorothea —but why always Dorothea? Was her point of view the only possible one with regard to this marriage?[1]

This is of course a direct assault on the reader, and an unfair one, in so far as the prejudice in favour of 'young skins that look bloom-ing in spite of trouble' is one which George Eliot has herself fostered. It would seem a merely clumsy way of shifting the point of view (and perhaps it is hard to accept it completely) if it had not been prepared for by a number of earlier shifts, less ostentatiously announced: most superbly, in the scene of the Casaubons' first quarrel. This episode (too long to quote) occurs in Chapter **XX**. Dorothea has inquired about her husband's studies, and hoped she may be of increasing use to him.

> 'Doubtless, my dear,' said Mr Casaubon with a slight bow. 'The notes I have here made will want sifting, and you can, if you please, extract them under my direction.'
> 'And all your notes,' said Dorothea, whose heart had already burned within her on this subject, so that now she could not help speaking with her tongue.[2]

—and Dorothea's enthusiasm then launches her into an intense plea that he will begin to write the book which will make his vast knowledge useful to the world.

The excessive feeling manifested would alone have been highly disturbing to Mr Casaubon, but there were other reasons why Dorothea's words were among the most cutting and irrita-ting to him that she could have been impelled to use. She was as blind to his inward troubles as he to hers: she had not yet learned those hidden conflicts in her husband which claim our

---

[1] *Middlemarch*, ch. 29   [2] Ibid., ch. 20

pity. She had not yet listened patiently to his heart-beats, but only felt that her own was beating violently. In Mr Casaubon's ear, Dorothea's voice gave loud emphatic iteration to those muffled suggestions of consciousness which it was possible to explain as mere fancy, the illusion of exaggerated sensitiveness: always when such suggestions are repeated from without they are resisted as cruel and unjust. . . . Here, towards this particular point of the compass, Mr Casaubon had a sensitiveness to match Dorothea's, and an equal quickness to imagine more than the fact.[1]

Dorothea is not being impertinent nor even, in one sense, thoughtless: her enthusiasm is genuine, and what she says is what she has long pondered, and intends as real praise. The sense of inadequacy that stings Casaubon is his own, because the inadequacy is his own, and we do not condone the quick temper with which he rebukes Dorothea. Yet at the same time this is the scene in which our sympathy first shifts towards him: Dorothea, we learn, 'was as blind to his inward troubles as he to hers'. This calm statement is all important. We do not retract any of our previous judgement of Casaubon: we learn, not that he is a better man than we'd thought, but simply that he is a man who suffers.

I give one other example of the treatment of Dorothea and Casaubon—probably the most moving of all. After Casaubon has learnt of his illness from Lydgate, and repulsed Dorothea's attempts at sympathy, she waits in the corridor to meet him as he goes to bed.

He started slightly on seeing her, and she looked up at him beseechingly, without speaking.

'Dorothea!' he said, with a gentle surprise in his tone. 'Were you waiting for me?'

'Yes, I did not like to disturb you.'

'Come, my dear, come. You are young, and need not to extend your life by watching.'

When the kind quiet melancholy of that speech fell on Dorothea's ears, she felt something like the thankfulness that might well up in us if we had narrowly escaped hurting a lamed creature. She put her hand into her husband's and they went along the broad corridor together.[2]

After the scene with Lydgate, and the account of the pride and fear with which Mr Casaubon greeted the knowledge of his danger,

[1] *Middlemarch*, ch. 20   [2] Ibid., ch. 42

his remark to Dorothea has an even greater power than out of context: it is Shakespearean in power. The image of the 'lamed creature', too, clashing with our feelings about Casaubon's earlier behaviour that day, echoes earlier and similar images, for a complex and moving effect. This, we see, is the happiness they might have together—this, and no more. It is the tame rescuing of happiness from bitterness, through a rescuing from egoism, which Mr Eliot offers his fallen couple in *The Cocktail Party*: 'the best of a bad job is all any of us make of it'. Not that George Eliot could ever have said that: Dorothea's higher hopes matter too much to her. It is this which gives the moment such tragic reverberations (Dorothea had hoped for so much more) beyond its human pathos.

One of the triumphs of the scene is the complete conviction which Casaubon carries. We cannot doubt that his behaviour to Dorothea has been cool and even cruel; but we have been made to feel what he has to bear. Perhaps the finest sentence of all gives the measure of his case: Lydgate, we are told 'was at present too ill acquainted with disaster to enter into the pathos of a lot where everything is below the level of tragedy except the passionate egoism of the sufferer'. Because we have seen that egoism so clearly, we can feel the fineness of this moment of communion, when he responds to Dorothea's companionship.

George Eliot's treatment of Casaubon is one of the first examples in literature of what Lionel Trilling calls 'the double truth'. The phrase comes in his story *The Other Margaret*, in which Stephen Elwin finds himself arguing with his thirteen-year-old daughter Margaret about their coloured servant, also called Margaret. The servant is dishonest and malicious, and contrasts painfully with their previous servant, Milly, who had been a good loyal person. The daughter finds it hard to admit this: she is a passionate liberal, and insists that because the other Margaret is coloured, 'It's not her fault. She's not responsible.' Here is Elwin's reflection on this:

> Had he been truly the wise man he wanted to be, he would have been able to explain, to Margaret and himself, the nature of the double truth. As much as Margaret he believed that 'society is responsible'. He believed the other truth too.[1]

—and the other truth is that wrong is wrong, and right is preferable. The Casaubon story seems to me the finest illustration of this point

[1] 'The Other Margaret'; *Partisan Review*, 1945

ever written. Never for a moment does George Eliot forget Casaubon's responsibility for the failed marriage: it is he who spurns Dorothea, who is quick to resent, who is locked up in his egoism. Yet from the time when sympathy begins to shift towards him, we are never allowed to look at him through the eyes of Celia, or Mrs Cadwallader, or Lydgate, even though we know they are right. A compassion is demanded of us—and is given—through whose clamour we can no longer attend to the voice that says 'He is responsible'. Both attitudes are total: they are incompatible, yet they exist alongside each other.

I hardly need to say, after this, that the portrayal of Casaubon is untouched by any of the deflections that may have come from the treatment of Dorothea. Let us turn now to the less clear-cut case of Will Ladislaw. Here, of course, the deflection would, if it is present, lead George Eliot to idealise him, and many critics claim that this is what happens. 'Who can forgive Dorothea,' asks C. S. Lewis, 'for marrying such a sugarstick as Ladislaw?' 'The author, who is evidently very fond of him,' writes Henry James,

> has found for him here and there some charming and eloquent touches; but in spite of these he remains vague and impalpable to the end. . . . He is . . . a woman's man.[1]

Now it is certainly not true that (as Leavis maintains) Ladislaw is presented more or less uncritically by the author. George Eliot likes him, but the liking is clear-sighted, not indulgent:

> Will was not displeased with that complimentary comparison, even from Mr Brooke; for it is a little too trying to human flesh to be conscious of expressing one's self better than others and never to have it noticed, and in the general dearth of admiration for the right thing, even a chance bray of applause falling exactly in time is rather fortifying.[2]

If we replaced 'expressing' by 'behaving', we could attach the sentence to Fred Vincy: it is exactly the tone in which George Eliot speaks of him. And Will during his journalist phase is no more idealised than Fred: 'it is one thing to like defiance,' says George Eliot as Will has to live up to his intentions, 'and another thing to like its consequences'. Even Will at Rome, though treated

---

[1] 'George Eliot: *Middlemarch*' (1873); reprinted in *Nineteenth Century Fiction*, December 1953
[2] *Middlemarch*, ch. 46

more sympathetically (for this is the beginning of Will the lover), is clearly enough seen. When his friend Naumann shows him Dorothea leaning against the statue of Ariadne, the love he is not yet conscious of emerges as very convincing ill-temper:

> 'Only think! he is perhaps rich, and would like to have her portrait taken. . . .'
> 'I didn't know they were coming to Rome.'
> 'But you will go to see them now—you will find out what they have for an address—since you know the name. Shall we go to the post? And you could speak about the portrait.'
> 'Confound you, Naumann! I don't know what I shall do. I am not so brazen as you.'[1]

This is detached, surely: we are more conscious of a defensive self-righteousness in Will's remark than of any real indictment of Naumann. And the chapter ends on one of George Eliot's characteristic and impressive generalisations:

> Why was he making any fuss about Mrs Casaubon? And yet he felt as if something had happened to him with regard to her. There are characters which are continually creating collisions and nodes for themselves in dramas which nobody is prepared to act with them. Their susceptibilities will clash against objects that remain innocently quiet.[2]

Ladislaw has had a bad press from the critics: if he had not been Dorothea's lover, he would have been widely praised as a portrait of a dilettante, drawn with sympathy well laced with irony. But he *is* Dorothea's lover, and in this we can see both the cause and the partial justification for the way critics have treated him. For although George Eliot does not sentimentalise Will noticeably, she does sentimentalise the love between him and Dorothea. The scene in which they finally come together is moving and convincing, and to wish it away would be cynically to refuse one of George Eliot's genuine successes. Yet such a scene does not end things: it should not replace—as it is more or less made to—a human relationship by an idealised ending. After this scene, there is no scrutiny of Dorothea's life. True, we can believe her second marriage was happy: but there is a great difference between a happy marriage realistically portrayed (or, since we are after all near the end of the book, convincingly hinted at), and the glow that suffuses the final pages of a

[1] Ibid., ch. 19   [2] Ibid., ch. 19

Victorian novel, to the public's satisfaction. Dorothea's second marriage, like that of Adam and Dinah, is merely a happy ending. And just as Adam had to grow shadowy with romance when he took on his final role as a lover, so Ladislaw, splendidly as he is elsewhere seen, blurs slightly as he becomes Dorothea's husband.

The reason for this may not be simply timidity and conventionalism on George Eliot's part, but (in part at least) something more interesting. When *Middlemarch* came out, the *Times* review asserted (with great insistence) that it was not feminist propaganda:

> There is a certain school which will find satisfaction in thinking that Dorothea's story involves some special impeachment of the fitness of the present female lot. We do not think that this is at all intended, and if it be intended it is certainly not justified. ...Her failures and mistakes are not due to the fact of her being a woman, but are simply those which belong to the common lot of human life. . . . The fetters she wore are too common to humanity, but the weight of them is felt far more by men than by woman.[1]

Now the *Prelude* makes it fairly clear that this is to be a book about woman's lot:

> Some have felt that these blundering lives are due to the inconvenient indefiniteness with which the Supreme Power has fashioned the natures of women: if there were one level of feminine incompetence as strict as the ability to count three and no more, the social lot of women might be treated with scientific certitude. Meanwhile the indefiniteness remains, and the limits of variation are really much wider than any one would imagine from the sameness of women's coiffure and the favourite love-stories in prose and verse.[2]

If Dorothea (let us put it at its crudest) could have become a doctor or a teacher, she wouldn't have needed Sir James Chettam's help to build the cottages; and she wouldn't have married Casaubon. Now there is only one passage which says this, or anything approaching this:

> For a long while she had been oppressed by the indefiniteness which hung in her mind, like a thick summer haze, over all her desire to make her life greatly effective. What could she do, what ought she to do?—she, hardly more than a budding

---

[1] Review of *Middlemarch* in *The Times*, 7 March, 1873
[2] *Middlemarch*, Prelude

woman, but yet with an active conscience and a great mental need, not to be satisfied by a girlish instruction comparable to the nibblings and judgements of a discursive mouse. With some endowment of stupidity and conceit, she might have thought that a Christian young lady of fortune should find her ideal of life in village charities, patronage of the humbler clergy, the perusal of 'Female Scripture Characters', unfolding the private experience of Sara under the Old Dispensation, and Dorcas under the New, and the care of her soul over her embroidery in her own boudoir—with a background of prospective marriage to a man who, if less strict than herself, as being involved in affairs religiously inexplicable, might be prayed for and seasonably exhorted. From such contentment poor Dorothea was shut out.[1]

This is feminism, surely: it shows Dorothea 'alternating between a vague ideal and the common yearning of womanhood'—and finding both as unsatisfactory as the author finds them. There seems to her no way that the ideal can be made less vague: that 'thick summer haze' is woman's lot. How understandable then that Dorothea should convince herself that the two will meet in marriage to Mr Casaubon.

Yet the *Times* reviewer was right. George Eliot does not develop this point, and is very anxious to portray Dorothea's lot as belonging 'to the common lot of human life'. During the marriage, it was possible, even necessary, for George Eliot to drive away, or ignore, the feminist hare she had started: for whatever made Dorothea marry Casaubon, the marriage once it has taken place is itself—as a human relationship—her subject. But with Dorothea a widow and in love with Will, the question must arise whether her 'active conscience and great mental need' would really be satisfied in marriage, even happy marriage. The evasive glow with which the marriage is presented is George Eliot's way of avoiding this question.

Not that it is completely avoided: and in the Finale George Eliot allows herself one or two remarks that the comfortable reader had better not linger on too carefully (as the *Times* reviewer no doubt did not):

Dorothea could have liked nothing better, since wrongs existed than that her husband should be in the thick of a struggle

[1] Ibid., ch. 3

against them, and that she should give him wifely help. Many who knew her, thought it a pity that so substantive and rare a creature should have been absorbed into the life of another, and be only known in a certain circle as a wife and mother. But no one stated exactly what else that was in her power she ought rather to have done.[1]

For Dorothea could neither write novels, nor edit the Westminster Review, nor help in the founding of Girton College. The feminist ghost that the author had called up and then banished has briefly returned. That George Eliot was uneasy about this seems clear from the second last paragraph of the novel. As it now stands, this has a reference to the pressure of society that is typical of George Eliot and not at all feminist: the 'determining acts of her life' were 'the mixed result of young and noble impulse struggling amidst the conditions of an imperfect social state'.[2] In the first edition this was spelt out in more detail, and the imperfections of the social state listed; and the second item on the list is 'modes of education which make a woman's knowledge another name for motley ignorance'.[3] In the original manuscript,[4] though there was more detail than now remains, this phrase was not there. She must have added it in proof, then deleted it on a later revision. George Eliot did not, as novelists go, rewrite much; and we can surely conclude that she was uncertain about this paragraph because she could not decide how explicitly she should mention woman's contemporary lot. The uncertain protestations of *The Times*, then, are not surprising: their seeds lay in the author herself. If we feel any embarrassment about Dorothea's second marriage, it may be due as much to this as to a deflecting emotional identification of author with heroine.

Having made this concession, then—and conceding too that there are occasional passages where enthusiasm for Dorothea strikes a false note (for this is a very long book, after all)—I reassert that George Eliot's identification has not caused her to falsify, distort or evade; the personal interest is not a deflecting one. What then do Leavis' criticisms come to? If we look at them again, we can notice that not all his phrases concern truth or falsehood: he speaks of 'immaturity', of 'emotional confusions and self-impor-

---

[1] Ibid., Finale [2] Ibid., Finale
[3] Quoted in Gordon Haight's notes to the Riverside edition of *Middlemarch*
[4] Add. MS 34037, British Museum

tance of adolescence', of 'indulgence'. If Mr Brooke or Sir James
Chettam or Mr Casaubon were articulate enough, and masters of
modern terminology, they would say the same.

The disagreement between Leavis and George Eliot is in fact an
ethical one. The heart of Leavis' criticism does not concern falsity
in the author's vision, but the value of the Theresa-complex. So
it is not surprising that all his criticisms have been anticipated by
George Eliot and put into the mouth of one or other of her characters. It is Mrs Cadwallader who describes Dorothea as 'a girl who
would have been requiring you to see the stars by daylight' and who
says that 'marriage to Casaubon is as good as going to a nunnery'.
There is no reason why the reader should not agree with her, as
Blackwood, the book's first reader, agreed totally with Celia, yet
did not find this a sign of weakness. Most critics who have defended
George Eliot against Leavis have done so by accepting his ethical
premise, and denying his reading of the treatment of Dorothea. I
want to shift the emphasis not towards stressing the irony with
which Dorothea is portrayed, but towards defending Saint Theresa
against the concept (a central one in Leavis' criticism) of maturity.
The presence of a noble nature, generous in its wishes, ardent in
its charity, *does* change the lights for us; loving heart-beats and
sobs after an unattained goodness ought to have a more complex
fate, as the adolescent matures, than simply to be outgrown; and
maturity is a virtue within the range of some very dreary people,
and beyond the range of some very fine ones. Leavis, in short,
has made not an artistic but an ethical criticism. Valuing the
Theresa-complex less than George Eliot does, and maturity more,
he has passed off his ethical disagreement as if it were the discovery
of an artistic flaw. This is why Daiches' defence of the book seems
to me the wrong one: he, like Leavis, seems to have a very qualified
admiration for Theresas, and so to make the book acceptable has
imposed on it a moral that is not quite George Eliot's. I want to
put myself with George Eliot against both these critics, even if it
means being called immature. There are worse charges.

4 'The Mill on the Floss': Which is the Way Home?

Finally, *The Mill on the Floss*. I have kept this to the last,
though it is the earliest of the novels here discussed: not because it is
the most complex book, but because the problem it raises has to be

settled in the most complicated way. *The Mill on the Floss* can be analysed in the same terms as I have already used with Romola. Its central episode raises the moral issue that I have called self and other. In running off with Stephen Guest, Maggie has been obeying only selfish impulses: to marry him would be to buy her happiness at the cost of others, above all of Lucy's, to whom Stephen is engaged. The language in which she says this to Stephen is sternly and outspokenly moral:

> We can't choose happiness either for ourselves or for another: we can't tell where that will lie. We can only choose whether we will indulge ourselves in the present moment, or whether we will renounce that, for the sake of obeying the divine voice within us—for the sake of being true to all the motives that sanctify our lives.[1]

Romola, in leaving Tito, tried to choose happiness, if only negatively; and if this reasoning of Maggie's were to succeed, we could feel she had won the same kind of Pyrrhic victory that Savonarola wins over Romola's personality. But we are now at the climax of the action, and Maggie's victory must be complete. The axis of self and other is therefore crossed with that of duty and impulse.

Maggie's elopement with Stephen, as I have already pointed out —as indeed is obvious—was a surrender to impulse.

> Stephen spoke with deep, earnest pleading. Maggie listened— passing from her startled wonderment to the yearning after that belief, that the tide was doing it all—that she might glide along with the swift, silent stream, and not struggle any more.[2]

That 'tide' is carefully poised by the author between literal and figurative. A real tide has swept them along, and also a tide of feeling, and the two are deliberately blurred in this image. This tide however has led Maggie to act selfishly. She sees this almost immediately, but sees it only with her reason.

> Oh, it is difficult—life is very difficult! It seems right to me sometimes that we should follow our strongest feeling; but then, such feelings continually come across the ties that all our former life has made for us—the ties that have made others dependent on us—and would cut them in two.[3]

[1] *The Mill on the Floss*, B. 6, ch. 14
[2] Ibid., Bk. 6, ch. 13   [3] Ibid., Bk. 6, ch. 11

It is clear then how the struggle must culminate: Maggie must *feel* that she ought to go back. The clash between self and other must be translated from a clash between impulse and duty to a clash between two impulses. This is what happens: the needs of Lucy and Philip come to life in Maggie's imagination, and speak with the same urgency as her own longing.

> Stephen—don't ask me—don't urge me. I can't argue any longer—I don't know what is wise; but my heart will not let me do it. I see—I feel their trouble now; it is as if it were on my mind.[1]

Maggie will now have the strength to go back, we realise: duty has been translated into a language that speaks to the whole personality. This is confirmed when Lucy comes to see Maggie. Perhaps in execution this scene is not very successful: there are too many assurances of Lucy's sweetness and 'heart-piercing' tenderness. But it was the right scene to have, for it sets a human positive against Maggie's love for Stephen. It shows us that Stephen is given up not merely for a principle but for something that can also take the form of impulse. We realise, in fact, that to translate duty into feeling is easier for some forms of duty than others. An abstraction could not speak to the imagination in this way: not in the world of George Eliot, perhaps not in that of any novelist, though poetry might bring it to pass. Duty which takes the form of the needs of others—other individuals, known to you—can clearly come to life as principle hardly can, and Maggie's love for Lucy and for Philip can be enlisted against her love for Stephen. It is no longer a question of love versus renunciation. Renunciation alone would be too weak to conquer feeling.

But this last sentence must give us pause: surely it does not do justice to the psychological complexity of the episode. For there has not been a simple contrast in Maggie between renunciation and impulse. Renunciation itself has been one of her strongest impulses, and it has neither followed reason nor led her to act for others. If Maggie's impulses have been self-regarding, they have sometimes regarded a strange, even a perverted self. As Tom realises.

> I never feel certain about anything with *you*. At one time you take pleasure in a sort of perverse self-denial, and at another

---

[1] Ibid., Bk. 6, ch. 14

you have not resolution to resist a thing that you know to be wrong.

There was a terrible cutting truth in Tom's words—that hard rind of truth which is discerned by unimaginative, unsympathetic minds.[1]

We could fit this point into our scheme by calling Maggie's impulsive renunciations selfish. They represent a surrender to a twisted but genuine selfishness, and therefore have nothing in common with her final achievement in learning the needs of others. But if we do this, we confess the inadequacy of the scheme for analysing Maggie's psychology, for her pleasure in perverse self-denial and her drifting along the warm tide of her feeling for Stephen have so little in common that it must be misleading to class them together.

Maggie breaks free of the book that contains her: she has a kind of independent existence that I can best indicate by saying that the terms in which the action of the book is best analysed (the terms that show the parallel with *Romola*) do not tell us much about her. Her development does not fit these terms as Romola's does. Romola, as we have seen, is given three awakenings—from Stoicism to love, from self to other (with a reversion on the first axis) and her final awakening to the love of others. But Maggie never needs to awaken from restraint: the Maggie who surrenders totally to impulse is there from the beginning. This is the Maggie who cuts off her hair, pushes Lucy in the mud, begs Tom for forgiveness, feels the 'bitter sorrows of childhood, when sorrow is all new and strange', and who makes of the first two books of *The Mill on the Floss* perhaps the most vivid and compelling childhood story in English fiction. Maggie's intensity is shared by her creator, and is communicated to us. It does not, any more than Dorothea's, result in an inability to see her objectivity (what hostile critic of the book has ever hit the Maggie-nail so neatly on the head as Tom does in the passage above?): but it does lead us into a very deep identification with her.

Identification like this does not speak in moral terms. The commitment to impulse and feeling that follows from our sympathy with Maggie does on occasion serve the author's moral purpose, but that is not its cause. It serves a moral purpose when, for instance, Maggie is led to protest against the cursing of Wakem:

[1] *The Mill on the Floss*, Bk. 6, ch. 4

'Write as your father, Edward Tulliver, took service under John Wakem, the man as had helped to ruin him, because I'd promised my wife to make her what amends I could for her trouble, and because I wanted to die in th'old place, where I was born and my father was born. Put that i' the right words—you know how—and then write, as I don't forgive Wakem for all that; and for all I'll serve him honest, I wish evil may befall him. Write that.'

There was dead silence as Tom's pen moved along the paper: Mrs Tulliver looked scared, and Maggie trembled like a leaf.

'Now let me hear what you've wrote,' said Mr Tulliver. Tom read aloud, slowly.

'Now write—write as you'll remember what Wakem's done to your father, and you'll make him and his feel it, if ever the day comes. And sign your name Thomas Tulliver.'

'Oh, no, father, dear father!' said Maggie, almost choked with fear. 'You shouldn't make Tom write that.'

'Be quiet, Maggie!' said Tom. 'I *shall* write it.'[1]

Here we are completely on Maggie's side, and we believe Maggie is right. Yet if we are to be honest we must admit this is, in the end, a coincidence. Mr Tulliver is following impulse as much as she is, and there is something compelling about his urge towards revenge. Of course George Eliot prefers Maggie's impulse because it is not cruel, not vengeful, and of course we do too: but its goodness does not follow from the fact that it is Maggie's, and we share it not primarily because it is good but because we have by now identified so closely with her. Hence we share her attraction to Stephen—or rather, the reason we don't share it is that Stephen is such a dummy. What we share is the yearning that takes her to Stephen, the need that causes her to see so much in him. George Eliot understood this: she meant us to share the yearning, whatever our reservations about Stephen (and she knew well enough what a provincial dummy Stephen was, 'with his diamond ring, attar of roses, and air of nonchalant leisure, at twelve o'clock in the day').

If anyone speaks for the moral scheme of the book it is surely Dr Kenn: but he never speaks to us as Maggie does. We give one kind of assent to Dr Kenn when he decides to do his best for Maggie; we give quite another kind of assent to Maggie when she pushes Lucy into the water.

The moral pattern of *The Mill on the Floss* does not square with

[1] Ibid., Bk., 3, ch. 9

the creation of Maggie. They often overlap—often enough for the discrepancy not to show too obviously—but they lead independent lives. This becomes clear at the one point when the discrepancy does show: in the ending. It is not surprising that this has been the most criticised part of the novel.

In the final chapter, Maggie goes through the last phase of her struggle. She has received a letter from Stephen, urging her to marry him; and she feels 'as if her real temptation has only just begun'. Dr Kenn has just told her that it is best for her to leave St Oggs: this has made her prospects more desolate than ever, and the letter offers her a way back to life that she finds it almost impossible to resist. Now I have to admire George Eliot's honesty in inserting this episode. It is another example of the truthfulness of fiction: artistically, the climax of Maggie's story came when she left Stephen and came back to St Oggs, but life may not respect artistic climaxes, and George Eliot has therefore shown us that Maggie may be visited by another and drearier temptation. Yet the effect of this episode of the letter is to undo much of the climax. Now again we see her renunciation of Stephen as perverse. Stephen's letter ties it to the perversity we have already perceived in Maggie. He calls it a 'useless sacrifice', a 'perverted notion of right', when set against his 'single over-powering passion, that worship, which a man never gives to a woman more than once in his life'. And the image of Maggie in the cavern has the same effect:

> At the entrance of the chill dark cavern, we turn with unworn courage from the warm light; but how, when we have trodden far in the damp darkness, and have begun to be faint and weary —how, if there is a sudden opening above us, and we are invited back again to the life-nourishing day?[1]

This is not one of George Eliot's finest images—too conventional and (perhaps) too melodramatic to be wholly convincing. But what force it has works on the side of Stephen's plea and against the 'damp darkness': it is too easy to see this exploration as perverse. Other details have the same effect.

> No—she must wait—she must pray—the light that had forsaken her would come again: she should feel again what she had felt, when she had fled away, under an inspiration strong enough to conquer agony—to conquer love.[2]

[1] *The Mill on the Floss*, Bk. 7, ch. 5   [2] Ibid. ,Bk. 7, ch. 5

She should feel again what she had felt: at this moment Maggie's decision is wholly theoretical, working against her personality, her deepest needs. Self is yielding to mere reason. Appropriately, she picks up Thomas a Kempis, and finds support for her decision in 'the little old book that she had long ago learned by heart'— the book whose teaching we have now learned to see as slightly unhealthy for Maggie, as part of her 'perverse self-denial'. What positive is there to set against the sour taste of this renunciation? Only the suffering caused to others. To this Stephen has already said 'there are ties that can't be kept by mere resolution. . . . Would they have thanked us for anything so hollow as constancy without love?' The only possible reply to this is that Stephen will come to love Lucy again, and Maggie has to say this: 'Forgive me, Stephen! It will pass away. You will come back to her.' Maggie has to say it, and George Eliot has to believe it, or the sacrifice must seem perverse. George Eliot is too honest however to believe it with the full weight of the novel, and therefore she has had to confine herself to a sentence on the last page:

> One of them visited the tomb again with a sweet face beside him—but that was years after.[1]

What could be less plausible than this one 'happy ending' sentence, imbued with all the vagueness of a final page? It surely convinces us that George Eliot could never have written the chapter that this sentence ought to be summarising, and as a counterweight to Stephen's very convincing rejection of hollow constancy it has no effect at all.

Maggie's final rejection of Stephen, then, comes as close to mere renunciation as anything in the book. It is a pure application of duty, without even the advantage of using an acceptable standard of duty. And at this moment, at Maggie's darkest hour—

> At that moment Maggie felt a startling sensation of sudden cold about her knees and feet.[2]

From then on all is rapid. The flood has come, Maggie takes a boat to find Tom, and the two of them are drowned together, not divided in their death.

This conclusion is tremendously moving, and we can see why. The full power of the book is at last released. The flood has been

[1] Ibid., Conclusion   [2] Ibid., Bk. 7, ch. 5

prepared for in two ways. In the first place, by a careful accumulation of details. To reread *The Mill on the Floss* is to see admiringly the dozens of small touches which anticipate the end. There are those details which are meant to work unseen—images of water and of being swept away—and those which are meant to be seen but not noticed—Mrs Tulliver's constant fear that her children will be drowned, or the historical gossip of St Oggs:

> And now, for the last two days, the rains on this lower course of the river had been incessant, so that the old men had shaken their heads and talked of sixty years ago, when the same sort of weather, happening about the equinox, brought on the great floods, which swept the bridge away, and reduced the town to great misery.[1]

This comes in the very chapter we are considering, and is a good example of how by dropping into the casual vein of filling in 'background' George Eliot can anticipate her climax while appearing to digress. These details are well done, and remind us what a skilled craftsman George Eliot was. But the flood is also prepared for by more direct emotional means. It is the supreme image for being swept away—for just that state of being in Maggie to which we most fully respond. Maggie's behaviour is as unhesitating as the waters: she is swept away figuratively as well as literally. And in this new unhesitating state, frightened but exhilarated, carried over the flooded fields, she is moving towards being the old Maggie again.

> 'O God, where am I? Which is the way home?' she cried out, in the dim loneliness.[2]

That is surely a very successful image. In her bewilderment, Maggie may not even be clear what she means by 'home', but it is nonetheless what she might well have said. This uncertainty gives the remark a generalised quality that leads straight into the completely generalised, figurative sense that the cry clearly has if we take it out of its context—Maggie's question about her own identity: the generalised 'dim loneliness' adding to this.

And so the fulfilment Maggie finds when she fetches Tom is the completest fulfilment she ever has. Acting with her whole self, in a way that seems to sweep self along, she has been reunited to her earliest love. Her death is indeed her 'supreme moment', and is a

---

[1] *The Mill on the Floss*, Bk. 7, ch. 5   [2] Ibid., Bk. 7, ch. 5

complete contrast to the moment of renunciation in which she first felt the sensation of sudden cold about her knees and feet. Fittingly, the book ends on an image of childhood, on the emotional fulfilment that it offers, to us in memory, to Tom and Maggie in strange ironic fact:

> The boat reappeared—but brother and sister had gone down in an embrace never to be parted: living through again in one supreme moment, the days when they had clasped their little hands in love, and roamed the daisied fields together.[1]

I have already, I hope, anticipated the conclusion I now want to draw. What is wrong with this ending? Is anything wrong with it? The moral scheme of the book—the scheme George Eliot had so earnestly laboured to establish—has been undermined and then pushed aside. Our emotions, so carefully invested in the renunciation of Stephen, have been battered until we have lost all our previous confidence in its rightness. And at that very moment we are offered Maggie's final experience, an experience of pure self-fulfilment. It is true that her final union with Tom is the victory of love over estrangement, but these terms are misleading. Once again, we have to say that if fulfilment coincides with morality it is a coincidence. Maggie did not take a moral decision in fetching Tom, she acted on a level below that of moral concepts. The occasional hints that it was otherwise (the 'almost miraculous divinely-protected effort') jar and ring false. What makes Maggie fetch Tom is what made her cut her hair off, run away to the gipsies, meet Philip Wakem, protest at the bible oath—the fact that she is what she is. 'Which is the way home?' The answer is, the way to yourself.

And now suppose a critic objects to this compelling and moving ending: what exactly is his objection? It is not simply an artistic objection. Drawing on all that is deepest and most powerful in the book, it would be absurd to call it an artistic failure. Nor is it simply a moral failure: our identification with Maggie, I have already suggested, is below the level of moral approval and disapproval. It is an objection that mingles artistic and moral points, mingles them inextricably. There is even a passing resemblance between the complaints of some of the contemporary reviewers of *The Mill on the Floss*, and that of some modern critics. The critic of *The Saturday Review* said plaintively of the last book 'what does

---

[1] Ibid., Bk. 7, ch. 5

it all come to except that human life is inexplicable, and that women who feel this find the feeling painful?'[1] *Macmillan's Magazine* made a similar complaint:

> It is *not* right to paint *Maggie* only as she is in her strong, unsatisfied, erring youth—and leave her there, her doubts unresolved, her passions unregulated, her faults unatoned and unforgiven: to cut her off ignobly and accidentally. . . .[2]

This is too openly moralistic for our sophisticated methods, yet it has something in common with—say—F. R. Leavis' well-known criticism:

> Something so like a kind of daydream indulgence we are all so familiar with could not have imposed itself on the novelist as the right ending if her mature intelligence had been fully engaged, giving her full self-knowledge.[3]

No doubt the maturity that Leavis wants is very different from the moral soundness that the Victorian critics wished to see. Yet both are tracing artistic flaws back to a moral inadequacy in the author's attitude, and one remark in *The Saturday Review* is as shrewd as any modern critic: 'the conduct of the story always affords an opening to escape from the responsibility of definite thought'. The flood is 'the dreamed-of perfect accident,' says Leavis, '. . . that shall vindicate us against a harshly misjudging world'. Are they not making the same point: that having raised certain moral issues, George Eliot is not entitled to sweep them aside in mere identification with the heroine.

It is an artistic flaw, since the book raised expectations, by the subtlety of the moral analysis, that it is now not fulfilling, But it is an artistic triumph too, as the full power of George Eliot's expression is released at the end. Power is purchased by the neglecting of purpose. It is hard to wish that it hadn't been done—as hard as to wish that Shakespeare had not spoiled *The Merchant of Venice*, by letting Shylock smother his intention; or that Milton had not spoiled *Paradise Lost*.

[1] 'The Mill on the Floss', *Saturday Review*, 14 April, 1860; reprinted in *George Eliot and her Readers*, ed. Lerner and Holmstrom

[2] 'To Novelists—and a Novelist', *Macmillan's Magazine*, April, 1861; reprinted in the same

[3] *The Great Tradition*, ch. 2, § 1

CONCLUSION

CONCLUSION

THE reason I have taken *The Mill on the Floss* last may now be clear: it is George Eliot's one subversive book—the one book in which she let herself go completely. Morality is not translated into impulse in this book, as it is in *Romola*: it is replaced by impulse. What this impulse leads to overlaps largely with what reason approves, but it is only an overlap—or, as I have been calling it, a coincidence. Is there any guarantee that the flood will bear us to what the book (or society, or conscience) requires? The 'immorality' of *The Mill on the Floss* is the first inkling of the more radical immorality of Lawrence: I want that pound of peaches.

It is on this final ambivalent status of impulse that I want to end: by suggesting, very briefly, that it is an ambivalence that Romanticism made inevitable. For if there is any single element that lies at the centre of the Romantic movement, it is surely the liberation of impulse. For some critics (F. L. Lucas, for instance) this is the very definition of Romanticism: for those who have elaborated more thorough and complicated definitions, it is a clear corollary. Perhaps the most authoritative conception that recent scholarship has offered us is that which Morse Peckham extracted from the area of agreement between Lovejoy and Wellek:

> What then is Romanticism? Whether philosophic, theologic, or aesthetic, it is the revolution in the European mind against thinking in terms of static mechanism and the redirection of the mind to thinking in terms of dynamic organicism. Its values are change, imperfection, growth, diversity, the creative imagination, the unconscious.[1]

The shift to a dynamic—organic view of the world naturally directs attention to what is dynamic in man: and the liberation of forces in the self is a consequence which follows very naturally from every element in this list. From change, since the great forces of change are within, or at least speak to something within. From imperfection, since the perfect man will have none of the instability that presses forces to release themselves. Growth is internally propelled. Diversity is encouraged if we let ourselves go. The creative

[1] Morse Peckham, 'Towards a Theory of Romanticism', PMLA, 1951

imagination and the unconscious are, to us, inseparable—certainly since Freud, and even, if we use the wisdom of hindsight, since Wordsworth—and the unconscious is the very source of those forces whose release the Romantics saluted:

> *Ah! from the soul itself must issue forth,*
> *A light, a glory, a fair luminous cloud*
>   *Enveloping the earth—*
> *And from the soul itself must there be sent*
>   *A sweet and potent voice, of its own birth,*
> *Of all sweet sounds the life and element!*[1]

It is easy and uncontroversial then to point to the Romantic acceptance of impulse. It raises controversy when we ask what the consequences of impulse are. Obeying the forces that have been liberated, what do we find they have told us to do? Have they led us in a way that reason approves, or have they defied reason?

Perhaps this is the most important cleavage in the Romantic movement. To describe it I turn to another part of Peckham's article, in which he describes 'negative Romanticism':

As various individuals, according to their natures, and their emotional and intellectual depths, went through the transition from affirming the meaning of the cosmos in terms of static mechanism to affirming it in terms of dynamic organicism, they went through a period of doubt, of despair, of religious and social isolation, of the separation of reason and creative power. It was a period during which they saw neither beauty nor goodness in the universe, nor any significance, nor any rationality, nor indeed any order at all, not even an evil order. This is negative romanticism, the preliminary to positive romanticism, the period of *Sturm und Drang*. As the nineteenth century rolled on, the transition became much easier, for the new ideas were much more widely available.[2]

'As the nineteenth century rolled on.' But opening our eyes to that rolling on, we see things becoming harder, not easier. The separation of reason and creative power was not an uncomfortable growing pain, but a serious and permanent consequence of the liberation of impulse: some would say, *the* serious and permanent consequence.

When forces are liberated in the self they may help us to win the goal that reason aims for, to attain what the self had always intended

---

[1] Coleridge, 'Dejection, an Ode', ll 53-58
[2] Peckham, op. cit.

but could not achieve without such liberation; or they may be dangerous and destructive forces, forces that reason and tradition fear, though they may be hailed with joy. To point to the hostility to reason and tradition, let us call this subversive liberation.

The distinction between reasonable and subversive liberation, between positive and negative Romanticism, is partly chronological, partly national, partly it defies patterning. Chronological, because the first generation of Romantics (in England at least) show little sign of subversion: Blake is perhaps one kind of exception, and Rousseau another. National, because there is no great Romantic subversive in England in the nineteenth century: apart from the partial case of Blake, there is only the minor (though fascinating) example of Swinburne. The great nineteenth century subversives are Baudelaire, Dostoyevsky and Nietzsche.

To point the distinction, we want a positive Romantic who is English, lived early in the nineteenth century, is a great writer and believed in release. Wordsworth is the obvious example, and against him we can set Nietzsche.

What Wordsworth learned from his early upbringing is recorded in *The Prelude*; and the title of the eighth book is almost enough, by itself, to establish our point. 'Love of Nature leading to love of Man': from his childhood experiences among the mountains were nurtured the sympathetic impulses, the feelings that bound him to his fellows:

> *first I looked*
> *At man through objects that were great or fair;*
> *First communed with him by their help. And thus*
> *Was founded a sure safeguard and defence*
> *Against the weight of meanness, selfish cares,*
> *Coarse manners, vulgar passions, that beat in*
> *On all sides from the ordinary world*
> *In which we traffic.*[1]

The presence that disturbs him with the joy of elevated thoughts in *Tintern Abbey* has taught him that trust in his deepest feelings is also

> *The anchor of my purest thoughts, the nurse,*
> *The guide, the guardian of my heart, and soul*
> *Of all my moral being.*[2]

I do not want to suggest that Wordsworth's profound understand-

---

[1] *The Prelude*, Bk. 8, ll, 315-322   [2] 'Tintern Abbey', ll. 109-111

ing of how his sensibility grew is glibly moralised in the telling. The greatest passages in *The Prelude* are accounts of episodes that take place below the level of moral judgement and moral concepts: the stealing of the boat, the stealing of the birds, the skating, the boy who called to the owls, the sight of the mountains reflected in the still water, the ascent of Snowdon—all these marvellous re-creations of the moments when his whole self is drawn into harmony with the world around him: they are moments at which moral concepts and reasoning processes do not exist, when no sentiments exist save awe, surrender and a kind of holy fear. Yet what these experiences taught is what he would have wanted to learn, if he had chosen; and when he looks back on them from adult life, he realises that in being shown 'the bond of union between life and joy' he was being given something to live by, a knowledge that would carry him through the despair brought by London, by the weight of ages that descended on his heart.

It is as a matter of fact not quite true that the early experiences are independent of moral concepts: at least one of them seems to describe the growth of conscience. This is the stealing of the birds in Book I.

> *Ere I had told*
> *Ten birth-days, when among the mountain-slopes*
> *Frost, and the breath of frosty wind, had snapped*
> *The last autumnal crocus, 'twas my joy*
> *With store of springes o'er my shoulder hung*
> *To range the open heights where woodcocks run*
> *Among the smooth green turf. Through half the night,*
> *Scudding away from snare to snare, I plied*
> *That anxious visitation;—moon and stars*
> *Were shining o'er my head. I was alone,*
> *And seemed to be a trouble to the peace*
> *That dwelt among them. Sometimes it befell*
> *In these night wanderings, that a strong desire*
> *O'erpowered my better reason, and the bird*
> *Which was the captive of another's toil*
> *Became my prey; and when the deed was done*
> *I heard among the solitary hills*
> *Low breathings coming after me, and sounds*
> *Of undistinguishable motion, steps*
> *Almost as silent as the turf they trod.*[1]

[1] *The Prelude*, Bk. 1, ll. 307-325

This is Wordsworth at his most genuine and his most imaginative. It is hard to imagine the play of Latinate against Saxon diction more brilliantly used:

> *I plied*
> *That anxious visitation;—moon and stars*
> *Were shining o'er my head.*

That sudden break into plain and huge statement places the scene before us with true Wordsworthian simplicity, the simplicity that can write of the great natural objects, sun, moon, stars, as if no-one had ever written of them before. We see that this passage takes its being from the sense of a grandeur independent of Wordsworth's own presence, a grandeur that he even troubles—the grandeur of the motion and the spirit that impels all thinking things. The interaction between that and his own anxious thoughts determines what he takes from the moment, and this interaction turns into an alienation after he has done wrong and stolen the birds. I don't think we need pay too much attention to the Augustan touch

> *—a strong desire*
> *O'erpowered my better reason,*

for there is a stronger, deeper, less obvious desire to be at peace with the scene around him which forms the true subject of the passage. When the interaction led to the fear so marvellously rendered in the last lines, he had experienced guilt as no moral teaching could ever have led him to experience it.

The great passages of *The Prelude* show the growth of the poet's sensibility through a dropping of inhibitions, a learning to trust in his own deepest self. What he derived from this is sometimes, though not often, presented in directly moral terms; and when the adult poet looks back on it in the light of what man needs, he then realises that reason and morality are glad of what Nature taught.

I have chosen Wordsworth but might equally have chosen Shelley—or such lines as these, in which music

> *. . . Such enlarged passion brought*
> *That love, hope, rage, and all experience,*
> *Were fused in vaster being, fetching thence*
> *Concords and discords, cadences and cries*
> *That seemed from some world-shrouded soul to rise,*

Some rapture more intense, some mightier rage,
Some living sea that burst the bounds of man's brief age.[1]

These lines are unimaginable before the English Romantic movement: the 'vaster being', the cadences 'that seemed from some
world-shrouded soul to rise', the final culminating image of release
—these are what Wordsworth taught to English poetry, though the
lines could never be taken for Wordsworth. They are too poetic,
lacking in the sturdy matter-of-factness that is his strength and his
weakness. They could, however, be taken for Shelley, who is fond
of 'raptures intense' and 'world-shrouded soul': they are in fact by
George Eliot. *Jubal*, from which they are taken, is her most Romantic poem (despite the couplets): Jubal could take his place in the
long line of solitary figures who stand as emblems for Romanticism
itself, Alastor, Endymion, the Scholar Gipsy, the Ancient Mariner
and the solitaries of Wordsworth. The poem tells how Jubal, third
son of Cain, discovered music and made the first lyre; then left his
people and wandered into years of solitude to find further inspiration; then in old age came back and found them worshipping his
name. 'The little pulse of self' drives him to declare himself,
but no-one will believe him; he is first laughed at, then beaten:

The immortal name of Jubal filled the sky
While Jubal lonely laid him down to die.[2]

It is an ironic version of the theme of the choir invisible: the transcending of self in the universality of art. Self, however, must
accept this, must consent to become its admirers.

Jubal is a figure for Romanticism itself because of the nature of
his discovery of music. His aim is to capture 'the music of the
World': if he can release his own deeper self he will come in touch
with it. It is as different as can be from the music of the spheres, an
idea understood by the intellect, and to be heard only by the sinless.
Neither intellect nor virtue teaches Jubal the music of the world,
but sensitivity, wise passiveness, impulses from the vernal world
and the drawing out of his own unconscious responses to nature.
Even discipline is not a subduing of nature but a drawing out: the
'guidance sweet' of the rules of music simply teaches

the blissful Right,
Where strictest law is gladness to the sense.[3]

[1] George Eliot, 'Jubal', in *Jubal and Other Poems*
[2] Ibid.   [3] Ibid.

If we think again of the couplet

Some rapture more intense, some mightier rage,
Some living sea that burst the bounds of man's brief age

we can see a direction into which George Eliot might well have taken her myth. If music releases such rapture and such rage, could they not get out of control? There would have been a nice irony if Jubal had been destroyed by the wild power that he himself had summoned up; but George Eliot is interested only in the irony of the situation, not in any irony arising out of the nature of the rapture. She therefore draws no connexion between the mocking of Jubal and the music that the mockers had just been playing: they 'beat him with their flutes', but this is a mere ironic detail in passing— they do not beat him with their flutings. And if we turn back to that so Romantic couplet already quoted, we can notice that the living sea 'burst the bounds of man's brief age'. 'Burst the bounds' is as clear an image of liberation as one could ask for, but it is only liberation from time, not from restraint: not a *real* bursting of bounds. The line is less violent than it looks. There is nothing destructive in this impulse.

Writing about the discovery of music, the Romantic poet does not pause to approve this discovery by reasoned comment: he shows it to be a discovery of the music of the world. Harmony with nature becomes a criterion of approval. Here perhaps is the basis for believing that impulse takes us where reason beckons. If you hold an organic conception of the universe, you can naturally believe that one's deepest impulses will bring one into contact with that, which is itself the basis of all right reason.

Yet it will be best to avoid such terms as basis, for they seem to assume too intellectualist a view of causation. I do not wish to invoke the devil of causation at all—it carried off the scrupulous soul of Lovejoy and of many lesser men, and it imposed a gross Sunday-school moral on *The Ancient Mariner*. All we need to say is that the organic conception of the universe, which everyone agrees is Romantic, naturally goes with a belief that reason and impulse are in harmony. This wording enables us to move comfortably from poetry to the novel. Novelists do not go in for a sense sublime Whose dwelling is the light of setting suns, nor for cadences and cries That seemed from some world-shrouded soul to rise, nor for the abyss that shouts 'Heaven, hast thou secrets? Man unveils me; I have none.' Yet the release of deeper forces in the self is as much a part of the Romantic movement if it happens in Lowick or St Oggs or Wessex or Cossethay as it would be while ascending Snowdon or waiting for sunrise in the Vale of Chamonix.

Against all this we can set the subversives: those whose art is dedicated to the release of impulses which frighten, repel or disgust. Subversive Romanticism is often most powerful, as one would expect, when some opposing force (aesthetic, moral, traditionalist) blocks the impulse, gives it something to push against. Thus Dostoyevsky takes off the lid in *Notes from Underground*, but keeps a running possibility of Christian disapproval and redemption beneath the surface of the story. Or Baudelaire releases lust, cruelty and the stench of *Une Charogne*, but in impeccable formal uniform. Nietzsche, being further from art and nearer to the discursive, has not the same apparatus of restraint to hand: his substitute is the restless dialectic that causes him to contradict, with equal eloquence, almost everything he asserts.

Beyond Good and Evil and *The Genealogy of Morals* are perhaps the most eloquent statements of subversive Romanticism that the nineteenth century produced. They urge the release of impulse, but in a world that is no longer an organic, an harmonious whole. The aristocrat is preferred to the slave because his uninhibited morality does not bottle up impulses in order to give them a twisted expression in the concept of evil as in belief in Hell.

> When a noble man feels resentment, it is absorbed in his instant-aneous reaction, and therefore does not poison him. . . . Such a man simply shakes off vermin which would get beneath an-other's skin.[1]

Slave-morality ('rancour turning creative and giving birth to values') is far worse than the aristocratic morality of triumphant self-affirmation. The Nietzschean aristocrat affirms himself like the Byronic hero, and if tradition judges the result to be wicked, that places tradition. Hence Nietzsche defends cruelty: 'In the days when people were unashamed of their cruelty life was a great deal more enjoyable than it is now in the heyday of pessimism.' He defends it with great subtlety and proto-Freudian shrewdness, but he is very firm on what he is defending: 'Practically everything

---

[1] *Zur Genealogie der Moral*, Pt. I, § 10

that we call "superior culture" rests on the intellectualisation and deepening of *cruelty*.'

Lawrence too defends cruelty, and often in highly Nietzschean language though without Nietsche's shrewdness. The comparison is hard on Lawrence, since his discursive writings seldom have the probing subtlety of his fiction: but I must, briefly, make it, since it places Lawrence in the tradition he most belongs in. Lawrence's essay on Dana (in *Studies in Classic American Literature*) is one which must have embarrassed many of his admirers, yet it is not an accident or an aberration: we cannot afford to look the other way when Lawrence embarrasses us. There is a description of a flogging in *Two Years Before the Mast* that must move most of its readers to the same helpless fury it drew from Dana: a wanton display of cruelty by a captain who was in a stupor of rage. Lawrence's account is far too long to quote in full, and I must ask the reader to turn it up, along with Dana's.

> You have a Sam, a fat slow fellow, who has got slower and more slovenly as the weeks wear on. You have a master who has grown more irritable in his authority. Till Sam becomes simply wallowing in his slackness, makes your gorge rise. And the master is on red hot iron.
>
> Now these two men, Captain and Sam, are there in a very unsteady equilibrium of command and obedience. A polarized flow. Definitely polarised.
>
> The poles of will are the great ganglia of the voluntary nerve system, located beside the spinal column, in the back. From the poles of will in the backbone of the Captain, to the ganglia of will in the back of the sloucher Sam, runs a frazzled, jagged current, a staggering circuit of vital electricity. This circuit gets one jolt too many, and there is explosion.
>
> 'Tie up that lousy swine!' roars the enraged Captain.
>
> And whack! Whack! down on the bare back of that sloucher Sam comes the cat.
>
> .   .   .   .   .
>
> The blood begins to go quicker. The nerves begin to recover their vividness. It is their tonic. The man Sam has a new clear day of intelligence, and a smarty back. The Captain has a new relief, a new ease in his authority, and a sore heart.
>
> There is a new equilibrium, and a fresh start. The *physical* intelligence of a Sam is restored, the turgidity is relieved from the veins of the Captain.

It is a natural form of human coition, interchange.

It is good for Sam to be flogged. It is good, on this occasion, for the Captain to have Sam flogged. I say so. Because they were both in that physical condition.

Spare the rod and spoil the *physical* child.

Use the rod and spoil the *ideal* child.

There you are.

Dana, as an idealist, refusing the blood-contact of life, leaned over the side of the ship powerless, and vomited: or wanted to. His solar plexus was getting a bit of its own back. To him, Sam was an 'ideal' being, who should have been approached through the mind, the reason, and the spirit. That lump of a Sam!

But there was another idealist on board, the seaman John, a Swede. He wasn't named John for nothing, this Jack-tar of the Logos. John felt himself called upon to play Mediator, Intercedor, Saviour, on this occasion. The popular Paraclete.

'Why are you whipping this man, sir?'

But the Captain had got his dander up. He wasn't going to have his natural passion judged and interfered with by these long-nosed salvationist Johannuses. So he had nosey John hauled up and whipped as well.

For which I am very glad.

．　　．　　．　　．　　．

After all, it was not so terrible. The captain evidently did not exceed the ordinary measure. Sam got no more than he asked for. It was a natural event. All would have been well, save for the *moral* verdict. And this came from theoretic idealists like Dana and the seaman John, rather than from the sailors themselves. The sailors understood spontaneous *passional* morality, not the artificial ethical. They respected the violent readjustments of the naked force, in man as in nature.[1]

The passage is probably improved by the heavy cutting I have had to do (the original is six times as long): and I therefore felt it necessary to include the excursus into Lawrence's crazy anatomy in the third paragraph. I will not pause to discuss its doctrines in any detail, or to trace them into Lawrence's own fiction, since that would be to go over ground already trodden. I have quoted the passage because it seems to follow so naturally out of Nietzsche: whether this is direct influence or a common tradition need not

[1] 'Two Years before the Mast'; *Studies in Classic American Literature*, ch. 9

concern us. Nietzsche's aristocratic morality is Lawrence's blood contact of life; his slave-morality is Lawrence's idealism. Nietzsche presents his system through a historical myth that has the same curious status as other historical myths—the social contract or the Freudian primal crime: it is neither an identifiable moment in the past, nor a mere allegory of psychological patterns in the present. Lawrence presents his through a physiological myth that is sheer nonsense, and adds little but an air of pretentiousness. Lawrence's passional morality despises idealism in just the same way as Nietzsche despised Christianity.

Yet the Lawrence serves too as a gloss, and a critical gloss, on Nietzsche's doctrine. For the cruelty of Dana's captain is not the contemptuous self-affirming egoism that Nietzsche so admired in his aristocrats; that Captain is not really like Mirabeau 'who lacked all memory for insults and meanness done him, and who was unable to forgive because he had forgotten'. If the animal innocence of the blond beast ever existed, it exists no longer: the cruelty that Dana depicts has its own kind of rancour. It's not that Lawrence has misunderstood Nietzsche: it is that he has subjected his doctrine to the one test that matters, the test of literary creation—he showed us what it looks like. The test is vicarious in this case, since the creator was Dana; but there is no lack of direct testing too.

The prime aim of this book has been to compare three novelists: if the scheme I have set up has any wider reference, it is because it represents three attitudes to moral experience. The typology is personal and ethical. But this short final note now enables us to append a historical dimension, or at least to suggest that we can reach out for the ghost of history. The typology can be made historical with delicious and dangerous ease: Jane Austen is a pre-Romantic; George Eliot is a positive Romantic; Lawrence is a Romantic subversive.

INDEX

This index is not exhaustive; its purpose is simply to help the reader to find the main discussions of each of the novels